HARVARD HISTORICAL MONOGRAPHS

XLII

Published under the Direction of the Department of History
from the income of The Robert Louis Stroock Fund

New Zealand, 1769-1840
Early Years of Western
Contact

by
HARRISON M. WRIGHT

HARVARD UNIVERSITY PRESS
Cambridge, Massachusetts
1959

Library of Congress Catalog Card Number 59–12979
Printed in the United States of America

To my wife

PREFACE

This book discusses aspects of the history of northern New Zealand before 1840 from the point of view of the interaction between the Maori and Western societies. The explorers, traders, whalers, missionaries, and other Westerners who visited New Zealand in the early years are considered primarily as the agents of change in the Maoris, and the Maoris are considered as they and their environment altered the expectations and activities of the Westerners who came to live among them.

Most of the discussion revolves around the Bay of Islands, which was the area most continuously subjected to Western pressures before 1840. The South Island is rarely mentioned: while the character of Maori-white history there was in several respects quite unlike that of the North Island, the South Island had only a very small percentage of the Maori population. The terminal date, 1840, was picked partly because the character of white immigration and Western pressures began to change shortly after that date, partly because New Zealand historians have more thoroughly examined the later years, and partly because 1840 is a convenient and well-known historical milestone. It should be pointed out that although dealing to some extent inevitably with anthropological problems the book is history and as closely as possible adheres to historical methods of presentation.

A note about the use and spelling of certain words: There is no entirely accurate and satisfactory term for the various non-Maori individuals who came to New Zealand before 1840. Except in places where one or another is obviously necessary, I have used "white man," "Westerner," and "European" more or less interchangeably. Although the Maori language is fairly well stabilized, the spelling of proper names (particularly of early people and places) often varies, and I have used wherever possible that adopted by J. R. Elder for his index to *The Letters and Journals of Samuel Marsden,* Dunedin, 1932. Quoted passages are copied as exactly as possible, however, and consequently have a variety of spelling inconsistencies.

I am indebted to many people for assistance in the writing of this book. A number of them have read all or part of the text and have given me the benefit of their special knowledge, although they are not responsible for the use to which I have put it. Among them are Professor R. G. Albion of Harvard University, Professor F. M. Keesing of Stanford University, Mr. A. Osborn of Harvard University, and Professor H. D. Skinner of the University of Otago in Dunedin, New Zealand. I am particularly obligated to Professor David Owen of Harvard University, who was the director of the thesis which resulted in this book, and to the Department of History at Harvard, which made its publication possible. Thanks are also due the Faculty Research Committee of Swarthmore College for its aid. Members of many library staffs, particularly Mrs. Linda Rodda, of the Hocken Library in Dunedin, have been most helpful. I am happy to acknowledge my indebtedness to the United States Educational Foundation in New Zealand for a Fulbright Scholarship. Above all, I am thankful for the opportunity to have worked under Dr. Angus Ross, Senior Lecturer in History at the University of Otago, when I was in New Zealand. Dr. Ross not only directed my first enthusiasm for the topic, but has read the manuscript at every possible stage since it was begun. His generous aid has been indispensable.

Harrison M. Wright

Swarthmore, Pennsylvania
February 1, 1959

NOTE

Certain official publications and periodicals used frequently in the notes have been abbreviated as follows:

CMP	*Church Missionary Proceedings*
CMR	*Church Missionary Record*
HRNZ	*Historical Records of New Zealand,* ed. by R. McNab, 2 vols., Wellington, 1908–14
JPS	*Journal of the Polynesian Society*
MR	*Missionary Register*
PP, 1836, **VII**	*Parliamentary Papers,* 1836 (538), VII. Report From the Select Committee on Aborigines.
PP, 1837–38, XXI	*Parliamentary Papers,* 1837–38 (680), XXI. Report from the Select Committee of the House of Lords, Appointed to Inquire into the Present State of New Zealand . . .
PP, 1844, **XIII**	*Parliamentary Papers,* 1844 (556), XIII. Report from the Select Committee on New Zealand . . .
PP, 1846, **XXX**	*Parliamentary Papers,* 1846 (337), XXX. Papers Relative to New Zealand.
TPNZI	*The Transactions and Proceedings of the New Zealand Institute*

No reference has been made in the notes to the particular station at which a missionary letter from the Bay of Islands was written, unless it differed from that missionary's accustomed station. Following is a list of the stations of the missionaries whose letters from the Bay of Islands before 1840 are most frequently cited:

Butler, John:	Kerikeri, 1819–23
Clarke, George:	Kerikeri, 1824–1831; Waimate, 1831——
Davis, Richard:	Paihia, 1824–31; Waimate, 1831——
Hall, William:	Rangihoua, 1814–1825
Kemp, James:	Kerikeri, 1819——

Kendall, **Thomas:**   Rangihoua, 1815–1823
King, **John:**   Rangihoua, 1814–32; Tepuna, 1832——
Williams, **Henry:**   Paihia, 1823——

Since most of the letters referred to were addressed to one of the secretaries of the Church Missionary Society in London (usually Josiah Pratt before 1824, and Dandeson Coates after), no reference has been made in the notes to the recipient of a letter, unless it was other than a Church Missionary Society secretary. All manuscript letters are located in the Hocken Library, Dunedin, New Zealand, unless otherwise mentioned.

Many of the sources for quotations can be found in several places: manuscripts, missionary periodicals, and other published works. The references in the footnotes generally rely on manuscripts and missionary publications, except for the well-edited collections of the letters and journals of John Butler and Samuel Marsden.

Contents

PART ONE: THE WHITE PENETRATION

Introduction. The First Contacts   3

Chapter I. The Maori Background   9

Chapter II. Traders and Whalers   19

Chapter III. The Missionaries   38

PART TWO: THE DEPOPULATION OF THE MAORIS

Chapter IV. Maori Health   57

Chapter V. New Means of War   81

PART THREE: CHANGING PATTERNS OF BEHAVIOR

Chapter VI. The European View   105

Chapter VII. The Maori Domination   115

Chapter VIII. The Maori Conversion   141

Chapter IX. The Christian Maori   166

Conclusion. New Zealand in 1840, and After   187

BIBLIOGRAPHICAL ESSAY   203

INDEX   217

PART ONE

The White Penetration

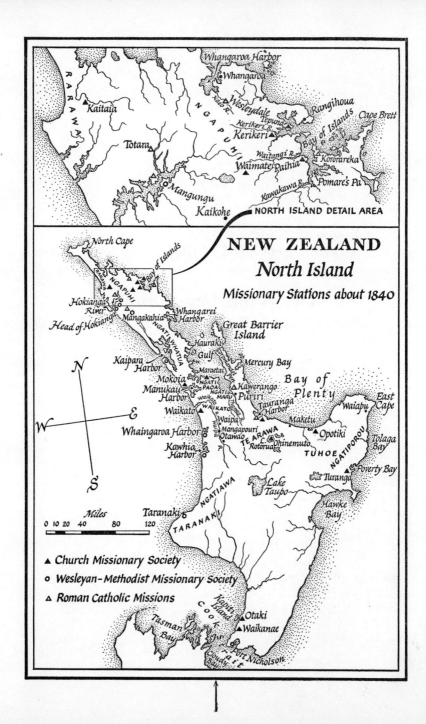

NORTH ISLAND DETAIL AREA

Whangaroa Harbor
Whangaroa
Wesleydale
Rangihoua
Kaitaia
Kerikeri R.
Cape Brett
Tepuna
Totara
Kerikeri
Bay of Islands
Kororareka
Waitangi R.
Mangungu
Waimate
Paihia
Kawakawa R.
Pomare's Pa
Kaikohe

NEW ZEALAND
North Island
Missionary Stations about 1840

North Cape
Bay of Islands
NGAPUHI
Hokianga River
Whangarei Harbor
Head of Hokianga
Mangakahia
NGATI WHATUA
Great Barrier Island
Hauraki Gulf
Kaipara Harbor
Mercury Bay
Mokoia
Maraetai
Bay of Plenty
Manukau Harbor
NGATI PAOA
Kawerango
Puriri
East Cape
Waikato
NGATI MARU
Tauranga Harbor
Waiapu
Waipa
Maketu
Whaingaroa Harbor
Mangapouri
WAIKATO
Opotiki
Kawhia Harbor
Otawao
TE ARAWA
Rotorua Ohinemuto
TUHOE
NGATIPOROU
Tolaga Bay
Lake Taupo
Turanga
Poverty Bay
NGATIAWA
Hawke Bay
Taranaki
TARANAKI

Miles
0 10 20 40 80 120

▲ Church Missionary Society
○ Wesleyan-Methodist Missionary Society
△ Roman Catholic Missions

Kapiti Island
Otaki
Waikanae
Tasman Bay
COOK STRAIT
Port Nicholson
Cloudy Bay

Introduction

First Contacts

The first meeting of white men and Maoris was brief but violent. When the Dutch explorer Tasman discovered New Zealand in December 1642, he was not even able to get ashore. One of the several canoeloads of natives who had paddled out inquisitively to his anchorage attacked the cockboat shuttling between his two ships. Four Dutch sailors were killed. Tasman considered himself lucky to rescue the rest of the men and to escape without greater loss of life. He traveled north, sounding and charting, but made no further attempts to land. The strip of coast he had sailed along was put on charts, eventually, but there was no one with the inclination to return there, and it was left alone to its strange and ferocious inhabitants for more than a century.

Evidently no white man saw New Zealand again until Captain Cook reached it in October 1769. But within five years of that date French and English navigators had thoroughly explored its coasts. They stayed in New Zealand for months at a time, charted its headlands and harbors, inspected its natural resources, and studied its natives with all the disinterested curiosity of the eighteenth-century explorers. Cook himself spent nearly half a year circumnavigating New Zealand on his first visit in 1769–70, and he had been there only two months when a Frenchman, Jean de Surville, also arrived and began exploring the North Island bays and river mouths—in fact the two men barely missed each other on the western coast. Another Frenchman, Marion Dufresne, visited New Zealand in 1772. The Maoris at the Bay of Islands, however, after a month of friendly trading, massacred a landing party which included Dufresne. Two subordinate officers, du Clesmeur and Crozet, were only just able to save the ships, retaliate, and escape with the remainder of the crew. Captain Cook returned to New Zealand four times during his subsequent Pacific voyages of 1772–1775 and 1776–1780.

The first explorers found a great deal that was new to European eyes. They discovered that New Zealand was not part of the long-sought southern continent, a thing which many geographers had assumed it to be—largely because Tasman had sailed only along one coast. They found instead that it consisted of two large islands and several smaller adjacent ones—about 100,000 square miles in all—set in a great expanse of ocean. The southern and more desolate of the two main islands had long and jagged mountain ranges which ran its entire length. There were wide, flat plains extending to the east coast, while to the west were foothills and, where the mountains ran into the sea, deep fiords. The surface of the northern island was more broken and less extreme than that of the southern island. Its coasts, especially in the long northern (North Auckland) peninsula, were dotted with bays and sheltered river mouths. The climate of New Zealand was warmer in the north, but everywhere it was more equable, though wetter, than the climate to which the Europeans were accustomed.

The landscape was covered with a dense, green foliage—a somewhat sterile green, perhaps, because there were few deciduous trees or plants. The vegetation of ferns, grasses, and flowering trees was for the most part new to the explorers. There were few animals, but the forest was filled with a "great variety of Beautiful singing Birds which made the Woods ecco with their different Notes which made the greatest harmony." [1] Both Captain Cook and Johan R.

---

[1] William Bayly, "Extract from the Journal kept by William Bayly . . . ," *HRNZ*, II, 207. (Bayly was at Queen Charlotte's Sound in 1773.) For general comments on New Zealand and the characteristics of the Maoris at this time, see James Cook, *Captain Cook in New Zealand. Extracts from the journals . . .* , ed. A. H. and A. W. Reed (Wellington, 1951); M. Crozet, *Crozet's Voyage to Tasmania, New Zealand, the Ladrone Islands, and the Philippines in the Years 1771–1772*, ed. and trans. H. Ling Roth (London, 1891), pp. 5–78; and the accounts and journals of Bayly, Edgar, Monneron, l'Horne, Roux,

Forster, one of the naturalists, discussed the prospects of a colony,[2] and most of the men who wrote about New Zealand praised its natural charms.

The explorers found the Maoris living mostly in the north. They were impressed by the size, strength, and vigor of the males—the thick legs (from "their constant squatting"), fine teeth, and olive complexions.[3] The Frenchman l'Horne conceded that their "faces are not at all disgusting."[4] Crozet added: "The women are not so good-looking on close examination; they have generally a bad figure, are short, very thick in the waist, with voluminous mammae, coarse thighs and legs, and are of a very amorous temperament, while on the contrary the men are very indifferent in this respect."[5] Some of the Maoris' faces were completely tattooed with blue-black spiral patterns, and the Maori women often had a few lines etched below their lower lips. Hair was straight and black, tied in a topknot, anointed with an oil and deep red dyes, and frequently decorated with feathers. Bright ear ornaments impressed the Europeans; so did the colorful skirts and mats of flax and the feather blankets with their rich designs.

The explorers saw villages and gardens where the Maoris grew *kumaras* (sweet potatoes) and, in the northern districts, yams and taros. There were apparently no domestic animals except a fox-like, barkless dog. While the Maoris themselves lived in small huts, there were large structures, such as the meetinghouses, which were sometimes twenty feet high and over sixty feet long. There were also stockades, or *pas,* of heavy trees, so skillfully constructed that villages might hold out indefinitely against attack by other Maoris.

du Clesmeur, etc., *HRNZ,* II, 201–481. The following paragraphs are based primarily on these sources.

[2] Cook, *Captain Cook in N.Z.,* p. 141; for J. R. Forster see George Forster, *A Voyage Round the World in His Britannic Majesty's Sloop, 'Resolution'* . . . (London, 1777), I, 522–23.

[3] "Extract from the Journal of Pottier de l'Horne . . . 1769 to 1773," *HRNZ,* II, 204 *passim.*

[4] "Extract from the Journal of Pottier de l'Horne . . . 1769 to 1773," *HRNZ,* II, 317.

[5] Crozet, *Voyage,* p. 28.

New Zealand was reminiscent of, yet quite unlike, Tahiti and other central Pacific islands.

Actually, the first white men to visit New Zealand had so much to look at that they could not keep their minds for long on any single thing. Their attention jumped from one unassimilated interest to another, and they made disconnected catalogues of whatever seemed most interesting. They described novel green stone tools, which they had not come across on other Pacific islands; well-designed spears and stone clubs; the dances and cries of the Maoris; the curious carvings and small stone *tikis,* or images. They remarked on polygamy and the Maoris' easy assumption of premarital intercourse. A Frenchman concluded that this was due to the "consumption of so much fish, which is a very heating food. . . ."[6]

Estimates were made as to how many inhabitants there were: Forster thought about 100,000 in the North Island.[7] Cook hazarded a guess as to the origin of the Maoris and the South Pacific peoples— that it "certainly is neither to the Southward nor Eastward, for I cannot perswaide myself that they ever came from America. . . ."[8] Joseph Banks, the scientist, was particularly interested in the preserved heads, which remained in good condition after a process of steaming and smoke drying, and he forced some of the Maoris to sell him one.[9] For all these men, and for geographers throughout the world, the opening of New Zealand was accomplished with an eager and many-sided curiosity.

It is recorded that before 1769 the Maoris thought New Zealand comprised all of the habitable part of the earth except for "Hawaiki," their half-mythical, half-remembered home.[10] One can scarcely guess what the white men must have seemed to them. A secondhand account of Cook's landing, if not entirely trustworthy, is suggestive: One Maori said that when his people saw Captain

---

[6] Roux, "Journal," *HRNZ,* II, 401.
[7] Forster, *Voyage,* I, 515.
[8] Cook, *Captain Cook in N.Z.,* p. 150.
[9] Cook, *Captain Cook in N.Z.,* p. 145.
[10] G. L. Craik, *The New Zealanders* (London, 1830), p. 341.

Cook's ship, the *Endeavour,* come over the horizon they thought at first that it was a huge bird, "and many remarks passed among them as to the beauty and size of its wings. . . ." Soon they discovered a smaller, unfledged bird—one without sails—descending to the water. And when they saw "a number of party-coloured beings, but apparently in the human shape, also descending, the bird was regarded as a houseful of divinities. Nothing could exceed the astonishment of the people." [11] When Cook came ashore, the Maoris ran in terror. Later, when they tried to assert themselves by force, an English sailor shot and killed a Maori. "The manner of his unseen death was ascribed as a thunderbolt from these new gods; and the noise made by the discharge of the muskets was represented as . . . thunder. . . . Many of these natives observed, that they felt themselves taken ill by only being particularly looked upon by these Atuas." [12]

After a little contact with Europeans, French or English, the Maoris generally began to see that these strange creatures were actually human beings. Once on board, wrote Roux, "they regarded us with great care and considered the whiteness of our skins as something extraordinary, and forthwith a cry of surprise would escape them. They took great pleasure in looking under our clothes, to see if we were of the same colour underneath." [13]

There was always enthusiastic trading after the first tentative exchange of clothing. Every European ship experienced a rush of

[11] Joel S. Polack, *New Zealand: Being a Narrative of Travels and Adventures . . . ,* new ed. (London, 1839), I, 15. For other alleged accounts of the Maoris' conception of the first white men, see John White, *Ancient History of the Maori, his Mythology and Traditions* (Wellington, 1887–90), V, 120–28; William Baucke, *Where the White Man Treads* (Auckland, 1905), pp. 58–72; and the journal of Mrs. Sarah Mathew in Felton and Sarah Mathew, *The Founding of New Zealand. The Journals of Felton Mathew, First Surveyor-General of New Zealand and his Wife, 1840–1847,* ed. J. Rutherford (Dunedin, 1940), p. 150. Presumably none of these interpretations of Maori thoughts has more authenticity than any other. Cook's activities for the first few days can be easily found, however, in *Captain Cook in N.Z.,* pp. 33–39.

[12] Polack, *New Zealand,* I, 15.

[13] Roux, "Journal," *HRNZ,* II, 369.

eager and curious Maoris. The Maoris would give almost anything
the Europeans asked, including daughters, for even a nail or two,
but they would also "dextrously pick our Pockets of our handker-
chefs or steal anything they could." [14] Whatever was removable on
the ships was in danger of being taken, since almost everything the
Europeans had the Maoris thought that they could use themselves.
They watched whatever the Europeans did with eager interest,
and looked on perplexedly as the explorers planted corn, beans, and
other Western plants and tried to make them understand the value
of these foods. The Europeans left samples of whatever they could
behind, and every ship that came unfolded new wonders of the
white man to the Maoris.

There were three human components in the history of New
Zealand before 1840: the Maoris, who might have gone on living
as they had been more or less indefinitely, if in 1769 the first repre-
sentatives of the Western world had not arrived, and two types of
white people—one commercial, one religious—who brought their
different but characteristically Western ways of life to test the Stone
Age culture of the Maoris.

[14] Bayly, "Extract," *HRNZ*, II, 203.

Chapter I

The Maori Background

Ever since the time of the first explorers, historians and anthropologists have been trying to uncover information about the Maoris who lived before 1769. But there is not much to go on, and the early years of the Maoris can be only dimly discerned in the difficult deciphering of traditions and in the very scanty archaeological remains.

Maori traditions tell of occasional Polynesian visits to New Zealand from about the tenth century A.D. and say that New Zealand was not finally settled by the Polynesians until the middle of the fourteenth century, when seven long canoeloads of voyagers arrived at the North Island from their home, "Hawaiki," possibly Raiatea in the Society Islands. It is difficult to determine to what extent this corresponds to actuality. The fourteenth-century Polynesian voyagers, if any existed, evidently did not make the first human contact with New Zealand: most anthropologists state that there were humans already living in New Zealand by the middle of the fourteenth century. But it is unknown who these earlier people were. Because it appears that they had fuzzy hair and artifacts typical of the western Pacific but not Polynesia, the great ethnographer of the Maori, Elsdon Best, believed they were Melanesians.[1] Another famous anthropologist, Sir Peter Buck, however, felt that the Maoris had "pure" Polynesian blood, and he argued that all New Zealand groups originated in central Polynesia.[2]

A New Zealander, Andrew Sharp, has recently propounded a theory about the origins of the Maoris which criticizes the basic

[1] Elsdon Best, *The Maori* (Wellington, 1924), I, 44.
[2] Peter H. Buck, *The Coming of the Maori* (Wellington, 1949), pp. 65–73.

premises of the older views. Sharp argues that no one came to New Zealand deliberately at any time, that there were no mass migrations and no planned settlement, and that such ideas come only from the overselective reading of traditions. According to Sharp, New Zealand, like the other Polynesian islands, was settled because of the limitations, not the virtues, of Polynesian navigational techniques. It was stumbled upon accidentally by a lost canoe, or canoes, which may have come from anywhere in any century. In this theory Sharp helps account for the lack of two-way voyages and the absence of pigs and other Polynesian animals which one might expect in a purposeful voyage. But no matter what people did drift to New Zealand, adds Sharp, those from eastern Polynesia set the basic culture pattern.[3]

Traditions say that the Maoris of the seven mythical canoes settled in different areas and became the founders of seven great families of tribes, and most Maoris today trace their ancestry back to one or another of the famous canoes. Each of the seven superunits can be easily divided by means of tradition into tribes and subtribes down to the community and extended kin groups which constitute the normal unit of Maori society. Most anthropologists, however, now tend to cut across the traditional ancestral lines and to divide New Zealand not into hereditary groups, but into tentative culture areas. Dr. H. D. Skinner, for example, has suggested four such areas for the North Island, based on material culture, dialect, and so on.[4] Whatever the means of organization, attempts to subdivide the Maoris are always admittedly arbitrary in detail.

By 1769, each group of Maoris had developed peculiar characteristics of its own. The Ngapuhi, for instance, who constituted the largest tribe in the North Auckland peninsula and the one with which most early white contact occurred, were particularly known for their personal independence. Whether this was due to the more favorable conditions for growing food or to the relative isolation which helped protect them from war, the fact is that they had much

---

[3] Andrew Sharp, *Ancient Voyagers in the Pacific* (Harmondsworth, Eng., 1957), pp. 163–85.
[4] H. D. Skinner, "Culture Areas in New Zealand," *JPS*, XXX (1921), 71–78.

less of the communal cohesiveness which characterized Te Arawa and other interior groups.[5]

The population of the pre-European Maoris is as difficult to determine as their origins. Depopulation began immediately after 1769, and the first explorers could not hope to give a definitive number. Forster's estimate of 100,000 was based only on what he could gather from his points of observation on the coasts, and no white man went into the interior of New Zealand until long after 1800. Since Cook's time the estimates have varied from the less than 100,000 of Dr. Skinner to the more than 500,000 of Dr. K. B. Cumberland.[6] Both of these men are contemporary New Zealanders, and both estimates are probably extreme. Dr. Skinner based his on the fact that the South Island population apparently grew after the introduction of the white potato and concluded that the North Island population must have increased also. But food in the South Island was so hard to obtain that its population might well have increased with the potato, while the North Island, with a more adequate food supply anyway, suffered depopulation from greater contact with the whites. Dr. Cumberland, a geographer, admittedly based his estimate of the population on New Zealand's geographical potential, not on what most anthropological and historical records indicate it to have been.

The usual estimate is that there were probably between 200,000 and 300,000 Maoris in 1769. I think it was, at most, 200,000. A number of different counts and estimates made at the time established the population as being from 100,000 to 150,000—say 125,000 Maoris —in 1840. Accepting this, and working back through the years of depopulation, one could scarcely place the 1769 figure below 175,000, while anything much above 200,000 seems too high for the number

---

[5] Much of this information was transmitted verbally by Prof. F. M. Keesing of Stanford University; see also Eric Ramsden, *Busby of Waitangi. H. M.'s Resident at New Zealand, 1833–40* (Wellington, 1942), p. 212.

[6] H. D. Skinner, "The Maoris," *Cambridge History of the British Empire,* vol. VII, pt. II (Cambridge, 1933), 19; and Dr. K. B. Cumberland, "Aotearoa Maori: New Zealand about 1780," *The Geographical Review,* XXXIX (July 1949), 417.

of archaeological relics and remains. This is especially the case since the constant shifting of tribes from site to site would tend to indicate a larger population than was actually there.[7]

The Maori population, whatever its exact amount, was unevenly distributed. The South Island, although it is the largest, had probably not a twentieth of the total number. Perhaps a quarter to a third of all the Maoris lived in the long peninsula stretching north of Auckland, around such well-known bays and river mouths as Whangaroa, Kaipara, the Bay of Islands, Hokianga, and Whangarei. Another quarter may well have been found in the bulge which forms the East Cape, and along the Bay of Plenty. The Waikato district was fairly well populated. One can assume that about a sixth or a seventh of the population lived there, with slightly less around Rotorua and slightly more around Taranaki. The southeast coast of the North Island was thinly populated as, except for Wellington, it is today.[8]

While the basis of the culture of the Maoris was obviously Polynesian, it did not maintain its Polynesian purity for long in New Zealand. The harshness of even northernmost New Zealand induced changes from the Polynesian norm which were still going on at the time of the European discovery.[9]

For one thing there was the question of food. Three Polynesian staples, the cocoanut, breadfruit, and banana trees, would not grow in the New Zealand climate. Furthermore, the taro and yam flourished only in the extreme north, and yielded but one crop a year.

[7] Gordon Lewthwaite, "The Population of Aotearoa: Its Number and Distribution," *The New Zealand Geographer,* VI (April 1950), 49, has made a very careful study and thinks there were "about a quarter of a million" Maoris in 1769. He relies to a greater extent than I on the remains of old hill forts, storage pits, drains, and the like. See also Edwin Harding, "Prehistoric Drains on the Kaipara, West Coast," *JPS,* XXXVII (1928), 367–68.

[8] See H. D. Skinner, "The Maoris," *CHBE,* vol. VII, pt. II, 19, for a similar estimate. Also Lewthwaite, "Population," *N.Z. Geographer,* VI (April 1950), 49–52.

[9] The following paragraphs are based, to a large extent, on Peter H. Buck, *Vikings of the Sunrise* (Philadelphia, 1938), pp. 259–83. See also the two articles by Ernest Beaglehole entitled "The Polynesian Maori." One is in *JPS,* XLIX (1940), 39–68, and the other in *The Maori People Today. A General Survey,* ed. I. L. G. Sutherland (London, 1940), pp. 49–74.

And the Polynesians successfully transferred to New Zealand only one of their domestic animals, the dog, leaving the pig and fowl behind or accidentally exterminating them before they had a chance to reproduce. Since New Zealand had no indigenous mammals except two species of bats, and only a few species of reptiles, there was a considerable shortage of meat. The Maori diet consequently changed, and *kumaras,* fern roots, and fish became the basic Maori foods. The Maoris learned to cultivate the large gardens which the first Europeans had seen and to store their food on platforms built on piles. They ate the dogs, and also rats, which had evidently stowed away in the first canoes and spread ashore. Cannibalism also became a source of protein. Since New Zealand had few predatory animals, it was a paradise for birds. Many of these plump and heavy creatures had lost the use of wings, and the Maoris easily caught them as well as others in a variety of snares and traps. The moa was probably nearly extinct by the time of widespread Maori settlement,[10] but the kiwi and the weka, both ground birds, as well as various parrots and pigeons, were eaten in large quantities.

As the Maoris had to adapt their food to new conditions, they also had to find new methods for protecting themselves from the cold. The paper mulberry did not thrive in New Zealand, so they took a native plant, a species of flax, and learned to make it into a new kind of cloth. They made cloaks from the dogs' skins and often built their huts into the ground for further warmth.

Meanwhile they came across the new, hard, and shiny minerals, like basalt and nephrite (greenstone), minerals not usually found on central Pacific islands, and carefully ground them into adzes and other tools. They cut canoes out of the immense trees; erected meetinghouses; carefully harvested crops; constructed fish nets, hooks, and traps for birds. Diseases were practically unknown, and because there was no contact with the outside world, none were introduced. It was a healthy and vigorous life.

Mentally the Maoris lived in a world which no one, who did not belong to it, can ever fully understand. It can be described as a

---

[10] Roger Duff, *The Moa-Hunter Period of Maori Culture,* 2nd ed. (Wellington, 1956), pp. xi, 280–81.

dream world, a subconscious world, a children's world, or an irrational world, but no phrase or analogy is entirely satisfactory. Such devices are suggestive only because the cultural potential of the Maoris was so much higher than its actuality: the experiences of the Maoris were limited, and they had no great variety of challenges or stimulation. They were isolated not only physically, but mentally—to all intents and purposes being, as they believed, the only people in existence. In 1769, except for the realm of spirits and the memory of Hawaiki, the range of their thoughts stopped at what they could see from the shores of New Zealand.[11]

Religion both dominated and was a reflection of the Maori way of life. It emanated from the everyday existence of the Maoris and at the same time gave that existence meaning. Except for occasional variations in detail, all the Maoris shared the same religious beliefs. They personified forces they could not understand and lived in a world filled with spirits. According to the Maoris, the major gods, or *atua,* were the offspring of the earth and the sky. Each represented a major department of life: one was the father of the flora and fauna, including man; another was the god of war; still another held sway over peace and agriculture; and so on. Besides the gods shared by all the Maoris, each tribe had a number of its own. Most tribes had a special war god, for example, since Tu, the major god of war, could not be expected to fight on both sides of a battle at once. There were gods of the sweet potato and the rainbow, gods of streams and gods of forests. And as the family was the basic unit of Maori society, so each family also had its own particular gods: everyday spirits which took care of what was left uncovered by the others.[12]

Every aspect of Maori life was in fact explainable through one

[11] An excellent presentation of the Maori character and personality is in Felix M. Keesing, *The Changing Maori* (New Plymouth, N.Z., 1928), pp. 22–39. For other intuitive interpretations see James Cowan, *The Maoris of New Zealand* (Christchurch, 1910), pp. 19, 102, 114, 142–43, 196; and William Baucke, *Where the White Man Treads* (Auckland, 1905), pp. 10, 22, 53. Information of a more specific and less imaginative sort is in Best, *The Maori;* and Buck, *Coming of the Maori.*

[12] Buck, *Coming of the Maori,* pp. 454–72, gives details about the gods.

or another of the gods. If, while being cut, a tree fell and killed a Maori, was it not because that Maori had not properly paid his respects to Tane, the father of the flora, or to one of the tribal or family gods? Did the crops fail? Rongo, who regulated agriculture, or some other god with the appropriate power, was angry. Was a war lost? The god of the other tribe had gotten the best of one's own. The results of the anger of the gods were visible everywhere: bad weather, poor catches of fish, wounded warriors, flooded villages, and disease.

Obviously the only way for a Maori to lead a successful life was to avoid angering the gods. This was extremely difficult to do. But eventually, from experience with different manifestations of the gods' displeasure, a complicated network of regulations and habits to help in this developed. Appropriate rites had to be performed in letter-perfect fashion to ensure successful undertakings; many things could not be done, or disastrous consequences would ensue.

The most important guide for conduct of the Maoris was the well-known *tapu*—a form of prohibition.[13] It forbade, in certain circumstances, any contact between particular persons, places, or things, and the rest of the world. Some things were *tapu* permanently, such as religious shrines; others only temporarily, such as weapons. Anything could be *tapued* to placate the gods associated with it. Chiefs and everything that pertained to them were *tapu*. If a chief blew on a fire, no other Maori could eat food cooked by it, because the fire was *tapu*. If a chief were tired of a feather cloak, it had to be destroyed, or some other unfortunate Maori might put it on. Places were *tapu*: sacred spots, burial grounds, special hunting areas, rivers, growing crops. Animals were *tapu*: certain birds could not be trapped at certain seasons, and fish were permitted to spawn in peace. Food was *tapu*. Like most primitive peoples the Maoris *tapued* most heavily the things they did not understand and could least effectively control: mothers in childbirth, sick people, and death.

When a Maori discovered he had violated a *tapu,* he knew that some misfortune would follow. Occasionally, it is said, Maoris died

---

[13] See for example Best, *The Maori,* I, 251–61.

from nothing more than the realization of what it was they had done. European visitors were constantly citing specific examples to prove their assertions about this apparently incredible fact. As late as 1840, one white settler told J. L. Campbell, then a newcomer, that he had once inadvertently informed a Maori girl she had just eaten a *kumara* from the burial ground of the great chief Te Rewi. "Lord! sirs, the *kumara* dropped from her hand as if she had been shot," he claimed to his skeptical audience, ". . . and *she* was a gone 'coon in eight-and-forty hours." [14] Maoris, on the other hand, often did not know that they had violated a *tapu* until misfortune came to them. Either way the explanation was the same. Wherever there was misfortune there was also a violation of the code of behavior and vice versa. The explanation was a closed circuit, and a satisfyingly simple one.

The mediums between the gods and ordinary humans were the *tohungas,* or priests. [15] They came in various grades and with different titles. Since they could communicate with the spirit world, it was they who decided what was *tapu* and what rites and ceremonies should be performed in any particular circumstance. The more important *tohungas* could perform acts of witchcraft and *maketu,* or magic. Some could make lightning strike, wither leaves, and kill a man from miles away. Their powers varied with the gods with whom they dealt. The higher *tohungas* were carefully trained, knew a great deal of tribal lore, studied the skies and the weather, and were in fact quite knowledgeable men. The lesser *tohungas* were occasionally only shams. The Maoris willingly accepted the authority of the *tohungas* over sacrifices, rituals, chants, and the other necessary devices for propitiating the gods.

The excessive restraints imposed upon the Maoris by their spirit world found vigorous outlet in other spheres of their activity. [16] In

[14] John Logan Campbell, *Poenamo. Sketches of the Early Days in New Zealand* . . . , "New Zealand" ed. (Wellington, 1953), p. 126. See also nn. 14 and 15, Chapter IV.
[15] Buck, *Coming of the Maori,* pp. 473–76, gives details on the *tohungas.* Also see Best, *The Maori,* I, 243–51.
[16] Keesing, *Changing Maori,* pp. 28–38, served as the basis for this paragraph.

their outward relations the Maoris were usually overpositive and self-assertive. The prominence of *mana,* or prestige, typified this characteristic.[17] Important people had a great deal of *mana;* slaves had virtually none. And since nothing succeeds like success, the more *mana* a Maori had, the easier it was for him to acquire it. The Maoris would cheat, lie, murder, enslave, and torture in order to increase their *mana* at the expense of others. Chiefs had little real control over tribes except in times of war. Feats of bravery, strength, and cunning were the proof, and at the same time the means, of increasing prestige.

The most prosaic social customs, no matter how they started in reality, soon became so imbued with religious connotations that there was something sacred in all of them. The most banal proceedings involved prestige. Maori customs which the missionaries so abhorred were therefore not simply unattractive pagan excrescences which could be removed to "civilize" the rest of Maori life.

War may have begun as a contest for lands or for some other utilitarian purpose. It finally evolved largely into a matter of *mana.*[18] Insults and defeats demanded avenging. Slaves were taken in battle to enhance prestige; the eating of enemies completed their degradation. Since the gods played a major role in explaining any victory or defeat, some of the most elaborate of all the Maori rites and ceremonies took place before and after every battle.

Cannibalism may well have originated from a lack of meat in the Maori diet. Slaves were often killed and eaten for apparently no other reason. But by 1769 cannibalism had also come to have a definite role in Maori religion, and was probably, in fact, practiced more as part of a ritual than for food. In the Taupo district the female half of the population was virtually excluded from eating human flesh.[19] Maori warriors ate the heart and eyes of the first of

[17] Keesing, *Changing Maori,* pp. 28–31. See also Best, *The Maori,* I, 386–90.
[18] See Buck, *Coming of the Maori,* p. 387; Cowan, *Maoris,* p. 247; Elsdon Best, "Notes on the Art of War," *JPS,* XII (1903), 39; as well as nn. 11–16 in Chapter VII.
[19] Best, "Notes on the Art of War," *JPS,* XI (1902), 71; Edward Shortland, *The Southern Districts of New Zealand; A Journal with Passing Notices of the Customs of the Aborigines* (London, 1851), pp. 69–74.

the enemy killed in battle. For one Maori to pick his teeth at another and so imply that he or his ancestors had eaten the ancestor of the other was often enough to start a war.

Slavery was ubiquitous. It was not determined by race or caste. Anyone could be made a slave. Slaves were captured in battle, bought, and sold. The number held was an indication of the wealth and prestige of those who owned them, while, in their enslavement, slaves lost whatever *mana* they had once possessed.[20] They were treated exactly as their masters wished. They could be forced to exhaustion in work or knocked on the head and eaten. Some were traditionally killed on the death of a chief. When desired, the women were taken as wives. If not freed by their master, slaves were doomed. Even if they escaped they were often looked down on by their fellow tribesmen for having lost their *mana*. The few slaves who died natural deaths were scarcely noticed. Their spirits were left to struggle toward the spirit world—which existed beyond the North Cape—as best they could.

Any list or description of Maori customs is in the end deceptive, however, because each element had too many ramifications and involvements to be comprehensibly isolated and defined. Maori behavior was the complement of Maori thought. Together they were both the actuality and the explanation of Maori existence.

[20] Buck, *Coming of the Maori*, pp. 401–402. But see n. 58, Chapter VIII.

Chapter II

Traders and Whalers

There was very little contact of any sort between the white people and the Maoris for almost forty years after Cook's last visit in 1777. Small whaling and extensive sealing trades developed around the South Island after the settlement of Australia in 1788, but it was an area in which there were only a few Maoris. Several explorers went near or to New Zealand, and a few traders stopped by for spars and flax. In 1793, Philip Gidley King, the lieutenant-governor of Norfolk Island—and later governor of New South Wales—briefly visited the North Cape, but did not get to the Bay of Islands, nor did he even land. Some whalers undoubtedly stopped for wood for their fires and for water before 1800, but there was little else to attract them; the pigs and potatoes, which later became important objectives, had been too recently introduced by Westerners to have multipled to any degree. Occasionally white men were stranded along the coasts and presumably lived among the tribes if they were not eaten. With few exceptions, however, they escaped whenever possible.[1]

It is important to discuss in some detail the nature of these early white contacts with the Maoris, and those of later years, not only because of the obvious bearing this had on the relations which ex-

[1] The most readily available sources of information for this period can be found in *HRNZ* and in Robert McNab's books about the early shipping. The most pertinent of these is *From Tasman to Marsden. A History of Northern New Zealand from 1642 to 1818* (Dunedin, 1914). References to individual white men living in New Zealand may be found in this book, pp. 94, 113; and in the letter of S. Marsden, Parramatta, June 23, 1813, Ms vol. 54, no. 9.

isted between the two races, but because of an interesting problem. Some New Zealand and Empire historians have stated that large numbers of lawless whalers and traders were living at the Bay of Islands and destroying the Maori society with their immoral activities by the time the missionaries arrived there in 1814. "So, by the second decade of the century," writes one, "a state of anarchy prevailed at the Bay of Islands, where several hundred white men and thousands of visitors . . . showed the barbarians what civilized man could be and do. Rum, disease, the traffic in girls . . . were at that time destroying the Maoris at an alarming rate." [2] And another writes: "In the north at the Bay of Islands . . . a notorious settlement of escaped convicts, whalers and the world's worst riff-raff debauched both themselves and the neighbouring Maori tribes. . . . It was not until 1816 that organized mission education first offered its guiding hand. . . ." [3] The writers generally go on from such statements to give the missionaries credit for their endeavors to save an already disintegrating Maori society. All this sounds very reasonable, and the only difficulty with it is that no early visitor seems to have left a record of any nonmissionary population at the Bay of Islands before, or even shortly after, 1814.

It is tempting to believe that this is because such a population

[2] I. L. G. Sutherland, "Maori and Pakeha," *New Zealand,* ed. H. Belshaw (Berkeley, 1947), pp. 54–55. See also J. B. Condliffe, *A Short History of New Zealand,* 2nd ed. (Christchurch, 1927), p. 31; Peter H. Buck in preface to Eric Ramsden's *Marsden and the Missions. Prelude to Waitangi* (Sydney, 1936), p. viii; and A. W. Shrimpton and Alan E. Mulgan, *Maori and Pakeha. A History of New Zealand* (Auckland, 1921), p. 29, for examples by New Zealand writers. Examples of the idea in Empire histories may be found in A. P. Newton, *A Hundred Years of the British Empire* (London, 1940), p. 71; Paul Knaplund, *The British Empire, 1815–1939* (New York, 1941), p. 294; and Eric Walker, *The British Empire, its Structure and Spirit, 1497–1953,* 2nd ed. (Cambridge, Mass., 1956), pp. 42–43. Among the exceptions to this interpretation have been the works of W. P. Morrell and, most recently, Keith Sinclair's *A History of New Zealand* (Harmondsworth, Eng., 1959).

[3] D. G. Ball, "Maori Education," *The Maori People Today. A General Survey,* ed. I. L. G. Sutherland (London, 1940), p. 270.

did not exist before 1814 and did not in fact even begin to develop until late in the 1820's. However, if one cannot blame the wicked living of white people for dislocating the Maori population and culture before the missionaries arrived, he must either look elsewhere for explanations of the dislocation, or conclude that it did not take place, or took place not so early. And he must seriously consider the effects of the activities of the missionaries on the Maoris. In any case he must, to begin with, unearth what he can about the character and extent of the nonmissionary white population.

By the turn of the century probably several ships a year stopped at the Bay of Islands for water or other reasons, but no accurate record remains of their names and where they went. In 1805, a doctor from New South Wales named John Savage spent a few weeks in the Bay of Islands and made no mention of a white settlement.[4] There really were not enough ships in the entire South Pacific to visit New Zealand in any numbers. American whalers, for instance, did not work their way around Cape Horn until 1791, and none evidently went so far west as New Zealand until after 1800.[5] Because of the monopoly of the East India Company, unlicensed British whaling in the neighborhood of New Zealand, although it existed, was illegal until after 1798, while trading was technically restricted until the acts of 1813.[6] And just as the numbers of British and American whalers and traders started expanding in the Pacific, the Napoleonic Wars and the War of 1812 brought activities to a halt.

Meanwhile the sporadic contact between the white people and the Maoris in the north of New Zealand had been already temporarily checked for other reasons. In 1809, the *Boyd,* a ship stopping to pick up spars on the way from Sydney to London, was captured by the Maoris of Whangaroa, who massacred almost everybody on board.

[4] John Savage, *Some Account of New Zealand; particularly the Bay of Islands, and Surrounding Country* . . . (London, 1807).

[5] McNab, *Tasman to Marsden,* pp. 97–98, 103.

[6] John M. Ward, *British Policy in the South Pacific, 1786–1893* (Sydney, 1948), pp. 14–30.

For several years afterwards, very few captains went to the harbors of the North Island, in spite of the fact that whaling increased in the nearby waters until shortly after 1812.

The effects of the famous *Boyd* massacre can be seen in the trials of Samuel Marsden, then the senior chaplain in New South Wales. In December 1814, Marsden achieved a long-standing dream by establishing a mission station at the Bay of Islands, but this was the result of years of waiting. Marsden had left England in 1809 with two lay missionaries whom he intended to send right on to New Zealand, but they arrived at Sydney in February 1810, just before the news arrived of the taking of the *Boyd*. The missionaries stayed in Sydney. There was no trade with New Zealand and no way to get them to the Bay of Islands. "I waited more than three years," Marsden wrote, "and no master of a vessel would venture for fear of his ship and crew falling a sacrifice to the natives." [7] Eventually Marsden had to buy his own ship, the brig *Active,* and send it on a trial visit, before he received the governor's permission to go himself and found the mission station.

The first permanent white population in New Zealand was established at the Bay of Islands by Marsden late in 1814. There were, admittedly, a few nonmissionary Europeans already living in New Zealand when the *Active* arrived. But they hardly constituted a "population." Marsden said that during his two months in New Zealand he came across six runaway convicts.[8] John Liddard Nicholas, a young English traveler who went along on the voyage, later said there had been only two Europeans of any sort.[9]

In any case, when the *Active* sailed from the Bay of Islands late in February 1815, it left behind, according to Marsden, twenty-one oddly assorted white people who were all associated in one way or another with the Church Missionary Society.[10] By 1819 the estab-

[7] *The Letters and Journals of Samuel Marsden,* ed. J. R. Elder (Dunedin, 1932), p. 62.

[8] Letter of Samuel Marsden, Parramatta, June 15, 1815, Marsden, *Letters and Journals,* pp. 139–41.

[9] J. L. Nicholas, *PP,* 1837–38, XXI, 5.

[10] Marsden, *Letters and Journals,* p. 140.

lishment had grown, through births and other persons sent over by Marsden, to forty-five. This figure does not include the family of the ex-captain of the *Active,* a Mr. Hanson, who had by that time left the employ of the Missionary Society.[11]

So infrequent was commercial shipping in the early years that Thomas Kendall, the unofficial head of the missionaries, reported only fourteen vessels visiting the Bay of Islands from 1816 to 1819. The captains of these vessels occasionally asked permission to leave with the missionaries escaped convicts who had stowed away in Sydney, but this was not granted. Some undoubtedly did get on shore anyway—whether they remained there or not.[12] In November 1819, Kendall wrote that the European inhabitants of New Zealand consisted of fifty-two people—the mission establishment and the seven Hansons.[13] He mentioned no others. A naval ensign who was in New Zealand for about ten months the following year explicitly stated that the Hansons constituted the only nonmissionary European population "established in New Zealand."[14]

Kororareka was a Maori settlement in the Bay which was later to become the source of much contention as the principal rendezvous of visiting whalers and the whipping boy of missionaries and their supporters. In September 1819, Samuel Marsden, then in New Zealand, visited "King George" (Te Uriti), an important Maori chief at Kororareka. "King George expressed his regret that there were no Europeans to reside with him; he said he wanted a carpenter, a smith, and a clergyman. We promised that he should have a European to live with him as soon as we could spare one."[15] Whalers that visited the Bay of Islands anchored at Kororareka, since it was

[11] Letter of J. T. Bigge to Earl Bathurst, February 27, 1823 (Commissioner Bigge's Report), *HRNZ,* I, 593.

[12] Letter of Thomas Kendall to Bigge, November 8, 1819, *HRNZ,* I, 444; letter of Kendall, January 19, 1816, Ms vol. 55, no. 45; see also *HRNZ,* I, 404, 408–409.

[13] Letter of Kendall to Bigge, November 8, 1819, *HRNZ,* I, 441.

[14] Alexander McCrae, "Evidence Given before Commissioner Bigge . . . May, 1821," *HRNZ,* I, 542.

[15] Marsden, *Letters and Journals,* p. 160. Marsden was at Kororareka for two days.

the most convenient spot, and the number of vessels which did so increased markedly about 1820. But the Bay was still hardly crowded.[16]

Only in 1824 did the first signs of a settlement at Kororareka receive special mention by the missionaries. There had evidently been occasional nonmissionary white men staying on and off there for several years. It was really not so much a settlement, however, as an exchange depot for crews. Henry Williams said that perhaps a hundred sailors in the course of 1824 had deserted their ships and that there were at least twenty living "on the other side of the Bay" at the time he wrote. But "the Captains do not hesitate to employ them immediately upon their wanting men." [17]

The white population at Kororareka apparently fluctuated around one or two dozen for several years. Early in 1827 there were two sudden, though small, increases of population. One was from the ship *Wellington,* which had been taken over by escaped convicts. When it was captured in the Bay of Islands in January 1827 over forty of the prisoners got away. However, all but six were quickly returned by the Maoris.[18] The other increase was occasioned by the appearance at New Zealand, late in 1826, of the ship *Rosanna,* sent out by a colonizing organization, the New Zealand Company, to take settlers to the Hauraki Gulf. The supposed hostility of the Maoris upset the design, and the ship left New Zealand early in 1827 after another unsuccessful attempt, at Hokianga, to discharge its passengers. A few Scotch mechanics were not intimidated, and

[16] Letter of Henry Williams, November 10, 1823, p. 39, typewritten copy of his letters, Hocken Library, Dunedin; letter of Mrs. Henry Williams, October 1, 1824, Ms extracts, 1822–24 (no paging), Alexander Turnbull Library, Wellington; Journal of John Butler, February 10, 1820, *Earliest New Zealand. The Journals and Correspondence of the Rev. John Butler,* comp. R. J. Barton (Masterton, N.Z., 1927), p. 68.

[17] Letter of Williams, December 31, 1824, p. 87, typewritten copy of his letters, Hocken Library.

[18] Journal of Mrs. Henry Williams, January 7, 1827, Hugh Carleton, *The Life of Henry Williams. Archdeacon of Waimate,* ed. and rev. J. Elliott (Wellington, 1948), p. 87; Augustus Earle, *A Narrative of a Nine Months' Residence in New Zealand, in 1827* . . . (London, 1832), pp. 126–30.

some of them settled down at Kororareka and also Hokianga.[19] After the increase of both the Scotchmen and the few convicts from the *Wellington,* Henry Williams later remembered only that "there were from ten to twenty Europeans always residing" at Kororareka in 1827.[20] In July 1827, Williams heard that "there are at least three and twenty runaway men and prisoners on the opposide beach. . . . our fears are far greater with respect to these characters, than of the Natives; tho we must acknowledge we have never received personally any thing but civility from them, as also whenever we go to the shipping. . . ."[21]

Other descriptions at this time are vague, but they do give the impression that the supposed characteristics of Kororareka were still somewhat unformed. For example, Augustus Earle, who was at Kororareka for nine months in 1827, once had occasion to round up "all the white men I could"—in order to destroy a Maori oven which was unfortunately in the process of roasting a little Maori girl. He could collect only six unarmed, if determined, rescuers, for there had been "not a single vessel in the harbour" for a month.[22]

Earle was a professional artist who supported himself by selling drawings of his travels around the world. He published a book about his stay in New Zealand in 1832. Since it contained a number of remarks which suggested certain mental, social, and spiritual inadequacies on the part of the missionaries, it was not particularly well received by those worthy men. It is nevertheless a valuable book. Earle's description of Kororareka in 1827 included a cottage or two, some building by the Scotch mechanics going on, a few beachcombers and convicts, whom the settlers at Kororareka protested

[19] Earle, *Narrative,* pp. 51–52.

[20] Letter of Williams, February 15, 1831, p. 226, typewritten copy of his letters, Hocken Library.

[21] Journal of Williams, July 24, 1827, N.Z. Ms Copybook, 1826–28, pp. 404–405, library of Church Missionary Society, London.

[22] Earle, *Narrative,* pp. 118–20. For other accounts of Kororareka at this time, showing its small size and Maori atmosphere, see Peter Bays, *A Narrative of the Wreck of the Minerva Whaler of Port Jackson* . . . (Cambridge, Eng., 1831), pp. 162–63; and M. J. Dumont D'Urville, *Voyage de la corvette l'Astrolabe* . . . *1826–29* . . . *Histoire du voyage* (Paris, 1830–33), II, 364.

they did not like, occasional jugs of grog being sold—generally a fairly peaceful and industrious little group of people.[23] Since Earle relished the picturesque, it is not likely that his description was toned down very much for public consumption. Kororareka was hardly a "plague spot of contamination" or an "Alsatia of the Pacific," as it has been called, in any case.

By 1827, the white missionary population at the Bay of Islands consisted of twenty adults and forty children. It probably totaled well over sixty by 1830.[24] In contrast to these figures, one missionary said that "in the beginning of 1833 there were, altogether, not more than from twenty to thirty white persons living at the Bay of Islands, exclusive of the Missionaries. About forty persons, supposed to be runaway convicts and sailors, were living at one of the *pas* before the arrival of the British Resident [James Busby]; but, on his coming, they had mostly disappeared. There were then only two or three boarded houses all round the Bay, besides those occupied by the Missionaries."[25] Mr. R. W. Hay, who collected information on New Zealand from the Colonial Office in 1832, said that including the missionaries and their families the white population of the Bay of Islands "must exceed one hundred," a figure which seems not out of line.[26]

So far as it can be determined (to come momentarily to some sort of conclusion), the missionary population at the Bay of Islands was larger than the nonmissionary population until after 1830. Of course, even in the late 1820's there were sometimes more whalers and

---

[23] Earle, *Narrative*, pp. 51–54, for example.

[24] *MR*, March 1828, p. 174, and January 1830, p. 43. Statistics are hard to find. See also the letter of Marsden, April 25, 1826, *Letters and Journals*, p. 445n. Other statistics are in the N.Z. Ms copybooks of 1826–28 and 1828–31, pp. 357, 532, and pp. 228, 236 respectively, library of Church Missionary Society, London.

[25] William R. Wade, *A Journey in the Northern Island of New Zealand: Interspersed with Various Information Relative to the Country and People* (Hobart Town, 1842), p. 182.

[26] R. W. Hay, "Notices of New Zealand. From Original Documents in the Colonial Office," *The Journal of the Royal Geographical Society of London*, II (1831–32), 135.

traders than missionaries in the Bay at one time, but these were the crews of ships which soon departed. The permanent nonmissionary population of the Bay (and this does not mean that any particular individuals stayed there permanently) began to overtake that of the missionary group only as the 1830's progressed.

The increase of the nonmissionary population in the 1820's and after was caused, to a great extent, by the growth of commercial interests. New Zealand had several natural products which brought ships to its coasts in numbers—particularly after the unexpected, continued existence of the missionaries had shown that the Maoris were not always so ferocious as they appeared.

The kauri tree, a tree of great height which grew almost exclusively in the North Auckland peninsula, provided traders with both gum and timber. Americans bought the gum, for the most part, and used it in making varnish.[27] British authorities expected the timber to be a valuable source of spars, important to the survival of the Royal Navy. In 1820, an ex-frigate, the storeship *Dromedary,* visited New Zealand on its way home from Australia with orders from the British government to gather kauri spars. The ship spent ten months in New Zealand with a success that was hardly noticeable, but the voyage did produce an interesting by-product. This was a book published by Major Richard Cruise in 1823, as comprehensive, accurate, and unbiased as anything written about New Zealand in the period.[28] In general kauri timber proved hard to get, no matter how attractive it looked while standing. Although the Maoris were willing to work long hours, they could not easily cut down trees one or two hundred feet long, drag them over rough country to the rivers, and float them down to European ships.

[27] Charles Darwin, "Journal and Remarks," in Captain Robert FitzRoy and others, *Narrative of the Surveying Voyages of His Majesty's Ships Adventure and Beagle . . . 1826–1836* (London, 1839), III, 510; Abel Du Petit-Thouars, *Voyage autour du monde sur la frégate la Vénus . . .* (Paris, 1839–41), III, 123.

[28] Richard A. Cruise, *Journal of a Ten Months' Residence in New Zealand,* 2nd ed. (London, 1824); see also Alexander McCrae, *Journal Kept in New Zealand in 1820 . . . ,* ed. Sir F. R. Chapman (Wellington, 1928). McCrae was on the same ship as Cruise.

A much more promising product was flax. The New Zealand variety, an indigenous plant, was used by the Maoris in making such things as mats, baskets, and fish nets. From the time of Cook, explorers and financiers assumed it would be the basis of New Zealand's economy. In fact, flax appeared for a while to be the solution to the rope problem of the Royal Navy. In 1831 the Navy contracted for eight hundred tons of it at £41.15s per ton, which was then sent to the ropemaster at Portsmouth. The resulting product, though tougher and stronger than rope made from European hemps, was brittle and swelled unusually in wet weather. A series of conflicting reports came in from the captains of vessels who were trying it out. Of those who were dissatisfied, some blamed the process of manufacture, others blamed the fibre itself. In any case, the contract was not renewed.[29] The peak year for New Zealand flax was 1831. The number of tons leaving Sydney for London jumped from 60 in 1828, to 841 in 1830, and 1062 in 1831. In 1832 it fell below 750 and declined steadily thereafter.[30]

While the flax and kauri trades helped increase the nonmissionary population in New Zealand generally, they did so to only a limited extent in the Bay of Islands, because the Bay of Islands was not a practicable depot for natural products. Surrounded by hills and placed in an awkward corner of New Zealand, it would have been absurd to try to collect things there from the interior by land, and cargoes once in ships were more sensibly sent direct to Sydney or to London. One New Zealand merchant said that a ton of flax

[29] Charles Terry, *New Zealand, its Advantages and Prospects, as a British Colony* . . . (London, 1842), pp. 239–41; G. B. Earp, *PP,* 1844, XIII, 92–95. A summary of the Admiralty reports is in *PP,* 1837–38, XXI, 157–59; see also C. Enderby, *PP,* 1837–38, pp. 71ff.

[30] For statistics see *MR,* January 1833, pp. 62–63; William Breton, *Excursions in New South Wales, Western Australia, and Van Dieman's Land* . . . *(1830– 33),* 2nd ed. (London, 1834), p. 287; Joel S. Polack, *Manners and Customs of the New Zealanders* . . . (London, 1840), II, 296. For flax decline see Wade, *Journey,* p. 62; Joel S. Polack, *New Zealand: Being a Narrative of Travels and Adventures* . . . , new ed. (London, 1839), II, 287ff. For general trade see James Busby, *Authentic Information Relative to New South Wales and New Zealand* (London, 1832), p. 59.

cost more at the Bay of Islands than it did at Sydney.[31] European flax and timber traders visited the Maoris at dozens of places along the northern coasts—such as the Hokianga River and the Hauraki Gulf—and the principal source of the population increase at the Bay of Islands must therefore be found elsewhere than in those trades.

The fact is that the particular attractions of the Bay of Islands pertained more to whalers than to traders. Almost inaccessible by land, the Bay was most convenient by sea, and an ideal port. The hills which blocked it off from the interior served to protect the ships which sailed into the long finger-like projections formed by several small rivers which ran into the sea. Rich whaling grounds were nearby. The popularity of the Bay of Islands as a whaling port only waited on sufficient refreshment for whalers, receptive inhabitants, and a supply of whaling ships in the vicinity. Refreshments had increased in variety and attractiveness as the potato, the pig, and other Western foods became common around the Bay after 1800. The attitude of the Maoris became more friendly as the whalers adjusted their articles of trade to the Maori demand.

The whaling ships themselves finally came from two sources. The Pacific sperm whaling industry grew with astonishing rapidity after the peace treaties were signed in 1814 and 1815, and the number of the deep-sea whalers at the Bay of Islands increased steadily. Another type of whaler arrived shortly after 1829 in the form of right, or "black," whalers, whose technique was to frequent the bays and river mouths of the South Island waiting for the right whales to enter in order to calve.[32] Unlike deep-sea whalers, the bay whalers stayed around the New Zealand coasts constantly, and some visited the Bay of Islands several times in the course of a year, in spite of settlements which also sprang up at Otago, Akaroa, Cloudy Bay, and other spots on the South Island. The demand for cheap oil and the desire for whalebone frameworks to keep the female torso rigidly in place and to form the skeletons of trunks, umbrellas, fish-

[31] Polack, *Manners and Customs,* I, 185.
[32] See Robert McNab, *The Old Whaling Days. A History of Southern New Zealand from 1830 to 1840* (Christchurch, 1913), pp. 83ff.

ing rods, and other manufactured goods precipitated the large-scale search for the right whale at this time.

In 1833, 89 ships visited the Bay of Islands—or, rather, 68 ships made a total of 89 visits. In 1834 there were 91 visits. By 1835 the figure had jumped to 103; and the next year it was 151. The proportion of whalers, and of American sperm whalers in particular, rapidly increased.[33]

As vessels arrived in growing numbers a permanent white population settled down to cater to them. When the traveler Edward Markham visited Kororareka in 1834, he described it this way: "I took up my quarters and surveyed Kororadica, Hell as the Missionaries call it. It certainly is a loose place when the ships are in Harbour. Some Sundays 300 Men, from Thirty Whalers, have been on Shore, with their ladies, and Many a Row takes place." [34] Markham, it might be added at this point, was a trader who spent nine months in New Zealand and wrote a short journal of his stay. As he strolled about the countryside gossiping on this and that with droll humor, he gathered an invaluable collection of facts and opinions—much of it evidently unprintable in New Zealand, because his fascinating manuscript has not yet been published.

Markham described Kororareka near the height of its very unstable population cycle. What the population was in off seasons—midwinter—is a matter of speculation. Usually over two thirds of the vessels that visited the Bay of Islands in the course of a year

[33] A. J. Harrop, *England and New Zealand* (London, 1926), p. 107, is the best printed source for these figures. More detail on American vessels, for later years only, is in *HRNZ*, II, 606–22, extracted from the National Archives, Washington, D.C.; John B. Williams, American consul at the Bay of Islands, 1842–1845, has left two interesting, if inaccurate, Ms accounts of New Zealand commerce. One is a purported description of shipping at the Bay of Islands from 1809, pp. 6–8 of the "Journal of John B. Williams in New Zealand, 1842–4," Peabody Museum, Salem, Mass. The other is a list of British imports of whalebone, sperm oil, black oil, and sealskins collected around New Zealand from 1828 to 1842. This can be found in the U.S. Consular Records, Bay of Islands, January 1, 1844, National Archives.

[34] Edward Markham, "Transcript of New Zealand or Recollections of it," Ms vol. 85, p. 94, Hocken Library.

did so between January and April. The ships provided a great addition to the permanent, or land-based, population. From May until December only a few ships stopped by a month.

The mid-1830's were the years when Kororareka probably lived up to its modern reputation. The pious whaler from New England, Knights, cried in outraged dignity against the "bare-faced villains" who lived among the Maori tribes selling rum to the whaling crews: "to give this beverage more stimulus they infuse into it a goodly portion of tobacco. When their victims get well crazed they persuade them to desert their vessel, & assist them to get their effects privately on shore; having thus far succeeded they keep them, untill they have eaten & drank what they consider the value of their clothes; then get them shipped, if possible, on board some other vessel. . . ." [35]

The number of escaped convicts, beachcombers, and other socially disreputable types was at its peak at this time. "There are many spirit-shops," wrote the ubiquitous Charles Darwin, who turned up at Kororareka on the *Beagle* late in 1835; "and the whole population is addicted to drunkenness and all kinds of vice." [36] The unknown author of the journal of the *Mermaid,* which visited the Bay in January 1837, reported: "Anchored at the lower anchorage off the native town called Corradiky, a filthy looking miserable place the residence also of several white people, whose principle occupation is to furnish Rum and Tobacco to the crews of the Whalers and other ships that visit here—The more respectable part of the white residents, reside apart from this place in various parts of the Bay." [37] Samuel Marsden was more explicit: "Here drunkenness, adultery, murder, etc., are committed. . . . Satan maintains his dominion without molestation." [38]

[35] "Journal of Brig 'Spy' of Salem. John B. Knights, Master," March–April 1833, Peabody Museum, Salem.

[36] Darwin, "Journal," in FitzRoy, *Narrative,* III, 500.

[37] "Journal of a voyage from Salem to New Zealand . . . in the Brig Mermaid. J. H. Eagleston, Master. October 1836–April 1839," entry for January 21, 1837, Essex Institute, Salem.

[38] Letter of Marsden, N.Z., March 27, 1837, *Letters and Journals,* p. 523; other brief Ms accounts of the Bay of Islands at this time may be found in the journal of the ship *Emerald,* by George N. Cheever, entry for April 21,

While the population of Kororareka multiplied after 1835, however, it was by no means the only nonmissionary settlement in the
Bay, as the remarks in the journal of the *Mermaid* suggest. Darwin
gathered that, "In the vicinity of the Bay of Islands, the number of
Englishmen, including their families, amounts to between two and
three hundred." [39] Kororareka he described as "the largest village."
Captain FitzRoy mentioned Kororareka, saying: "I think that it
was generally spoken of as the Principal [town]; but . . . it was a
mere Village. . . . The English Settlers are scattered round the Bay
at a good Distance from Kororarika. . . . The only Persons who live
there are Natives, and a few Shopkeepers who sell Spirits, and do
much Harm." [40] Other common meeting points of sailors were in
the *pas* of the chiefs, Pomare and Titore. From Samuel Marsden's
description in 1837, one could get the impression that more white
people lived in these places than at Kororareka.[41] There were also
five or ten traders and their families, such as the Clendons (he was
later the first American consul), scattered on different peninsulas
about the Bay.[42]

While the nonmissionary population of the Bay of Islands was,
in short, growing steadily during the 1830's, its size should not be
overestimated. This is especially important in respect to Kororareka.
The excessive behavior of the excessive numbers of sailors during
the seasons of their visits made it seem as though the permanent
population was bigger and more lawless than it actually was.
Kororareka did have the most convenient anchorage and was perhaps the best site for a village in the Bay. When the great influx of
settlers began, in 1839, most of the new people settled there. The
new settlers were a relatively respectable crowd, and while they
raised the land-based population to several hundreds at last, they

---

1835, and in Captain Eagleston's journal of the *Emerald* (bound with his
journal of the *Peru, 1830–33*), both in the Essex Institute, Salem.
[39] Darwin, "Journal," in FitzRoy, *Narrative,* III, 497.
[40] R. FitzRoy, *PP,* 1837–38, XXI, 164.
[41] May 6, 1837, *CMR,* April 1838, p. 118. B. Y. Ashwell, December 27, 1836,
CMR, March 1838, p. 84.
[42] FitzRoy, *Narrative,* II, 582.

also overwhelmed much of whatever lawlessness and crime existed. By early 1840, Kororareka was a relatively quiet seaport town and the Bay of Islands fairly filled with settlers.

The other places in the North Island where white people settled before 1840 can be discussed rapidly. The most important was the Hokianga River, across the peninsula from the Bay of Islands. This was really a poor harbor. Like most of the rivers on the west coast its mouth was swept by the sea, and the entrance was blocked by a shallow sand bar. The explorers did not investigate it. Probably no white man visited Hokianga until 1819, when Thomas Kendall and John King walked over to it from the Bay of Islands. Evidently the first ship to enter the harbor was a schooner, the *Prince Regent,* which successfully negotiated the bar in April 1820.[43] Hokianga, however, had an excellent supply of kauri trees and friendly Maoris. Once discovered, its settlement by enterprising Europeans was almost inevitable. And while the number of ships which risked visiting the river was always small, and there were many shipwrecks, the requirements of timber-cutting made the white population there more permanent than that of the whalers and traders at the Bay of Islands.

Earle wrote that a number of the Scotch mechanics of the Herd (*Rosanna*) expedition were at Hokianga in 1827.[44] Although possibly the first white people to settle there, they were joined almost immediately by others: sawyers, shipwrights, and missionaries.[45] R. W. Hay, in 1832, said: "The Wesleyan Mission resides here, about twenty miles from the mouth. A mile higher up is the settlement, for ship-building and other purposes, established originally by Messrs. Browne and Baine, now occupied by Mr. MacDowell. It still gives employment to about twenty mechanics, but the dockyard is abandoned. Total Europeans about fifty-two."[46] According

[43] Marsden, *Letters and Journals*, pp. 181; Cruise, *Journal*, pp. 85–86.

[44] Earle, *Narrative*, p. 27.

[45] Peter Dillon, *Narrative and Successful Result of a Voyage in the South Seas . . . to Ascertain the Actual Fate of La Pérouse's Expedition . . .* (London, 1829), I, 195.

[46] Hay, "Notices," *JRGSL*, II (1831–32), 136.

to James Busby and Edward Markham, the population grew to sixty or seventy by 1834.[47] The Europeans were scattered along the river banks where the kauri trees grew most abundantly. There were about one hundred white settlers, including the missionaries, in 1836.[48] "Several of the settlers are married to European females, who, without exception, have set an example to the native women . . . ," wrote one observer.[49] In 1837, Baron Charles de Thierry, an Anglo-French adventurer with traces of Belgian education, arrived at Hokianga with over fifty colonists whom he hoped to plant on a vast tract of land he said he had bought from two Maoris in England seventeen years before. While Thierry's claim was not exactly enthusiastically received by the local settlers, as one might expect, most of his party remained in the vicinity.[50] By 1840 there were at least two hundred Europeans settled along the shores of the Hokianga River.[51] It was the high point of white settlement in the area. As the cheap Maori labor disappeared and the kauri trees became harder to find, the river was eventually almost deserted by its white population.

After 1830 white men came to other parts of the North Island besides Hokianga and the Bay of Islands and settled in little groups along the coast, wherever there was timber to cut out or Maoris to trade with for flax and refreshments. Henry Williams first remarked on the appearance of these people in 1833, and said that

[47] Letter of James Busby to the Colonial Secretary, June 17, 1833, Ms correspondence, Alexander Turnbull Library; Markham, Ms vol. 85, p. 76, Hocken Library.

[48] Polack, *New Zealand*, I, 267; John Walton, *Twelve Months' Residence in New Zealand . . . 1837–8* (Glasgow, 1839), p. 18, gives figure for c. 1837–38.

[49] Polack, *New Zealand*, I, 267.

[50] J. D. Tawell, *PP*, 1837–38, XXI, 109–10.

[51] Ernest Dieffenbach, *Travels in New Zealand; with Contributions to the Geography, Geology, Botany, and Natural History of that Country* (London, 1843), I, 241; William Woon, October 23, 1838, *Report of the Wesleyan-Methodist Missionary Society*, 1839, p. 37. Du Petit-Thouars, *Voyage*, III, 155, gives a slightly higher figure for 1837–38, but his figures are not always accurate.

they had been arriving within the past few years.[52] There is little other record of white settlements made before that date, though several escaped convicts were supposedly at Kawhia in 1830, and bay whalers had already begun to live in the Cook's Straits area. (Port Nicholson, where Wellington is now situated, was however one of the spots rarely visited. There was little flax there, and evidently not sufficient tidal current to sweep the right whales into the harbor mouth.) Hay said in 1832 that there were thirty white men, mostly "idlers," on Kapiti Island—the home of Te Rauparaha, a famous chief—and perhaps eight or ten others in Taranaki.[53]

The number of white settlements soon began to expand. Joel Polack said that while in 1833 there had been hardly any white men at Mangakahia or Whangaroa, in 1837 "scarcely a river flows on either coast of the Northern Island whose banks are not possessed, in part, by our countrymen. . . ." [54] There were apparently eighteen whalers living at Tauranga in 1838. About a dozen Europeans, mostly sawyers, were found at Whangaroa around 1840. There was another dozen at Otawao, and perhaps forty individuals at the Kaipara estuary.[55]

There were very few white people, however, inland. Except for several missionaries, the only ones before 1840 were the "pakeha" Maoris, those independent individuals who went native and lived among the Maori tribes interpreting and helping in the contacts with other whites. The most famous of these was F. E. Maning, who came to Hokianga in 1833, and many years later wrote *Old New Zealand,* one of the best two or three books ever written about the country. Maning was *the* personification of the "pakeha" Maori.

[52] Letter of Williams, April 16, 1833, p. 270, typewritten copy of his letters, Hocken Library.

[53] Hay, "Notices," *JRGSL,* II (1831–32), 135; J. B. Montefiore, *PP,* 1837–38, XXI, 57. Information in parentheses is in Charles Heaphy, "Notes on Port Nicholson and the Natives in 1839," *TPNZI,* XII (1879), 32–33.

[54] Polack, *New Zealand,* II, 200–201.

[55] Markham, Ms vol. 85, p. 31, Hocken Library; Journal of William Williams, January 26, 1838, Ms in Alexander Turnbull Library; Dieffenbach, *Travels,* I, 237, 268, 318.

He married a Maori girl and became a favorite of the Maori tribes. ("He turned out a double-faced sneaking thief," wrote Markham, who was, however, no saint himself; ". . . Manning would have done Honor to the back Woods in America." [56]) The "pakeha" Maoris had their greatest importance during the 1830's—after the Maoris had seen the need for trade and before full-scale settlement made such agents unnecessary.

White visitors and missionaries made frequent and often wild guesses about the total white population in New Zealand. Several of the witnesses heard by the Select Committee of the House of Lords on New Zealand in 1838 estimated that there were about five hundred whites, of all types, in the North Island.[57] Most of their information was, by and large, a year or two old. George Clarke, in New Zealand in 1838, said: "The Whites in New Zealand for the most part consist of respectable industrious and useful settlers. . . . There are doubtless many prisoners of the Crown as there are some desparate characters of the Island the total number which has come under our view as computed in our letter March 1/38 about 1000." [58]

Although the missionaries did not approve of white people settling in New Zealand and disrupting their work, as occupation by Britain became imminent, white immigration could not be stopped. Early in 1839, Henry Williams made a detailed count of the white settlers in New Zealand:

Of the number of White Persons residing on the Northern Island, it is difficult to determine; but I should think there are not fewer than 1100—men, women, and children; not to mention those children born of Native Women to European Fathers. In this number I do not include any of the Mission Families. Those of the Church Missionary

[56] Markham, Ms vol. 85, p. 12, Hocken Library.

[57] J. Flatt (pp. 51–52), D. Coates (p. 264), J. Watkins (p. 14), *PP*, 1837–38, XXI.

[58] Letter of George Clarke, November 16, 1838, p. 380, typewritten copy of Henry Williams' letters, Hocken Library; see also his letter of March 1, 1838, p. 357. Two other general guesses on the white population in N.Z. are: Saxe Bannister, "On the Poulation of New Zealand," *Journal of the Statistical Society of London,* I (1839), 362–76; Du Petit-Thouars, *Voyage,* III, 93–95.

Society are, at this date, including Mr. Taylor and Mr. Hadfield, 169. Those of the Wesleyans, 37. Of the 1100 Whites, there are a few French, probably 20. Of Americans, say 50. The remainder are British Subjects. Of those not connected with the Mission there are, I believe, 26 families in the Bay of Islands, as traders. At Hokianga there are about 18 families; and at Wangaroa about 6 families, who may be regarded as fair-traders. The number of seamen running away from the shipping fluctuates. The grog-sellers in the Bay of Islands number about 50. The whole White Population is free from any constraint of the law. . . .[59]

As far as it can be determined, this is a fair estimate of the white population of New Zealand about 1839. Large numbers of white people did not settle in New Zealand until after 1830. Only then did the nonmissionary population at the Bay of Islands begin to overtake that of the missionaries and take on its traditional characteristics. After 1830, Europeans settled at other harbors and river mouths besides Hokianga and the Bay of Islands. Small groups might have been found anywhere along the coast. It was not, however, until just before the official acquisition of New Zealand that the white population jumped quickly to the thousand or fifteen hundred which it had at the time of the Treaty of Waitangi.

[59] Letter of Williams, January 11, 1839, *CMR,* December 1839, p. 288.

Chapter III

The Missionaries

Three bodies of missionaries worked in New Zealand before 1840. The first, always largest, and by far the most important was the Church Missionary Society. Organized by Evangelicals of the Church of England, it sponsored the original settlement at the Bay of Islands in 1814-15 under the supervision of Samuel Marsden. The second was the Wesleyan-Methodist Missionary Society, which had missionaries laboring at Whangaroa and then Hokianga after 1822; while the third consisted of a number of Roman Catholic missionaries, the first of whom arrived in 1838. The personalities and activities of the different missionaries and the disputes which arose among them and among the missionary bodies as each group competed with the others added to the confusion of the relations which existed between the Maori and European societies.

When Samuel Marsden left England for Australia in 1809, with his two prospective New Zealand missionaries, he also took with him the enthusiastic good wishes of a great many Englishmen, who expected that the next few years would witness a glorious transformation in New Zealand. There existed a growing feeling of confidence in England that Christianity could soften the most barbaric heathen customs, and the Maoris, who were particularly known as cannibals and for their ability to preserve human heads, seemed to be most appropriate subjects for conversion. While they were storybook savages, they did not, as did the Bushmen of South Africa and the aborigines of Australia, seem totally unadaptable to Western ways. They looked almost Caucasian, were obviously intelligent, and on the whole appeared quite capable of being quickly civilized. The well-wishers in England assumed that the Maoris would—as soon as the missionaries made them aware of the Word of God—reject their heathen pasts and turn in concert to Christian values and the Christian creed.

In the light of this expectation the early years of the mission in New Zealand were singularly disappointing. The five years it took to establish a mission station on the New Zealand coast were extended to over fifteen before there were any converts. In the meantime the mission seemed to fall apart, to become demoralized itself, rather than to purify the Maoris. Some of the missionaries engaged in musket trade, which was forbidden, while the immoral behavior of the two most responsible men was, to contemporaries, almost more in keeping with the savage character of the Maoris than with that of devoted English servants of the Lord. Throughout the entire time the missionaries argued among themselves and with Samuel Marsden in Australia.

Any account of the individual missionaries and their activities should begin with Marsden. He was the major personality of the early period of New Zealand history. And he was such a strong character that he achieved this distinction without ever having lived there. He made seven trips to New Zealand in all, the first being the one in 1814-15 and the last in 1837, when he was seventy-two years old. In 1820 Marsden was in New Zealand for over nine months; another time it was for only six days. Between his visits he kept authority over proceedings at the Bay of Islands by writing a voluminous correspondence.

Marsden was a short, heavy, imposing, humorless man, and, as one might expect, not a very amiable one. Vindictive, contradictory, stubborn, vain, often intolerant—he was all of these; and yet there was something so magnificent about him that one cannot possibly dislike him. His tremendous walks at an advanced age through untouched sections of New Zealand, his fearless behavior with the Maoris, his indifference to the sea—although he always got seasick and could not swim—his strength of will, his faith in his visions, and his conviction of his own infallibility, these were striking aspects of his remarkable personality.

Marsden was one of those people who can always support their positions with incontrovertible arguments. He was always right. This was one of his less endearing characteristics. If he wished to justify the establishment of the mission, he would write: "From my first knowledge of these people [the Maoris], I have always considered them the finest and noblest race of heathens known to the civilized world. . . ." [1] If he wanted to compare the present condition of the Maoris with what he assumed a little Christianity could make them, he would say, "I knew that they were cannibals—that they were a savage race, full of superstition, and wholly under the power and influence of the Prince of Darkness. . . ." [2] Marsden never was bothered by, nor admitted to, any inconsistency. Beneath his verbiage, however, he felt that the Maoris should be civilized before attempts were made to convert them, and to that end the whole paraphernalia of his mission was geared to bring them into the British (i.e., "civilized") way of life. In England in 1809, finding no clergyman willing to live in New Zealand, Marsden was happy to secure the services of a carpenter, a shoemaker, and a schoolmaster.

The schoolmaster was Thomas Kendall, an intriguing character and something of an enigma. He was recommended in 1809, arrived in Australia in 1813, and was given chief authority over the station in New Zealand in 1815, although neither of the other missionaries paid much attention to that fact. Kendall was interested in the Maori language, and without his efforts to write it down it could not have been retained in its relatively pure state. He was intelligent and sensitive. But eventually he became so absorbed with the Maoris that he began to live more with them than with his family; and when the interests of the Missionary Society and the Maoris differed, he tended to take the side of the Maoris. In 1823 Marsden dismissed Kendall from the New Zealand mission because his relations with a Maori girl had become a little too ardent. For a few years afterwards, however, the Kendall family lived on in the Bay of Islands.

[1] *The Letters and Journals of Samuel Marsden,* ed. J. R. Elder (Dunedin, 1932), p. 79.
[2] Marsden, *Letters and Journals,* p. 60.

William Hall, the carpenter, and John King, the shoemaker, were much less complicated people. Hall spent a good deal of his time complaining that he was being mistreated and that everyone else was mismanaging things. King, on the other hand, was a solid and unspectacular individual, earnest and plain. These two men, with Kendall, lived from 1815 to 1819 at Rangihoua, in the Bay of Islands.

In 1819 several other missionaries joined them. A new station, Kerikeri, was founded on one of the rivers, immediately under the protection of the famous and powerful chief, Hongi. Reverend John Butler, a new leader superseding Kendall, settled there. He was the first of the New Zealand missionaries also to be an ordained minister, but he was a curiously ineffective man and was resented by the others. Eventually he took to drink.

It is difficult to imagine a more depressing life than that spent by these four men in the years before 1823. Living with their families as far apart from each other as they could get, constantly insulting one another and complaining to Marsden—whom they did not like —bickering, badgering, accomplishing little: it must have seemed a futile existence indeed. "If I were but an hour in your company I would tell you absolute facts respecting the conduct of Mr. Kendall that would make your hair lift up your hat . . . ," wrote the not very gracious William Hall to his superiors in London. "Mr. Stockwell that convict that Mr. Kendall brought to N. Zealand with him was cohabiting with Mrs. Kendall, well known to all the Settlement except Mr. Kendall, self, and she actually brought forth a Son by Stockwell nothing like any other part of Mr. Kendall's family. . . . And since he [Kendall] came home from England he took a native girl into his house and sleeps with her in preference to his own wife, publicly known to both settlements. . . ."[3]

In 1823 Marsden dismissed Butler for drunkenness at the same time that he removed Kendall. While the musket trade was over-

---

[3] Letter of Hall, April 6, 1822, Ms vol. 67, no. 10. For other examples of friction see the correspondence in *Marsden's Lieutenants,* ed. J. R. Elder (Dunedin, 1934), pp. 119ff.; and *Earliest New Zealand. The Journals and Correspondence of the Rev. John Butler,* comp. R. J. Barton (Masterton, N.Z., 1927), entry for January 23, 1820, pp. 66ff.

looked in the handing out of judgments which took place, the appointment of Henry Williams to the head of the mission marked its end. Williams was a strong-willed man and ruled the missionaries honestly and soberly until long past 1840.

Williams gathered about him a corps of devoted and zealous men, among them his brother William Williams, who arrived in New Zealand in 1825, just out of Oxford and interested in medicine and the Maori language. Henry was the older, and had served for a number of years in the Royal Navy before turning to the ministry. He disagreed vigorously with Marsden's Maori policy, believing the Maoris should be taught the spiritual aspects of Christianity immediately, whether they were "civilized" or not. Although the two men argued, they managed to compromise their differences. As the years passed the mission policy gradually swung over to that of Williams, who was actually on the spot.[4]

Among the other men of the Church Missionary Society in New Zealand were three who are especially important because of the written material they left behind: James Kemp, George Clarke, and Richard Davis. Kemp came to New Zealand with Butler in 1819. A very pious individual, he stayed out of the ensuing social unpleasantries as best he could, and became storekeeper and schoolmaster. Clarke came to New Zealand in 1824. Though apprenticed to a gunsmith in England, he became in New Zealand, like Kemp, a teacher. His curiosity about the Maoris resulted in some excellent comments on Maori habits and behavior. In 1841, the first British governor, William Hobson, appointed Clarke "Protector of the Aborigines." Richard Davis came as an agriculturist. After 1830, when he began to farm inland at Waimate, he made valuable—if incidental—contributions to the information about the Maoris.

It would be too much to expect that among the eager and loyal missionaries in the years after 1823 there would be no failures. Such a one was William Yate. Yate arrived in New Zealand in 1828 and for a time was undeniably popular. He published a book in London

---

[4] Letter of Henry Williams, May 13, 1826, pp. 136–47, typewritten copy of his letters, Hocken Library, Dunedin; also later letters, as September 8, 1831, p. 240; and Marsden, *Letters and Journals,* pp. 130, 167.

in 1835, *An Account of New Zealand,* a most useful volume, and the only one published by a missionary before 1840. But in 1836 Yate was accused of immorality with the converted native boys and removed from his post.[5] After the scandal had broken the other missionaries forthrightly demonstrated their displeasure by (1) keeping a day of fast and penance to " 'avert the wrath of an offended God' "; (2) burning Yate's property; (3) renaming the place where he had worked the "Vale of Achan"; and (4) shooting his perfectly respectable horse.[6] "It need not now be withheld," wrote the Reverend William Wade, "that his book is looked upon here as a string of lies from beginning to end." [7]

The first baptism of a Maori in New Zealand took place near Paihia in 1825; the second did not follow until three years later. Only late in the 1820's did the missionaries find large numbers of Maoris even amenable to Christian instruction. At that point the entire missionary enterprise began to blossom.[8] It was a definite turning point.

In 1830 a mission station was established inland at Waimate. The three in the Bay of Islands, each of which had been in turn the missionary center, were no longer adequate. Rangihoua (1814), the original post, was quickly losing its Maoris through migration and disease; Kerikeri (1819) had ceased to have special significance with the death of Hongi in 1828; while Paihia (1823), the most important center, had as many missionaries as it could profitably employ. The

[5] While the charge was never proved, and Yate had some powerful supporters, it was undoubtedly sensible that he was removed. The case is discussed in detail in Eric Ramsden, *Marsden and the Missions. Prelude to Waitangi* (Sydney, 1936), pp. 20–44. Also see various letters of Marsden, *Letters and Journals,* pp. 518–19, 531, 534–35.

[6] Ramsden, *Marsden and the Missions,* p. 36.

[7] Letter of Wade, Waimate, September 28, 1836, Ms vol. 53, no. 25.

[8] William Williams, *Christianity Among the New Zealanders* (London, 1867), pp. 63, 100, 149, tells of first conversions. See also Journal of William Yate, April 6, 1828, N.Z. Ms Copybook, 1828–31, p. 260, library of Church Missionary Society, London. Though weak on statistics, the *MR* (1813——) and the *CMR* (1830——) give the general information on which most of the following account is based.

new station was on the trail to Hokianga, about twelve miles from Kerikeri. Good soil in the area was the main reason for its choice, once the increasing receptivity of the Maoris had permitted an inland location. The missionaries needed food and could not consistently grow crops down on the coast.

In 1830, also, the first adult Maoris "in full health and in the pride of life" were baptized.[9] And as 1831 and 1832 went by new missionaries—ministers, catechists, and general laborers—arrived. The Maoris around the Bay, even some of those who were not Christian, began to live with softened native traits. In 1833 over ninety Maoris were baptized at Waimate, which soon became the center of conversions.[10]

By 1833 there was enough success at the Bay of Islands, sufficient support in England, and the requisite number of missionaries to found new stations to the south. Some of the southern and interior Maoris had in fact already begun to ask for missionaries to be sent among them. At first a trial station was established at Kaitaia, which is in the northernmost part of the North Auckland peninsula. In October 1833, a group of missionaries left the Bay to settle as far up the Thames River as possible. They finally decided on and founded the Puriri station, in the middle of the Thames-Waikato district.

During the next year the missionaries explored the interior for other sites. The Maoris seemed almost universally anxious to have them. In 1835, four new stations were begun. There was Mangapouri, near the center of the Waikato district; Matamata, far up the valley of the Thames; Tauranga, on the coast of the Bay of Plenty; and Ohinemutu, in the midst of Te Arawa tribes at Rotorua.

In 1834-35, the missionaries brought a printing press to New Zealand and began to translate, print, bind, and distribute sections of the New Testament and the Book of Common Prayer. By 1835 the various mission schools had taught about eight hundred Maoris to read, were teaching four hundred more, and had care of two hundred and fifty children under eight years of age. There were then

[9] Letter of Mrs. Henry Williams, February 16, 1830, copied Ms extracts, Alexander Turnbull Library, Wellington.

[10] Report of George Clarke, Ms vol. 60, no. 98, Hocken Library.

nine mission stations, seven ministers, twenty catechists, a printer, and many unofficial female and native helpers. Over 1000 Maoris made a regular practice of worship.[11] In short, by 1835 missionary well-wishers in England could rest content with the progress that was being made, for the spread of the gospel was proceeding with uninterrupted success until, on Christmas Day, in 1835, a relative of the great chief Te Waharoa was murdered by a chief of Rotorua.[12]

A Maori war resulted in the middle of the southern mission area. The mission posts were raided, and the missionaries for a time were overwhelmed. They struggled to reach each other across the tangled swamps and hills of the interior; witnessed sights of cannibalism— saw baskets of human arms and legs and heads, which were jeeringly thrust before their eyes and carried off triumphantly to feasts. They tried to send their wives to safety and dispatch brief messages to home. While all of them escaped uninjured, the posts at Matamata, Tauranga, and Ohinemutu had to be abandoned to the war; and since the Mangapouri Maoris had migrated north, that post was also dropped. By the end of 1836 the church was no further ahead than it had been in 1834.

Eventually the war ran itself out and the missionaries spread again with even more success. By 1838 Tauranga and Rotorua had been resettled. Puriri was abandoned permanently, but two other stations near it were begun where there were more Maoris. Two mission posts founded on the East Cape were actually the result of the efforts of some Maoris who had independently begun to teach reading and the Scriptures among their tribes. And the pleas of other Maoris led to the establishment of two further stations in the southern part of the North Island, opposite the island of Kapiti, in 1839. Still another station was opened by an Englishman and a Christian native at Opotiki, across the island on the western shore of the Bay of Plenty.

In May 1838, the Church Missionary Society reported there were 178 Maori communicants, 1431 Maoris in school, and 2176 in church

[11] *MR*, March 1836, p. 157, based on information given by Yate.
[12] Letter of John Morgan, January 9, 1836, *MR*, October 1836, p. 487, tells of the murder. See also *MR*, June 1838, pp. 287–301.

congregations.[13] Less than two years later, Henry Williams, after a trip across the North Island, wrote that the Maoris who "assemble with us and receive instruction every Sabbath day, are not less than Eighteen Thousand Souls. . . . At whatever place I went to in that unknown part of the Island over which I have just traversed [Taranaki, etc.], our Prayer Book was in universal use. . . ." [14] And by July 1840, he thought: "The natives attending our instruction are not less than 30,000, and the baptized far more numerous than you have ever reported; I think at this time not less than 2,000. . . ." [15] The missionaries baptized over four hundred Maoris in the last six months of 1839 alone.

Meanwhile the Wesleyan-Methodist Missionary Society had been established in New Zealand by Samuel Leigh in 1822. Leigh originally intended to settle in the Thames Valley, but Hongi, the Ngapuhi chief, advised against it, saying he was about to kill the Maoris there (as, indeed, he was), and suggested the Methodists turn further to the north instead. The spot finally chosen was "Wesleydale," near Whangaroa Bay—itself the site of the *Boyd* massacre thirteen years before. The Maoris in that area were still unsettled, however, and since few ships visited the harbor, the missionaries and their families soon found themselves in precarious circumstances and short of food. Finally, in January 1827, Hongi and his army went to Whangaroa, the Maoris became upset, and in the confusion the little mission station was destroyed by a gang of marauding Ngapuhi, and the missionaries were forced to leave. They fled to Kerikeri and then left for Australia. "Thus terminated, for the present," wrote Leigh's enthusiastic biographer, "one of the most noble, best sustained, and protracted struggles, to graft Christianity upon a nation, savage and ferocious, which the history of the Church of Christ supplies." [16]

---

[13] *MR,* April 1839, p. 197.

[14] Letter of Williams, January 23, 1840, p. 405, typewritten copy of his letters, Hocken Library. (Slightly different version in *MR,* November 1840, p. 509.)

[15] Letter of Williams, July 25, 1840, p. 418, typewritten copy of his letters, Hocken Library.

[16] Alexander Strachan, *Remarkable Incidents in the Life of the Rev.*

The mission was re-established in New Zealand before the end of the year. In October and November 1827, James Stack and John Hobbs returned and settled, permanently this time, at Mangungu on the Hokianga River, among a branch of Ngapuhi closely related to that of the Bay of Islands.

In 1831 the Methodists baptized their first Maori, and from this time their work spread as rapidly and successfully as was happening across the peninsula at the Bay of Islands. By 1834 they were used to congregations of two hundred and fifty or three hundred every Sunday, although there were only four ministers in all. In 1834 they decided to establish a station in the Waikato River district. Two posts were begun and were soon drawing combined congregations of about five hundred natives, but because of a misunderstanding with the Church Missionary Society the stations were withdrawn in June 1836. The Methodist society did not attempt to expand again until 1837 when two posts were organized on the west side of the North Auckland peninsula at Mangakahia and the "Head of the Hokianga." In 1839 the stations on the west coast were reopened, and by the following year there were eight or nine Methodist stations in operation.[17]

By this time the Roman Catholic missionaries had also arrived in New Zealand. Pope Gregory XVI, in 1835, instituted the Vicariate of Western Oceania, and during the next year appointed a French priest, the Reverend J. B. F. Pompallier, the Vicar Apostolic. Pompallier was intelligent, honest, hard-working, and shrewd. He left for the Pacific with a few assistants in 1837, and after dropping off missionaries at several small Pacific islands arrived at Hokianga in January 1838 with one lay brother and a priest. On January 13, these

---

Samuel Leigh . . . (London, 1853), p. 280. See also *MR*, February 1825, pp. 103–104, March 1826, pp. 164–65, and August 1827, pp. 337–42.

[17] First baptism took place on February 16, 1831. For this see J. Stack, *Report of the Wesleyan-Methodist Missionary Society,* 1831, p. 43. See later issues of this *Report* for general Methodist growth; see also B. T. Smith, "The Wesleyan Mission in the Waikato, 1834–1841," an unpublished thesis, 1948, Auckland Univ. College Library; and Edward Markham, "Transcript of New Zealand or Recollections of it," Ms vol. 85, p. 66, Hocken Library.

men celebrated what they believed to be the first mass in New Zealand.[18]

Pompallier saw almost immediately that there were better missionary opportunities for him at the Bay of Islands, but he remained at Hokianga to learn the English and Maori languages. About two months after his arrival he baptized a Westernized Maori couple who wanted a Catholic wedding. He also built a small chapel with the help of some of the local white Catholics. In 1839 new priests arrived, and this permitted Pompallier to go to the Bay of Islands —or more exactly, Kororareka—at the end of June. At Hokianga he left a priest with sixty converts and fifteen hundred students. A third post was organized at Whangaroa, now peaceful, early in 1840. Shortly afterward the Catholics began to preach at Mangakahia and at Tauranga.

With three groups of missionaries in the same small area, there was bound to be hostility between them. Each church believed in its own conception of Christianity and followed its own method of propagation. And so in spite of the religious sincerity of these men, or rather, perhaps, because of it, a series of misunderstandings arose.

The Methodists and Anglicans enjoyed mild dissension. The first signs of difficulty were found in the conflicting spheres of interest which each had marked out for itself when the two churches began to expand to the south. Before then there was only friendliness and cooperation—as when the Anglicans helped the Methodists after the Whangaroa station had been destroyed. This friendliness was perfectly natural: the two religions were still much alike. Methodist missionaries in New Zealand used the Church of England services which had been translated into Maori not only because of the convenience and to avoid confusion among the Maoris, but because there was little difference between the services in any case.

When the Methodists settled in Hokianga, they assumed the Church Missionary Society would take jurisdiction over the east coast of the North Island, while they superintended the west. The

---

[18] Jean B. F. Pompallier, *Notice historique et statistique de la mission de la nouvelle zélande* . . . (Anvers, 1850), pp. 71–82, 124ff., for this and following paragraph.

Church Missionary Society, however, did not agree to this. Both groups wanted to work in the heavily populated Waikato district. They argued back and forth on their priority of intention, first visits, and ability to occupy. Eventually, in 1835, Henry Williams severed all communication with the Methodists. The Methodists withdrew their posts from the Waikato, but only when a treaty was signed in 1837 between Nathaniel Turner and Williams was agreement reached. By this treaty the Methodists were permitted to preach in the harbors of Raglan and Kawhia and their immediate hinterlands.[19]

By and large, the Anglicans criticized the Methodists for what Henry Williams called their "indiscriminate mode of baptism." [20] The Methodists were, admittedly, in New Zealand only to save souls. Perhaps they were a little less strict than the Anglicans in their criteria for the administration of baptismal rites. In 1838 they once held back the performance of a number of different ordinances in order to stage a gigantic weekend meeting. At this extraordinary event at the end of August, 700 Maori adults gathered together. On the Saturday night the missionaries married 21 couples, and the next day, for a suitable climax, baptized 129 specially prepared candidates of all ages.[21] This sort of grand-standing did not please the Anglicans particularly and neither, one suspects, did the occasional Methodist revival meetings. The first of these was in 1835. "A Love-Feast has been recently held at this Station," reported the Reverend Mr. Orton, "at which were present 200 natives, of whom upwards of forty spoke, in an affecting and satisfactory manner, of the work of grace in their hearts." [22]

The Anglican-Methodist rift might have become more serious

[19] Letters of Henry Williams for these years, typewritten copy of his letters, Hocken Library; Smith, "The Wesleyan Mission," Auckland Univ. College Library, pp. 93ff.; see also Rev. J. G. Turner, *The Pioneer Missionary: Life of the Rev. Nathaniel Turner* . . . (Melbourne, 1872), p. 181.

[20] Letter of Williams, September 24, 1838, p. 369, typewritten copy of his letters, Hocken Library.

[21] Nathaniel Turner, November 30, 1837, *MR*, December 1838, pp. 545–46.

[22] October 26, 1835, *Report of Wesleyan-Methodist Missionary Society*, 1836, p. 21; see also the numbers listed in Turner, *Pioneer Missionary*, pp. 164, 169–72, 178, 189, 203–204, *passim*.

than it actually did if the Catholics had not appeared in New Zealand, but the arrival of the Catholics immediately brought the two Protestant sects together. In the 1830's Catholics in general were regarded by English missionaries with much the same horror as Satan himself, and French Catholics were usually suspected of being agents of the French government as well.

Bishop Pompallier must have understood exactly how he would be received in New Zealand if only because of the difficulty he had finding a ship to take him from Valparaiso across the Pacific. Certainly once he had arrived he made no concessions to the Protestants. On the first Saturday after his arrival he accosted a number of Maoris who were on their way to the Methodist church. "Dressed in gaudy vestments," reported a startled observer, "and surrounded by his priests, he stood solemnly in the still air of the morning, mysteriously lifting up a large crucifix and an image of a woman and infant child." The Maoris were astonished. "In open view was a large tree with spreading branches. He pointed to its grand old trunk, and said it represented the Church of Rome, which had withstood so many storms. The large arms were the Church of England, and the small decaying boughs, the Wesleyan Church. With unmingled wonder and anger at what they had heard the natives sought their religious teachers." [23]

Their religious teachers evidently suggested throwing the entire Catholic establishment out of New Zealand—at least that is what the Maoris said when they came to perform that particular service on their way home from church the following week. However, everything turned out satisfactorily. Pompallier told the Maoris that he and the priests "were the ministers of the true God and of His church." [24] Upon this, the feelings of the Maoris changed. Several of the females seemed especially overcome with emotion and lifted their eyes up to heaven and clapped their hands and exclaimed,

[23] Nathaniel Turner quoted in R. A. A. Sherrin and J. H. Wallace, *Early History of New Zealand* (Auckland, 1890), p. 423; see also Turner, *Pioneer Missionary*, pp. 190–91.

[24] Jean B. F. Pompallier, *Early History of the Catholic Church in Oceania* (Auckland, 1888), p. 38.

" 'Oh! is it possible that these strangers are so good, and that we wished to kill them!' " [25] Somehow Pompallier always managed to survive in the atmosphere of intolerance which persisted around him.

The Protestants felt that the Bishop had eased himself into an area which had already been prepared by twenty years of Protestant labor: he was able to approach a group of heathen who were already half-civilized and certainly no longer dangerous. To some extent this was so. They argued also that he catered to the Maoris' tastes, demanding no "living proofs" of grace, but wishing only to baptize as many Maoris as he could as quickly as possible. The English missionaries said that the Catholics tried to associate the Virgin Mary with the wife of a Maori culture hero, and Pompallier himself admitted to considerable evasiveness before deciding that certain forms of dancing were not really proper.[26] Polygamy and tattooing were not necessarily prohibited for the Catholic neophyte. All this was hardly according to the rules of the game as the English missionaries played it. But on the other hand the Catholics were only being true to their faith, and they made no attempt to conceal their unpopular devotion to celibacy nor to pretend to believe that the Bible had the importance that the Maoris thought it did.

Henry Williams maintained that the Catholic mission resulted from the efforts of Satan. "The Popish Priests are invading us from all sides," he wrote; "we hear of thirty being at hand." [27] Richard Davis pleaded, "May the Lord, in mercy, deliver the Natives from the iron grasp of this fatal delusion!" but later confidently added that the "Lord has a Church and people here, against which Satan and his emissaries will never be able to prevail." [28] William Woon, a Methodist, planned to distribute a pamphlet among the Maoris entitled *Antichrist: A Conversation between a Teacher and his*

---

[25] *Early History*, p. 38; see also Pompallier, *Notice historique*, pp. 75–79.

[26] *Early History*, pp. 51, 70–71. Arguments of the English are expressed in Williams, *Christianity*, p. 253; *MR*, December 1839, pp. 553–55, and October 1842, pp. 477–80.

[27] Letter of Williams, July 25, 1840, p. 418, typewritten copy of his letters, Hocken Library.

[28] Journal of Davis, April 4 and April 11, 1839, *MR*, December 1839, p. 554.

Pupil. It was designed to expose such Catholic errors as "image-worship, forbidding to marry, transubstantiation, prayers to saints, intercessors, etc." [29] This must have made a pleasant half-hour of light reading. According to Pompallier, Protestant missionaries in the south once persuaded some indecisive Maoris to join their church by saying that the Bishop had recently thought it all over, finally seen the light, and decided to become Protestant himself.[30]

The French, on the other hand, thought that the English missionaries, as Laplace expressed it, "are distrustful, egotistical, parsimonious in the midst of plenty, and that they show neither the evangelical charity with which priests of all religions honor themselves, nor that noble and generous helpfulness common to their compatriots." [31] Unencumbered by wives, children, or personal property, the Catholic missionaries were free to devote their entire time to the conversion of the Maoris.

In any serious contest for converts, however, the Catholics were bound to be left far behind. The Protestants were backed by missionary societies with banks of money. English trading and whaling vessels in the harbors lent nominal support. Sydney itself was only two weeks away. And the Protestant societies were generally less stringent in their requirements for missionaries, and so had many more on hand.[32]

A major antidote to Catholicism was printed religious matter. "The press," said Woon, "will be a mighty engine in exposing the errors of their system. . . ." [33] This form of proselyting had a re-

[29] Letter of Woon to W.M.S., November 24, 1838, *Wesleyan Missionary Notices,* new series, no. 9 (September 1839), p. 141.

[30] Pompallier, *Notice historique,* pp. 116–17; see also letters of J. B. F. Pompallier and M. Servant, May 14 and March 5, 1840, *Annales de la propagation de la foi,* XIII (1841), 47, 41.

[31] C. P. T. Laplace, *Voyage autour du monde . . . sur la corvette de l'état la Favorite . . .* (Paris, 1833–39), IV, 34, 150–51; see also Abel Du Petit-Thouars, *Voyage autour du monde sur la frégate la Vénus . . .* (Paris, 1839–41), III, 22, 41–45, 92–93; Pompallier, *Notice historique,* p. 112.

[32] These fairly sound arguments are based on Pompallier, *Notice historique,* pp. 93–97, and *Early History,* p. 44.

[33] Letter of Woon to W.M.S., November 24, 1838, *Wesleyan Missionary Notices,* new series, no. 9 (September 1839), p. 142.

markable boom during the early 1840's, when large numbers of
Maoris had become able to read and eagerly sought anything in
print. In the five years before 1840, William Colenso turned out
roughly three and a half million pages of religious material, and
in 1840 alone he added over two million pages more.[34] The pressure
of the Catholics and the enthusiasm of the Maoris then brought the
British and Foreign Bible Society into the lists. In 1841 this society
printed twenty thousand New Testaments (another seven million
pages) which it distributed through the Protestant missionary
bodies. In 1843, and again in 1845, other lots of twenty thousand
were printed.[35] There was by this time at least one Maori New
Testament for every two Maoris in New Zealand, a proportion
which compared well with any country in the world.

[34] Colenso's reports in *MR*, November 1840, p. 512, and November 1841,
p. 519. My calculations.
[35] George Browne, *The History of the British and Foreign Bible Society . . .*
(London, 1859), II, 451–55.

PART TWO

The Depopulation of the Maoris

Chapter IV

Maori Health

There was no doubt among early white visitors to New Zealand that the Maori population was decreasing. In their letters and journals and in their books, they were almost unanimous in this respect. There was disagreement among them, however, when it came to analyzing the causes of the depopulation.

Joel Polack said, "I think the principal Cause is Infanticide. I have seen many Women who have destroyed their Children, either by Abortion, or, after their Birth, putting them into a Basket and throwing them into the Sea, after pressing the Frontal Bones of their Heads." [1] Edward Markham felt that "Rum, Blankets, Muskets, Tobacco, and Diseases have been the great destroyers . . . ," [2] while Charles Terry wrote in 1842 that the "causes have arisen from two sources,—some, from the barbarous customs and gross superstitions of the natives,—others, from their food and habits, and consequent diseases." [3] The Bishop of Australia, who visited the mission stations in 1839, thought it was "a most remarkable circumstance, that wherever we went, the children were very few; very few, indeed, compared with the number of adults. . . ." [4] And Captain FitzRoy, of the *Beagle*, argued that "Change of habits, European diseases, spirits, and the employment of many of their finest

[1] Joel S. Polack, *PP*, 1837–38, XXI, 84.

[2] Edward Markham, "Transcript of New Zealand or Recollections of it," Ms vol. 85, p. 149, Hocken Library, Dunedin.

[3] Charles Terry, *New Zealand, its Advantages and Prospects, as a British Colony* . . . (London, 1842), p. 178.

[4] Letter of Bishop of Australia, March 28, 1839, *CMR*, December 1839, p. 293.

young men in whale-ships . . . combine to cause this diminution."[5]

The Europeans generally accepted disease as an important cause of the decline in population, but they disagreed about the type of diseases themselves. A surgeon who visited the Bay of Islands briefly in 1834 wrote that venereal disease "has more Effect in destroying the Constitution of the Natives than perhaps any other Disease to which they are subject."[6] Joseph Matthews, a missionary at Kaitaia, thought the diseases could be partially explained by the Maoris' "change of diet" to Western foods and the "improper use of blankets."[7] Another missionary could account for some of the epidemics only as being the result of the Lord's displeasure at the Maoris for their barbarity and wars.[8]

Disagreement on the details of the Maori depopulation was to be expected of the contemporary Europeans. Most of them were acquainted with New Zealand only for short periods of time, and that usually spent around the Bay of Islands. Even the missionaries tended to stay near their posts, and they discussed what they had experienced within those narrow limits. To get a balanced picture of the depopulation of the Maoris one must draw on records covering the course of many years and a variety of places.

The Maoris were very healthy before they came in contact with the Europeans. There were evidently no epidemics in New Zealand before the white people introduced them. There were indeed some cases of scrofula and a few rare instances of leprosy. Warts, eczema, and boils were quite common, and sore eyes frequently resulted from the smoky huts in which the Maoris lived. But these were all inconsequential illnesses. If the Maori survived his birth, his neglected childhood, and his wars, he usually lived for a long time.

[5] Robert FitzRoy and others, *Narrative of the Surveying Voyages of His Majesty's Ships Adventure and Beagle . . . 1826–1836* (London, 1839), II, 569.

[6] J. Watkins, *PP*, 1837–38, XXI, 31. See also letter of Richard Davis, November 18, 1834, Ms vol. 66, no. 41.

[7] Letter of Matthews, March 4, 1839, *CMR*, December 1839, pp. 287–88.

[8] Letter of George Clarke, Waimate, November 16, 1838, p. 378, typewritten copy of Henry Williams' letters, Hocken Library.

The number of old Maoris particularly impressed the earliest European explorers. Captain Cook noticed that the Maoris "seem to enjoy a good state of Health, and many of them live to a good old Age." [9] Du Clesmeur thought the New Zealand fern root was specially nutritious since "we saw so many old people . . . ," [10] while Crozet observed that "their teeth are more used up than spoilt." [11]

But however healthy the Maori society may have been in 1769, it was at the same time extremely susceptible to foreign diseases. In their isolated island community the Maoris had developed no resistances, and the most commonplace European illnesses consequently affected them with undiminished strength.

Combined with this initial disadvantage, there were unusually favorable conditions for the spread of infection. The Maoris paid little or no attention to cleanliness and sanitation. One of the earliest observers wrote: "These people are extremely dirty. They eat the lice produced by dirtiness of the body, but they do not eat the lice from the head. I have seen several suffering from eczema, and a kind of ulcer or itch, which I think is brought on by uncleanness." [12] The dwelling places of the Maoris were small and dirty huts. The body of a dead chief was left unburied for several days or a week while friends and even whole tribes gathered to press noses and wail at his death. In war the Maoris traveled long distances and brought back slaves which were eaten or left to live among the members of the tribe. The Maoris always liked to mingle. They prepared and ate their food communally, had community latrines, and packed together in crowded meetinghouses to sit for hours arguing and talking among themselves. The result was that when foreign diseases were introduced they almost inevitably affected an

[9] James Cook, *Captain Cook in New Zealand. Extracts from the journals* . . . , ed. A. H. and A. W. Reed (Wellington, 1951), p. 142.

[10] Du Clesmeur, "An Account of a Voyage in the Austral and Pacific Seas . . . ," *HRNZ*, II, 473.

[11] M. Crozet, *Crozet's Voyage to Tasmania, New Zealand, the Ladrone Islands, and the Philippines in the Years 1771–1772*, ed. and trans. H. Ling Roth (London, 1891), p. 66.

[12] "Extract from the Journal of Pottier de l'Horne . . . 1769 to 1773," *HRNZ*, II, 337.

entire village and usually spread rapidly among the neighboring villages and tribes.

The Maoris further increased the impact of foreign diseases by the methods they followed to cure them. The rites and ceremonies they had traditionally practiced and which had been relatively harmless in their healthy community became dangerous after the introduction of serious diseases.

Like many peoples the Maoris associated illness with religion. They believed it came from wrongdoing, or some violation of the *tapu*, when a demon, usually incarnated in an animal, would eat away the victim's insides. A cure had to be effected by the *tohunga*. This meant immersion in water and rites to determine the source of the affliction, its degree, and if possible, its cure.

For minor ailments, such as goiter, boils, warts, and minor wounds, the Maoris used rational procedures: boils were lanced; warts cut down; flesh wounds cauterized or swabbed with a botanical salve. A few medicinal herbs were known and used to cure constipation and diarrhea. Splints were used to set fractures—cannibals are likely to have a good sense of anatomy—and heat to ease the pains of childbirth.[13]

Against more serious disorders, against afflictions they had never met and could not see, the Maoris were helpless. The priest might spend all the hours of the night determinedly arguing with the evil spirits, but he did not cure his patient. When the priest could make no cure, the patient would be carefully isolated from the rest of the tribe, placed under a flimsy shelter, and left to starve.

This action was not for purposes of quarantine; the time for that was past. The isolation resulted from the fact that the Maori was not afraid to die. If he believed he had violated a *tapu* and that the *atua* was consequently destroying him, he could resign himself to it. When he was placed apart under a rigid *tapu*, both he and the tribe confidently expected he would die, and usually he did. The Maori was susceptible to the fatal melancholia which evidently destroyed a great many of the Polynesian people. As Yate said, "In all internal disorders, inflammation, consumption, etc., the patient

---

[13] Peter H. Buck, *The Coming of the Maori* (Wellington, 1949), pp. 406–407.

lies down, sends for a priest, despairs, and dies." [14] A whaler in
Queen Charlotte Sound described the phenomenon by remarking
that " 'When a Maori tells you he's a-going to die, by —— he will,
and no mistake about it. They takes the fit, and off they goes in
the sulks.' " [15] The fact was that the Maori felt no fear of the here-
after and had great respect for the power of his gods.

In many cases the Maoris aggravated a European sickness in their
attempts to cure it. One writer has stated that whole parties would
bathe in streams to remove the spots caused by measles.[16] Certainly
they turned to cold water to relieve the heat of a fever. The Tiami
Maoris told Samuel Marsden a story which reveals a great deal
about the Maori attitudes. It was said that "some time ago one of
their tribe went on board a ship where he ate some provisions contrary to their customs, when their god in his anger slew a great
many of them. . . . their tongues [were] . . . foul, and their whole
bodies in a burning heat. The natives, supposing the heat which
they experienced to proceed from a secret fire within them, threw
off all their mats, drank cold water, bathed themselves in cold water,
and exposed themselves as much as they could to cold, under the
idea that the cold would quench the heat which they felt." Marsden
told them they should have kept themselves warm, but they
"laughed at this idea, and supposed that this would increase their
complaint." [17]

With no immunity, having exceptional means of contagion, and

[14] William Yate, *An Account of New Zealand; and of the Formation and
Progress of the Church Missionary Society's Mission in the Northern Island*
(London, 1835), p. 89; see also William Brown, *New Zealand and its Aborigines . . .* (London, 1845), pp. 75–78; and Elsdon Best, *The Maori* (Wellington, 1924), II, 30–31, on this controversial matter.

[15] Quoted by Edward J. Wakefield, *Adventure in New Zealand From 1839
to 1844. With some Account of the Beginning of the British Colonization of
the Islands,* ed. R. Stout (Christchurch, 1908), p. 49.

[16] Archdeacon Walsh, "The Passing of the Maori: An Inquiry into the
Principal Causes of the Decay of the Race," *TPNZI,* XL (1907), 163. I have
seen no contemporary statement to this effect.

[17] Samuel Marsden, *The Letters and Journals of Samuel Marsden,* ed.
J. R. Elder (Dunedin, 1932), pp. 211–12; see also T. Kendall, *MR,* November 1819, p. 466.

using absurd methods of cure, the Maoris were inevitably cut down once European diseases were introduced. Records remain of epidemics which swept through New Zealand from 1769 to 1840. They are often impossible to diagnose, however, since symptoms were rarely adequately recorded and the diseases frequently produced unusual reactions among the unexposed population. The insufficiency of the records is particularly noticeable for those diseases which occurred before there were written accounts of white people to supplement the verbal exaggeration of the Maoris.

A tradition mentions an epidemic before the arrival of Captain Cook, but it can probably be discounted.[18] Modern authorities disagree about Maori traditions themselves, and one reference is hardly to be accepted. Evidently the earliest epidemics were two which swept over the North Island within a few years of each other, sometime between 1790 and 1800. One of these was known to the natives as *rewharewha,* or foreign disease, and the Maoris claimed, as plague victims often have, that in many villages it left not enough survivors to bury the dead. The traditions of this disease in Taranaki, Mercury Bay, and Tuhoe indicate its wide extent.[19] An epidemic in the North Auckland area occurred about 1810, according to the statement of a young Maori who lost his parents during it.[20] Another epidemic, without doubt, originated in the Thames area in 1820, from the visit of a European ship, and spread south with warring tribes. The missionary Colenso said it "destroyed nearly 3-5ths of the people of the more Southern parts of the Northern Island; in some villages and sub-tribes leaving only one or two individuals." [21]

---

[18] Ernest Dieffenbach, *Travels in New Zealand; with Contributions to the Geography, Geology, Botany, and Natural History of that Country* (London, 1843), II, 13–14.

[19] W. H. Goldie, "Maori Medical Lore: . . . as believed and practiced in Former times . . . ," *TPNZI,* XXXVII (1904), 84–85; S. Percy Smith, *History and Traditions of the Maoris of the West Coast North Island of New Zealand Prior to 1840* (New Plymouth, N.Z., 1910), pp. 269, 310; Arthur S. Thomson, *The Story of New Zealand: Past and Present—Savage and Civilized* (London, 1859), I, 219; Walsh, "Passing of the Maori," *TPNZI,* XL (1907), 163.

[20] Rev. B. Woodd, *MR,* February 1817, p. 72.

[21] William Colenso, "On the Maori Races of New Zealand," *TPNZI,* I

Such early epidemics as these may have involved dysentery, diphtheria, streptococcal infections, influenza, or other diseases. Whatever their nature, there is no question that they destroyed a large section of the Maori population—whether one accepts the figures of Colenso or not. Nor were these diseases restricted in their effects to any particular section of the island.

Venereal diseases were introduced by the explorers, traders, and whalers. It is not known what the specific varieties were. The only person, apparently, to make an observation on the subject was a doctor who implied that syphilis, at least, existed in 1833-34.[22] It is probable that the first contagion came with the first ship. Over forty members of Cook's 1769 crew had venereal disease on leaving Tahiti, which is only a short run from New Zealand.[23]

Venereal diseases were introduced at a number of points, spread rapidly, and had a severe effect at first, because of the premarital intercourse accepted in Maori society. By the 1830's, however, the Maoris were treating the diseases as a matter of course. Some Europeans reported venereal diseases to be widespread and virulent; others said they were infrequent and mild. Certainly they were more prevalent at the Bay of Islands than elsewhere: a surgeon who was in and about Hokianga late in 1837 came across only five or six cases.[24]

The Maoris contracted whooping cough from a ship which entered the Bay of Islands in September or October 1828. It spread quickly among them and among the young white children, killing large numbers of the Maoris, before disappearing early in 1829.[25]

(1868), 8 (paged separately); M. J. Dumont D'Urville, *Voyage de la corvette l'Astrolabe . . . 1826–29 . . . Histoire du voyage* (Paris, 1830–33), II, 168.

[22] J. Watkins, *PP*, 1837–38, XXI, 19, 31.

[23] See William Bayly, "Extract from the Journal kept by William Bayly . . . ," *HRNZ*, II, 204.

[24] J. D. Tawell, *PP*, 1837–38, XXI, 121. See also Richard A. Cruise, *Journal of a Ten Months' Residence in New Zealand,* 2nd ed. (London, 1824), p. 274; John Savage, *Some Account of New Zealand; particularly the Bay of Islands, and Surrounding Country . . .* (London, 1807), p. 88; Dr. Fairfowl, "Evidence Given before Commissioner Bigge . . . May 1821," *HRNZ*, I, 555; but see Joel S. Polack, *PP*, 1837–38, XXI, 89.

[25] Letters of Henry Williams, January 29, 1829, p. 193, typewritten copy

Respiratory diseases were becoming general around the Bay of Islands by 1820. Occasional epidemics of colds or influenza would come from a ship in the harbor and sweep through the nearby tribes. By the late 1830's such epidemics were commonly occurring every spring and autumn. There was a severe series of "influenza" cases in 1837.[26] In the autumn of 1838 a new streptococcus-like infection which caused a swelling of the jaws and other painful symptoms spread from the Bay of Islands north to the Cape and south into the interior of the island. The missionaries noted its progress as it swept past them—taking from May until July to reach the mission station at Matamata.[27] The following spring such a severe form of influenza hit the Bay of Islands that "Scarcely a Native was to be seen moving about at this time. . . ." [28] And this type of disease continued to strike at the vitality of the Maoris in the years following.

The diseases, however, did become less fatal as they became more common. The Maoris developed resistance and a few began to adopt the advice of Europeans: to stay out of water, to eat food, to keep quiet. The epidemic of December 1838 killed only three or four natives at Kaitaia out of two hundred who were seriously infected.[29] There were, also, a number of diseases the Maori never came in contact with before 1840. Small pox was one. Yellow fever, cholera, and typhus were others. It is possible that neither measles nor scarlet fever was introduced into the North Island until just about 1850.[30]

To give an accurate statement of the numbers of Maoris killed by European diseases is manifestly impossible: estimates of the original population itself vary so much to begin with. For the present, a clear

---

of his letters; George Clarke, November 22, 1828, Ms vol. 60, no. 25; and James Kemp, February 2, 1829, Ms vol. 70, no. 31, all in Hocken Library.

[26] D. Coates, *PP*, 1837–38, XXI, 199–200.

[27] Letters of S. H. Ford to C.M.S., June 1838, *CMR*, May 1839, pp. 101–102; Richard Davis, May 25, 1838, Ms vol. 66, no. 58; and William R. Wade to William Wade, Waimate, June 15, 1838, Ms vol. 53, no. 27. See also Journal of Rev. Brown, Matamata, July 21, 1838, *CMR*, December 1839, p. 279.

[28] Report of S. H. Ford, late 1838, *CMR*, December 1839, p. 286.

[29] Letter of Joseph Matthews, March 4, 1839, *CMR*, December 1839, p. 287.

[30] See J. Watkins, *PP*, 1837–38, XXI, 20; Thomson, *New Zealand*, I, 212. There was a measles epidemic in the South Island in the 1830's.

enough picture of the change in Maori health after the time of Cook can be found in the descriptions written by Europeans in the middle of the 1830's. At that time Dr. S. H. Ford reported, "You may look far and wide, and you can scarcely point out a single instance of a New Zealander being free from disease." [31] Yate wrote, "There are, comparatively, but few old people in New Zealand. . . ." [32]

Many things introduced by the Europeans indirectly affected Maori health, and consequently Maori population. European plants and animals, trade, liquor, clothing, and prostitution: to some extent they all disturbed the conditions under which the Maoris faced the new diseases. But of these influences, only plants and animals spread throughout New Zealand to the same degree as the diseases themselves, and plants and animals were the least destructive influence of all. This is because most of the harm that was done by European animals was compensated for by European plants.

It is unlikely that Captain Cook, as tradition has it, successfully introduced the pig into the North Island. He did leave a few pigs behind in New Zealand (along with other animals, such as goats and chickens), but they were probably killed. Pigs suddenly appeared around the New Zealand coast about 1810, and it is probable that they were descendants of the dozen pigs Governor King landed at the North Cape in 1793, or of the other pigs which trading vessels dropped off at his order in the years after. At any rate the pigs spread rapidly, finding unlimited quantities of fern root and thistle, and the Maoris quickly became aware of their trading potentiality. Ships which had to go to Norfolk Island for their pork in 1807 could buy all they needed at the Bay of Islands by 1812. There were pigs in all parts of the North Island by 1820.[33]

---

[31] S. H. Ford, November 14, 1837, *CMR*, April 1838, p. 111.

[32] Yate, *Account*, p. 163.

[33] Marsden, *Letters and Journals*, pp. 63, 254, 527n; [G. L. Craik], *The New Zealanders* (London, 1830), p. 91; letter of P. G. King to H. Dundas, March 10, 1794, *HRNZ*, I, 192; memorial of C.M.S., *HRNZ*, I, 419, 423; letter of Samuel Marsden, October 28, 1815, Ms vol. 55, no. 39; Robert

But though the pigs were valuable in many ways, their general effect was to disrupt the Maoris' food supply. On the coasts they were too important for trade to be eaten regularly. Yet they ate the Maoris' fern roots and went into the Maori gardens, uprooting the carefully laid out *kumaras* and destroying other crops. The Maoris built fences around their fields, but these were never entirely effective. As one traveler remarked, "The Pigs turn up all the face of the country . . . and are in the most beautiful order possible from it." [34]

The European dogs, which came off early trading vessels and shipwrecks, affected the Maoris in a similar manner. The Maoris ate them rarely, yet they destroyed the Maori dog, which had been used for food, and attacked ground birds and what poultry the Maoris could obtain from the missions.[35]

It was a similar story with the European rat. The first European rats were evidently the black or English rats which came off the earliest ships and immediately began to exterminate the smaller, herbivorous, Maori variety. These new rats were sometimes eaten by the Maoris, but the brown or Norway rat, which arrived later, was not. The Norway rats came into the northern peninsula from ships probably shortly after 1830, and by 1835 had all but annihilated the other two species in that area. And again, not only did they deprive the Maori of this source of food, but they attacked the potatoes and cornfields as well. This unusual example of survival

---

McNab, *From Tasman to Marsden. A History of Northern New Zealand from 1642 to 1818* (Dunedin, 1914), p. 104. A letter of Joseph Matthews, Kaitaia, April 8, 1837, in Marsden, *Letters and Journals,* p. 526, suggests that King's pigs also may well have been killed before they could reproduce. This would have postponed the date of the introduction of pigs a few years.

[34] Markham, Ms vol. 85, p. 21, Hocken Library; Augustus Earle, *A Narrative of a Nine Months' Residence in New Zealand, in 1827* . . . (London, 1832), pp. 14, 84–86; Marsden, *Letters and Journals,* p. 100; Brown, *New Zealand,* p. 52.

[35] Joel S. Polack, *New Zealand: Being a Narrative of Travels and Adventures . . . ,* new ed. (London, 1839), I, 65–66; Earle, *Narrative,* pp. 147–48; Cook, *Captain Cook in New Zealand,* p. 140; Colenso, "Maori Races," *TPNZI,* I (1868), 62.

of the fittest was noticed by Charles Darwin himself, when he stopped at the Bay of Islands in the *Beagle*.[36]

The cat was introduced about 1810 and was prized by the Maoris both as food and for its skin. It did, however, compete with the Maoris for the New Zealand birds. The cats never spread to the extent of the European pigs, dogs, and rats, and were insignificant in their effects on Maori health.[37] The other domestic animals were also unimportant before 1840. The first cows, horses, and sheep came with Marsden in 1814. Those which escaped from the whites and survived were negligible. Some of the cattle Marsden sent over were given to the Maoris to breed; others broke loose. A small herd was running wild in the bush several miles in back of the mission settlements by 1820, but could never be caught, and the Maoris did not make any use of it.[38]

If the Maoris derived little nutritional value from the European animals—who were in fact competing with them for a limited food supply—it was a different situation with the European plants. These were accepted at once and eventually became the basis of the Maori diet.

Potatoes were introduced by Captain Cook or Marion Dufresne and were quickly traded among the Maori tribes. They were so prolific and needed so little attention that they supplanted the taro and yam almost immediately and by the early years of the nineteenth century were a staple item of Maori food. Even the *kumara*

[36] Charles Darwin, "Journal and Remarks," in FitzRoy, *Narrative*, III, 511; Elsdon Best, *Forest Lore of the Maori* (Wellington, 1942), pp. 416–17; Markham, Ms vol. 85, pp. 64–65, Hocken Library; George M. Thomson, *The Naturalization of Animals and Plants in New Zealand* (Cambridge, Eng., 1922), pp. 13, 78–83; H. Williams, May 16, 1832, *CMR*, October 1834, p. 226.

[37] John L. Nicholas, *Narrative of a Voyage to New Zealand . . .* (London, 1817), II, 22; Marsden, *Letters and Journals*, pp. 271, 284; Polack, *New Zealand*, I, 314; Colenso, "Maori Races," *TPNZI*, I (1868), 62.

[38] Marsden, *Letters and Journals*, pp. 79, 238; Nicholas, *Narrative*, I, 171–73; Earle, *Narrative*, p. 31; letter of William Hall, November 10, 1821, Ms vol. 67, no. 7; Journal of William Hall, April 20, 1824, Ms vol. 67, no. 26, Hocken Library; also John Butler, *Earliest New Zealand. The Journals and Correspondence of the Rev. John Butler*, comp. R. J. Barton (Masterton, N.Z., 1927), pp. 157–61.

was discarded to some extent for them, and perhaps this was their only disadvantage. They were so easily grown that the Maoris neglected to cultivate the other plants they should have been eating as well.[39]

Indian corn was given to the Maoris by Governor King in 1794, if not earlier. Eventually it became nearly as popular as the potato, and the Maoris had carried it to the East Cape by 1820. They had a peculiar habit of letting it rot in stagnant pools for months before they ate it, a practice still followed occasionally today, and not, evidently, a harmful one.[40]

Many other European and American plants were brought to New Zealand by white people, particularly the missionaries. None of them were as important as the potato and corn. Peaches grew wild over most of the island by 1840. Gorse had been introduced. Pumpkins, turnips, and cabbages had spread rapidly in the early years of the century.

The European plants and animals replaced the Maori ones easily, and made little disturbance. One anthropologist has said that "the indiscriminate gorging of new varieties of foods"[41] was an important factor in the lowering of Maori resistance to disease. But the new foods were too much like the old for this to be so. To be sure the Maoris occasionally had feasts of pork, but this sudden influx of meat after long periods of fasting, followed the pattern of their old cannibal orgies—which were dying out. The Maoris ate only this one variety of new meat, and that rarely. The potatoes and *kumaras* were very similar to one another, and furthermore there was never enough food of any variety on which to "gorge indiscriminately."

A number of the Western influences on Maori health had only

---

[39] Thomson, *New Zealand*, I, 73, 216; McNab, *Tasman to Marsden,* p. 94; Savage, *Account,* pp. 35–36, 54–57.

[40] Markham, Ms vol. 85, p. 44, Hocken Library; Elsdon Best, *Tuhoe. The Children of the Mist* (New Plymouth, N.Z., 1925), I, 556; Thomson, *Animals and Plants,* p. 489.

[41] Felix M. Keesing, *The Changing Maori* (New Plymouth, N.Z., 1928), p. 55.

local effects before 1840. These were factors which did not have the
reproductive qualities of germs and plants and animals, factors
which were unable to spread rapidly across the North Island by
means of propagation. The harmful effects of liquor, excessive
trade, prostitution, and European clothing were significant only
so far as the coastal harbors and a few areas immediately behind
them were concerned—where the Maoris and white people were
in continual contact over a period of years. It is particularly important to emphasize the fact that liquor and prostitution had little
influence on the population of the Maoris at this time because of the
general impression which exists—and always has existed—to the
contrary.[42]

The fact is that the Maoris had to be taught to like liquor. They
did not take naturally to it. Originally they had no fermented
beverages. Members of the ships which carried Crozet (1772), Forster (1773), Savage (1805), Nicholas (1814-15), and Cruise and
McCrae (1820) as well as others to the Bay of Islands persuaded
occasional Maoris to try a drink, but found none who really liked
it. McRae, for example, said, "I never met with any New Zealander
that liked spirits, even of those who had lived on board the whalers";
while Cruise wrote that "they may be induced to taste wine or grog,
but it is with reluctance."[43] One of the missionaries believed that
the reason there was no liquor traffic with the Maoris was because
the ships that visited the Bay of Islands had none to spare.[44] But it
was not just a matter of quantity. The fact was that there had to
be a permanent drinking population settled among the Maoris for
some time, in places like Hokianga and the Bay of Islands, before
any Maoris would find alcohol attractive.

[42] See, for example, some of the passages referred to in nn. 3 and 4 in
Chapter II above. See also Keesing, *Changing Maori,* p. 55, *passim.*
[43] Alexander McCrae, "Evidence before Bigge," *HRNZ,* I, 548; Joseph
Thompson, "Evidence taken by Commissioner Bigge . . . December 8, 1820,"
HRNZ, I, 499; Crozet, *Voyage,* pp. 24, 25, 37; George Forster, *A Voyage
Round the World in His Britannic Majesty's Sloop, 'Resolution'* . . . (London,
1777), I, 205; Savage, *Account,* p. 17; Nicholas, *Narrative,* I, 301; Cruise,
Journal, p. 305.
[44] Letter of John Butler, October 16, 1821, Ms vol. 58, no. 12.

Changes in Maori taste took place slowly. In the 1820's a few groups at the Bay of Islands were learning to drink, and the sweeping generalizations of the early travelers that the Maoris would not consume alcohol began to have occasional exceptions. Lesson, the French explorer, said that "pure water is the only drink of these people; they loathe strong liquors; and if some of them, or some of their girls, drink brandy, this pernicious habit has come to them during their stay on board European ships." [45] Earle wrote that, "During my residence in New Zealand, I have known but very few who were addicted to drinking, and I scarcely ever saw one of them in a state of intoxication. . . ." [46]

The missionaries kept close watch on the condition of the Maoris at Kororareka, making frequent excursions for that purpose across the Bay. Until after 1830 they found little in the way of drinking to report. In 1831, for instance, Henry Williams saw "Very many sailors rolling about intoxicated. What a contrast to the natives." [47] The first detailed missionary reports of drunkenness among the Maoris at Kororareka were written late in 1832. "The poor, unhappy Natives connected with the dreadful place, Kororarika, have lately taken to drink ardent spirits. . . ." [48] In 1834 some of the missionary natives came down to the Bay from Waimate and got drunk. [49]

Meanwhile a situation comparable to that at the Bay of Islands was developing at Hokianga. Markham, in 1834, said that the Maoris "gave me some Whi-pi or Good Water, as Rum is no longer called Why-Pecker, or Stinking Water." [50] Because of the increasing

[45] René P. Lesson, *Voyage autour du monde . . . sur la corvette la Coquille* (Paris, 1839), II, 361. My translation.

[46] Earle, *Narrative,* p. 251.

[47] Journal of Williams, November 27, 1831, p. 65, typewritten copy of his letters, Hocken Library.

[48] Yate, *CMR,* October 1834, pp. 229–30.

[49] Journal of George Clarke, April 26, 1834, Ms vol. 60, no. 97, Hocken Library. For more on Maoris' turning to alcohol see letter of Richard Davis, November 18, 1834, Ms vol. 66, no. 41.

[50] Markham, Ms vol. 85, p. 55, Hocken Library. See also his comments on pp. 30, 41, 94; and letter of James Busby to the Colonial Secretary, June 17, 1833, Ms correspondence, Alexander Turnbull Library, Wellington.

drunkenness of both Maori and white, the chiefs at Hokianga were induced to agree, in September 1835, to a law which prohibited the importation of spirits. It had little effect.[51]

A temperance society was formed at the Bay of Islands, about the same time, by the missionaries and some of the more respectable settlers. As at Hokianga, the object was to prohibit the importation of spirits. The missionaries wanted to reduce the lawlessness and brutality of the English settlement and felt that liquor brought harm to the Maoris. But when they asked James Busby to help them secure the agreement and assistance of the chiefs, whom Busby was at that time trying to organize into an informal confederacy, the Resident would not cooperate. He argued that liquor was not general among the Maoris of the Bay, and that the chiefs should not be given control over a problem which, he said, had "exclusive reference to British subjects." [52]

Furthermore, it was obvious that there was no way that the importation of liquor could be stopped. In the years after 1835 some of the Maoris between the Bay of Islands and Hokianga did become addicted to alcohol, and it was cheap rum and low-grade spirits which, to the excess they were taken, presumably weakened them physically and lowered their adaptability to the changes which were going on about them.

Yet it must not be supposed that drinking became universal in this area before 1840, let alone that it existed anywhere else to any great extent. Commodore Wilkes may have been exaggerating about the Bay of Islands Maoris when he reported that "The vice of drunkenness does not exist among them to any degree . . . ," [53] and

[51] *New South Wales Government Gazette,* Sydney, October 28, 1835; Eric Ramsden, *Busby of Waitangi. H.M.'s Resident at New Zealand, 1833–1840* (Wellington, 1942), pp. 111–21.

[52] Letter of Busby to the Colonial Secretary, September 10, 1835, Ms correspondence, Alexander Turnbull Library; *The Colonist,* Sydney, January 21, 1836; *Report of the Formation and Establishment of the New Zealand Temperance Society* (Paihia, N.Z., 1836), pp. 1–8; William Williams, *PP,* 1837–38, XXI, 188.

[53] Charles Wilkes, *Narrative of the United States Exploring Expedition during the Years 1838, 1839, 1840, 1841, 1842* (Philadelphia, 1845), II, 397.

perhaps William Brown was overstating the case in the same year (1840) when he wrote that "Even in the neighbourhood of settlements the number who give way to such indulgence is inconceivably small." [54] But the missionaries themselves testified that the use of liquor spread slowly, because the Maoris took so long to become accustomed to it.[55]

Even in the decades following 1840, the relative temperance of the Maoris was a constant subject for remark. A few observers thought that this was only because the Maoris could not readily acquire liquor. Most agreed it was because the Maoris did not like the stuff. J. L. Campbell said he lived in New Zealand a "score" of years "before I ever saw the spectacle of a native in a state of intoxication." [56] G. B. Earp said he knew of only two Maoris who were addicted to alcohol.[57] In the 1840's George Clarke and his son agreed the Maoris were temperate and uninfluenced by the white example.[58] And so it went. "Up to the time I left New Zealand in 1846," said James Stack, who though he was then only eleven had traveled a great deal around the North Island, "I had never seen a drunken Maori." [59]

Except in the case of the venereal diseases themselves, the sexual vices of the Europeans produced results scarcely more widespread than did the consumption of liquor. The sexual promiscuity of the transient whites, those in ships who visited the Bay of Islands or elsewhere for two or three weeks, increased in such places the Maori practices of abortion and infanticide. Such things were going on in the harbors about New Zealand from the arrivals of the first

[54] Brown, *New Zealand*, p. 52.

[55] J. Flatt, *PP*, 1837–38, XXI, 45; D. Coates, *PP*, 1837–38, XXI, 182.

[56] John Logan Campbell, *Poenamo. Sketches of the Early Days in New Zealand . . .* , "New Zealand" ed. (Wellington, 1953), p. 86.

[57] G. B. Earp, *PP*, 1844, XIII, 108.

[58] G. Clarke, *PP*, 1844, XIII, appendix, p. 344; and G. Clarke, Jr., *PP*, 1844, XIII, appendix, p. 124. E. Dieffenbach, *PP*, 1844, XIII, p. 617, also comments on Maori temperance.

[59] James W. Stack, *Early Maoriland Adventures of J. W. Stack*, ed. A. H. Reed (Dunedin, 1935), p. 262.

ships. But again it must be emphasized that promiscuity, abortions, and infanticides increased only in a few localities. In the areas where there were no white visitors the Maoris' practices remained unchanged.

Nicholas noticed a difference between the attitudes of the Maori girls at the Bay of Islands and those of other parts of the North Island in 1815.[60] By 1820 Maori chiefs at the Bay would let their daughters go out to the ships and offer what terms they could make with the Europeans for muskets or blankets. At the same time, however, "In the places that have not been frequented by Europeans, at the River Thames for instance, the chiefs would not allow their daughters to prostitute themselves, but only the slaves." [61] Adultery, which had been punishable by death, slowly became a less serious crime.

While promiscuity grew with increased shipping, permanent settlers tended to keep one woman for an extended period of time. It was not safe, even in the Bay of Islands, to jilt a Maori girl and stay around. Many white settlers found that marrying into a tribe gave them protection and preference in trading that they would not otherwise have. In the interior this was even more necessary. The pakeha Maoris discovered that the best way to survive among hostile tribes was to go native. There was no reason for excessive licentiousness in the interior, and there is no reason to think that it existed.

Abortion and infanticide were known before the arrival of the Europeans. A number of bizarre reasons were put forward by the curious European observers to explain infanticide, which most of them had never known before. Some believed the Maoris only killed female babies, on the theory that they were regarded with less favor than males. Slaves, especially those involved in polygamous marriages, were thought to kill their children rather than have them brought up by another woman or at a disadvantage. A Maori testifying before the House of Lords said infanticide was practiced to keep a family from growing too large. Some wives supposedly

[60] Nicholas, *Narrative,* I, 187–88.
[61] McCrae, "Evidence before Bigge," *HRNZ,* I, 541.

killed their children in fits of jealousy or anger. Whatever the specific causes, it is apparent that infanticide was well established in the cultural milieu of the Maori.[62] Abortion was not spoken of so freely, but it was evidently also practiced before the arrival of the Europeans. The Maori women used native herbs and primitive devices to accomplish it, and they spoke as though it were a matter of course.[63]

Infanticide and abortion certainly increased in the Bay of Islands and at other harbors along the coast after the arrival of the traders and whalers. Considering the amount of intercourse, half-caste children were conspicuously absent. It was not to be expected that Maori chiefs would assist in rearing these neglected offspring, and obviously the European fathers were not around to do it. Married Maori women, especially, were likely to prevent the birth of their illegitimate children or have them killed once born.[64]

As in the case of the intercourse which produced it, however, the European effect on infanticide and abortion was local and flourished only in a few places. And in those places it seems not to have been a cause of depopulation so much as a means of preventing the growth of a new, or half-caste, population, although some women must, in the profitable circumstances, have found it convenient to have no children whatsoever.

While the young women at the Bay were generally too busy entertaining whalers to bother raising families, they were defended by some contemporary writers who implied that there was no depopulation as a result of their activities. One writer said Maori girls liked and kept their half-caste children, and would not be

---

[62] Polack, *New Zealand*, I, 380–83; Journal of John King, September 22, 1822, Ms vol. 73, no. 11, Hocken Library; Nayti, *PP, 1837–38*, XXI, 113; Cruise, *Journal*, pp. 273–75; McCrae, "Evidence before Bigge," *HRNZ*, I, 539; letter of Richard Davis, January 25, 1834, Ms vol. 66, no. 37; Dieffenbach, *Travels*, II, 25.

[63] William B. Marshall, *A Personal Narrative of Two Visits to New Zealand, in His Majesty's Ship Alligator, A.D. 1834* (London, 1836), p. 13; Polack, *New Zealand*, I, 383; Cruise, *Journal*, p. 274.

[64] Cruise, *Journal*, pp. 273–75; McCrae, "Evidence before Bigge," *HRNZ*, I, 539.

separated from them.[65] Another felt that there was less infanticide where Europeans settled, since the Maoris tended to follow the European example.[66] The most ingenious suggestion was put forward by Earle: that in prostitution Maori girls had at last found a profitable function and that therefore young female babies had become too valuable to kill.[67]

These peripheral statements, however, do not really affect the central facts: Increased sexual intercourse caused no depopulation directly. But by increasing infanticide and abortion among the women of child-bearing age and keeping them occupied outside of their families, it probably affected the population indirectly at a few coastal points. What sexual promiscuity, abortion, and infanticide existed in the interior was the result of Maori custom, not white influence.

Though the debaucheries of the traders and whalers did not contribute materially to the decline of the Maori population, the trade they maintained had somewhat more serious effects. The efforts which Maoris made to acquire the European muskets, iron tools, and blankets changed the pattern of their lives completely, and left many of them ill-prepared to face the rigors of the European diseases.

Before the arrival of the Europeans the Maoris lived in *pas* on the tops of hills, which were comparatively dry and sanitary. They worked regularly at cultivation and never too strenuously, because they had to grow only enough for themselves. Growing crops were ordinarily unmolested, and in the season between planting and harvesting, the Maoris often migrated to the coast to fish, make artifacts, and prepare for war.

European trade at first consisted of a variety of knickknacks and

[65] "Journal of Brig 'Spy' of Salem. John B. Knights, Master," March–April 1833, Peabody Museum, Salem; see also "The Polynesians: and New Zealand (by a New Zealand colonist)," *Edinburgh Review*, XCI (1850), 461–63.

[66] Ernest Dieffenbach, *New Zealand, and its Native Population* (London, 1841), p. 26.

[67] Earle, *Narrative*, pp. 243–44.

iron tools exchanged for Maori carvings and mats. Muskets were
not introduced in quantity until after 1810, but soon became the
principal article of trade, and for a while the Maoris would accept
nothing else. The Maoris around the Bay of Islands would give a
large pig for a ten shilling axe in 1814. They offered eight pigs and
one hundred fifty baskets of potatoes for a musket.[68] And as muskets
increased, the price did not drop. Eight large hogs and three tons
of potatoes were procured for a musket in 1827.[69] At Hokianga
they were each worth up to a ton of cleaned flax.[70] European traders
shipped over five thousand tons of New Zealand products to Sydney
alone in 1830:[71] masts, spars, flax, kauri gum, and Maori curios.
The hundred or more whaling ships a year at the Bay of Islands
after 1835 demanded hogs and potatoes.

To produce goods for the Europeans, Maoris starved themselves
and worked to exhaustion. As early as 1805 Savage noticed that the
Bay of Islands Maoris reserved their potatoes for barter with European ships.[72] In 1820 Alexander McCrae wrote that these Maoris
suffered noticeably from lack of food in contrast to the Hokianga
Maoris, who had not yet begun European trade.[73] Pigs evidently
were not eaten except on special occasions; they were too valuable.
"The self-denial of the natives is wonderful," Earle wrote, "though
very fond of animal food, they sell the whole to us Europeans for
the means of war. . . ." [74] By the late 1830's there were so few pigs
around the Bay of Islands that Maori and white traders were able
to make a profit by shipping them there from others parts of the
island. For their own diet the Maoris at the Bay by then were often

[68] Letters of Samuel Marsden, June 15, 1815, and August 16, 1813, vol. 55,
no. 3, and vol. 54, no. 13.
[69] George Bayly, *Sea-Life Sixty Years Ago* (London, 1885), p. 127. Other
statistics may be found elsewhere, but all contribute to the same general
picture.
[70] F. E. Maning, *Old New Zealand* (Wellington, 1948), p. 188.
[71] James Busby, *Authentic Information Relative to New South Wales and
New Zealand* (London, 1832), p. 59.
[72] Savage, *Account*, p. 56.
[73] Alexander McCrae, *Journal Kept in New Zealand in 1820 . . .* , ed. Sir
F. R. Chapman (Wellington, 1928), p. 23.
[74] Earle, *Narrative*, p. 135.

reverting to fern root or rotted foodstuffs which the Europeans would not take.[75]

To some extent the lack of food resulted from the increase of warfare, caused by the European muskets. When, in the 1820's, large armies went to war, crops in some places were not grown. Unlike earlier times, fields were despoiled. In 1823 a Waikato chief, according to Marsden, was upset that Hongi "had such means for continual war which occasioned such great public calamities, famine, and distress everywhere, as all their pork and potatoes were destroyed and their farms neglected." [76] An intensification of cannibalism only partially made up the deficit, and that primarily for the warrior group.

As well as eating less, the Maoris near the coasts overworked themselves for trade. The new *kumara* plantations and fields of potatoes and corn which sprang up wherever there was room testified to unparalleled toil. The Maoris sweated to fell and prepare timber and clean flax. Consider the effort involved in earning a hundred muskets for a tribe, Maning wrote, "one hundred tons of flax, scraped by hand with a shell, bit by bit, morsel by morsel, half-quarter of an ounce at a time." [77]

Not only did the underfed coastal Maoris strain themselves for European trade, but they changed their place of habitation. Instead of retiring to the hilltop *pas* at night, they moved down to the low grounds where they worked. To some extent this was due to the changing character of their wars. Muskets made the *pas* untenable without a great deal of alteration, and growing crops were no longer safe from war parties. But also the Maoris had no time to spend traveling back and forth.

They built their stuffy huts on the swampy valley floors where the flax grew most abundantly. The air was moist, the water stagnant, and sewage had no proper means of draining from their

[75] Markham, Ms vol. 85, p. 45, Hocken Library. See also J. Watkins, *PP,* 1837–38, XXI, 20, and William R. Wade, *A Journey in the Northern Island of New Zealand: Interspersed with Various Information Relative to the Country and People* (Hobart Town, 1842), p. 170.

[76] Marsden, *Letters and Journals,* p. 386.

[77] Maning, *Old New Zealand,* p. 188.

makeshift villages. They worked waist deep in swamps and streams to cut out timber and float it down to European ships.

There is no question that this kind of living lowered their resistance to disease. Because there were more white men in the north, conditions were most serious there, spreading south only with the advance of trade in the late twenties and thirties. Yet even so, poor living conditions had a more widespread effect than liquor and the results of sexual promiscuity. Liquor spread slowly since the Maoris did not like it, and both it and promiscuity flourished only where there were large numbers of whites. But any coastal Maori tribe would change the order of its life to get the tools and muskets of the Europeans, whether or not the Maoris ever saw the Europeans at all.

Clothing and blankets—introduced largely by the missionaries— constituted another element of European life which indirectly affected the health of the Maoris. Blankets were James Busby's gift of welcome in 1833, and undoubtedly those which Hobson distributed persuaded a number of the Maori chiefs to accept the Treaty of Waitangi. The native girls on board the ships at Kororareka were often given secondhand finery from Europe as well. But these were insignificant sources of clothing and blankets compared to the streams which flowed through the mission stations at the Bay of Islands and Hokianga.

The missionaries had well-intentioned reasons for the introduction of these goods. In part it resulted from their ambition to civilize the Maoris, for to them clothing was a necessary symbol of the civilized man. "I hope the time is not far distant," wrote John Butler, "when they will all be clothed, and in their right mind, sitting at the feet of Jesus, and hearing His holy word." [78] Butler was, really, quite enthusiastic. "Happy day," he later cried, "when all the natives shall be clothed in European garments, and act toward each other upon the principles of the Gospel!" [79] From the first days of the mission, the missionaries distributed clothes as gifts

[78] Butler, *Earliest New Zealand,* entry for April 29, 1820, p. 79.
[79] Butler, *Earliest New Zealand,* entry for July 27, 1821, p. 142.

or rewards and to cover the naked bodies of the few natives who hung around the mission settlement.

The missionaries also wanted to find some alternative to guns and ammunition that the Maoris would accept in exchange for pork and the other foods which were necessities of mission life. After 1823 blankets slowly became the most important article of missionary trade. Henry Williams expressed the missionary attitude in a letter to Dandeson Coates: "The natives will give a good payment for a good blanket—with them also they can do no harm. Axes, etc., are comparatively seldom called for; if three-fourths of our expenditure in this way were in blankets, it would be far better—with a blanket we can buy anything . . . [and it] will soon require to be renewed, which is another advantage." [80]

The trade in clothing and blankets spread with the missionary settlements, as the Maoris became anxious to follow the English fashion and less willing to spend long hours making feather caps and skirts of flax. By the middle of the 1830's, some sort of European garment, perhaps a blanket or a poorly fitting shirt, was fairly common dress of the Maoris between the Bay of Islands and Hokianga. R. G. Jameson, who traveled to Waimate from the Bay of Islands in 1840, found scarcely any Maori without some such manifestation of the European influence.[81]

But however well intentioned the missionaries had been, the introduction of clothing ultimately proved an injury rather than a blessing to the Maoris because they had no conception of the proper way to wear it. The larger and thicker a blanket, the more it appealed to them. When a Maori had several blankets, he wore them all—in cold weather or midsummer. "We were surprised," wrote FitzRoy in the summer of 1835, "at seeing almost every native wrapped up in a thick blanket, perhaps even in two or three blankets, while we were wearing thin clothing." [82] When the Maoris

[80] Letter of Henry Williams, July 25, 1827, pp. 178–79, typewritten copy of his letters, Hocken Library.

[81] R. G. Jameson, *New Zealand, South Australia, and New South Wales* . . . (London, 1842), p. 248.

[82] FitzRoy, *Narrative*, II, 569; Markham, Ms vol. 85, pp. 28, 46, Hocken Library.

became hot, they would plunge into streams and let the clothes and blankets hang wet upon them.

They would not take their European clothing off, and it became tattered, ragged, and filthy. Dieffenbach said the Maoris' blankets were infested with vermin and dirt.[83] Darwin saw "a chief, who was wearing a shirt black and matted with filth; and when asked how it came to be so dirty, he replied, with surprise, 'Do you not see it is an old one?' "[84]

It was unfortunate that the good intentions of the missionaries resulted only in more sickness for the Maoris, but in the areas to the north where the European clothes and blankets were distributed, and later in the south, that was the case. Worn without regard to temperature or weather, soon more filthy than the native garments, they would have been better left at home.

Yet still, European clothes and blankets were only little more than local in their influence. Because they were articles of trade they spread further into the interior than the white-inspired abortion, infanticide, or drunkenness. But they did not kill directly, nor did they sweep across New Zealand like animals and plants or like the introduced diseases.

[83] Dieffenbach, *Travels,* II, 18.
[84] Darwin, "Journal," in FitzRoy, *Narrative,* III, 501. See also Polack, *New Zealand,* I, 62–63; G. B. Earp, *PP,* 1844, XIII, 106; and G. Clarke, Jr., *PP,* 1844, XIII, Appendix, p. 124.

Chapter V

New Means of War

The uncontrolled spread of contagious diseases was not the only important cause of the Maori depopulation. Because the introduction of European muskets and other weapons provided a means of destruction such as had never before been realized in New Zealand, to fatalities from diseases must be added the large number of deaths resulting from new means of making war. Wars in which European weapons were used began late in the second decade of the nineteenth century. They grew to a climax in the 1820's in the north, extended southward well into the 1830's, and killed Maoris in the tens of thousands. The explosive and violent nature of these wars resulted from the fact that a warlike people was suddenly given —and seized upon—an improved means of expressing its warlike nature.

The pre-European Maori wars were relatively small affairs with never more than a few hundred warriors on a side, and they lasted but a short length of time. They consisted of only a series of raids which took place when the Maoris had sufficient free time to engage in them. But nevertheless warfare and the warlike attitude were woven into the fiber of the Maori culture.

The long Maori tribal histories are in large part the record of wars, revenges, and individual feats of bravery. Maori boys were trained with meticulous care from the time they could walk to know the stylized patterns of fighting and the uses of the different weapons. They learned intricate religious rituals to ensure the preservation of strength and agility. Countless war cries, chants, prebattle rites, and all the postures, feints, and poses used in actual combat became second nature to the young Maori warriors, while the adult Maoris when not in battle spent much of their time training the boys, making weapons, and strengthening their hilltop *pas.*

Though stylized, the pre-European Maori battles were unquestionably hard fought. There was no sling and no bow and arrow. Although a throwing stick which helped propel darts was known, the weapons used almost exclusively were spears and clubs, infinitely varied in material, shape, and design. Maori warriors practiced sound, elementary strategy which included feints and different kinds of attacking formations. The advantages of surprise were usually exploited when possible, although sometimes the armies would meet formally to watch a single combat which they thought might determine the ultimate victor. They usually judged victory itself by the number of persons killed and taken captive. Being killed outright was generally thought preferable to being taken prisoner and made a slave.

There was no lack of causes and excuses for going to war. According to Sir Peter Buck, the acquisition of territory was a reason from the earliest times.[1] By 1769 it was no longer very important. Most wars at this time stemmed ultimately from the fact that the Maoris were extremely sensitive to insult. Affronts to their *mana,* or prestige, demanded *utu,* or revenge. Murder of a member of one tribe by a member of another, an act of adultery, a boast of superiority, a posture of contempt—these actions and countless others provided sufficient cause for not one, but for a series of wars, because the Maoris never forgave defeats and cherished their visions of revenge through generations.

A tribe not powerful enough to win its own battles would usually try to secure the assistance of a related tribe or else attack a weaker ally of the enemy. This inconsiderate procedure immediately extended the area of conflict by involving new groups of tribes. In

---

[1] Peter H. Buck, *The Coming of the Maori* (Wellington, 1949), p. 387. See also Apirana T. Ngata, "Maori Land Settlement," *The Maori People Today. A General Survey,* ed. I. L. G. Sutherland (London, 1940), p. 100. Buck, pp. 387-403, has been useful in preparing the passages relating to pre-European war.

the labyrinthine intertribal relations of alliance and opposition which grew up during the centuries there was unceasing agitation for revenge, one round of wars breeding the next, with allies and enemies changing relations in inextricable confusion.

The principal reason that deaths were relatively few in pre-European wars is that all the Maoris used the same or similar weapons. The relative equality meant, in the first place, that battles, while often bloody, very rarely resulted in massacres. More importantly, it meant that tribes with grudges often hesitated to attack each other because the outcome was so likely to be in doubt. But by the nineteenth century the different Maori tribes and sub-tribes had interminable backlogs of insults and battles which they were committed to avenge whenever it was possible.

The Europeans arrived to upset this precarious balance in two ways. In their everyday contact with the Maoris they increased the pressure for war by adding, intentionally and unintentionally, still further sources of irritation and insult to the Maori tribes. And then with the introduction of muskets they suddenly blew the lid off the suppressed intertribal antagonisms which had been building up.

European causes for wars could be found in the most unexpected places. Even the pigs which the Europeans brought with them had such effects. These strange and valuable animals were often made the particular possessions of different Maori tribes, which then became responsible for them. War was likely to result when the pigs went into nearby areas and destroyed the crops or violated the sacred *tapus* of another tribe. War as often came about when Maoris captured or killed a pig belonging to another tribe in their anxiety to have something to trade for muskets or for ammunition.

Another type of cause emerged when European captains put Maoris ashore on unfamiliar or hostile parts of the coast for various reasons: to have labor for cutting timber, to dispose of stowaways, to land Maori seamen before the trip to England, even to sell Maoris as slaves. About 1806, the English brig *Venus* abducted the sister and niece of a chief of the Bay of Islands, dropping one off at Tauranga and the other at the East Cape, and selling them for several mats apiece. As the result of quarrels these two women were eventually killed. The chief at the Bay of Islands, hearing of it, demanded revenge, and, though it took him until 1820, finally found the opportunity to attack the tribes which had bought and killed his relatives.[2] Maoris put ashore among already hostile tribes, of course, often fanned to flames a grudge which had been long smoldering. And the Europeans even caused wars by confusing one tribe with another: when the mistaken English retaliated against an innocent tribe for the *Boyd* massacre, they touched off a series of Maori conflicts.[3] The Europeans could scarcely come in contact with the Maoris without creating some small disturbance sufficient to upset the always tenuous peace between two tribes.

When muskets were introduced, the Maoris fortunate enough to acquire them began to pay off their old debts. The demand for muskets was slow at first. It began to spread more rapidly as the muskets reached increasing numbers of Maoris who had never known of them before and who in turn introduced them to others, until finally a craze for muskets swept over New Zealand like a contagious disease. To be without muskets became to court extinction, and as fast as the Maoris acquired them still more and more were demanded by others who were as yet unarmed. Only after twenty years was some sort of balance reached in that when all the surviving Maoris had muskets, had acquired immunity, so to speak, the wars began to diminish.

While wars with muskets multiplied the numbers of deaths, psychological factors were at first as responsible for this as the intrinsic efficiency of the weapons themselves. The early muskets were actually as poor as the traders thought they could dispose of, but they would have been fairly ineffective even if in perfect order. They were usually flintlocks, the type of gun in which a flint in the hammer strikes a spark, when the trigger is pulled, to ignite the charge. These muskets had to be tended carefully. The Maoris, not knowing at first how to take care of them, let them get wet and

---

[2] Samuel Marsden, *The Letters and Journals of Samuel Marsden*, ed. J. R. Elder (Dunedin, 1932), pp. 154–55, 172–73, 265.

[3] Marsden, *Letters and Journals*, p. 85.

unserviceable. Later, according to Earle, they were so fond of taking them apart and cleaning them that the working mechanisms soon became loose and eventually useless.[4] Meanwhile, powder was always in short supply, and stones often had to take the place of bullets. Unfamiliarly and awkwardly, the Maoris would take great lengths of time to load a charge, find a rest, and aim. Not infrequently they would blow themselves up or kill as many of their friends as of the enemy. Cruise, in 1820, said that "We have seen them, when about to shoot a pigeon, climb the tree where it was sitting . . . with a caution and address peculiar to themselves, and put the muzzle of the gun within a foot of the object, before they attempted to fire at it."[5]

Needless to say, such inefficiency would not have killed many Maoris by itself. In the early years the lethal effect of muskets was in the fact that they were mysterious and frightening. Maoris who had never seen muskets—and even those who had—tended to think there was something supernatural about them. Once fear took hold of an army's mind, the army was likely to collapse, and this in turn led to massacres and large numbers of captives. The more battles won through the agency of muskets, whether they actually did the killing or not, the more dread they inspired.

Of course the Maoris did not remain ignorant about muskets forever. As the number of muskets increased and as the Maoris overcame their superstitious fears, they slowly acquired the means and ability to shoot effectively. Before 1840 the flintlocks lost favor, and many of the now sophisticated Maori warriors would trade only for double-barreled percussion fowling pieces.

Like most elements of white culture, muskets were first introduced in numbers to the Bay of Islands, probably in the decade

---

[4] Augustus Earle, *A Narrative of a Nine Months' Residence in New Zealand, in 1827* . . . (London, 1832), pp. 72–73.

[5] Richard A. Cruise, *Journal of a Ten Months' Residence in New Zealand,* 2nd ed. (London, 1824), pp. 281–82; Earle, *Narrative,* pp. 108–109; William Yate, *An Account of New Zealand; and of the Formation and Progress of the Church Missionary Society's Mission in the Northern Island* (London, 1835), p. 127.

before 1800.[6] During the next ten years they grew steadily in prestige, and the Maoris grew more adept in handling them. The Maoris of Whangaroa may have used muskets at the massacre of the *Boyd* (1809), and Maoris definitely employed them against the retaliating English sailors in the following year. By 1814, when the missionaries arrived, Hongi had been able to teach himself to stock and mount a musket without assistance. He owned several.[7] John L. Nicholas thought that "Iron and firearms are by them held in greater estimation than gold and silver by us. . . ."[8] Although few inland had ever seen a musket, Maoris were familiar with them all along the coast from the North Cape to the Bay of Islands.[9]

As the European demand for New Zealand products grew, as more ships stopped by the Bay of Islands for pigs, potatoes, flax, and timber, the Ngapuhi held an increasingly advantageous position. They would take nothing else if they could get muskets and powder, and for these they would pay exorbitantly.

The missionaries at the Bay of Islands were in an awkward position. Set alone in their little settlement, they were expected by Marsden and the Missionary Society to survive as best they could, although small means had been made for their provisioning. Almost inevitably the missionaries were drawn into the musket trade: there was no other way for them to get the things they needed from the Maoris.

At first, or so it would seem, the missionary leaders placed no prohibition on giving muskets to the Maoris. In 1814, Samuel Marsden himself distributed them to favored individuals. When the *Active* sailed into the Thames River, Marsden permitted a Maori friend, Ruatara, to arm himself and twelve companions with muskets and pistols to impress the local tribes. Later he lent Ruatara a couple of pistols when his tribe was going to attack another near

[6] William Colenso, "On the Maori Races of New Zealand," *TPNZI*, I, (1868), 64.

[7] Letter of Whalers to Governor MacQuarrie, April 10, 1810, *HRNZ*, I, 300; letter of Thomas Kendall, Parramatta, September 6, 1814, Ms vol. 54, no. 66.

[8] John L. Nicholas, *Narrative of a Voyage to New Zealand* . . . (London, 1817), I, 164–65.

[9] Nicholas, *Narrative*, I, 254; Marsden, *Letters and Journals*, pp. 79–131.

the Bay of Islands.[10] Marsden, however, decided against the wisdom of permitting such goings on by the time he left New Zealand, early in 1815. He not only prohibited the missionaries from trading in muskets, but induced the settlers to say they would refrain from any private trade whatsoever.

But to trade with the Maoris without muskets was almost impossible. The infeasibility of procuring food in any other way was testified to by missionary and visitor alike. Only a few months after Marsden's departure, Thomas Kendall wrote that the Maoris had offered the settlers no food in four weeks. "We have procured some flax, but the natives like muskets much better than they do axes. Ships which come here and will spare muskets, will have a great advantage over us in point of trade." [11] In 1820 William Hall reported that: "The natives will not bring [timber] . . . for our mode of payment, neither will they sell us any pork scarcely. They save it all for the shipping that gives them muskets and powder." [12] Ensign McCrae, whose ship traded as Marsden wished in 1820, said his ship was "never able to procure by barter a fresh meal during the whole time that we were in New Zealand," [13] while Richard Cruise, on the same ship, remarked it was impossible to get the spars they wanted with the goods they had to offer.[14] In 1826, Henry Williams wrote: "The natives are quite indifferent to assist us: they are very unsettled: war occupies all their thoughts and the obtaining of muskets and powder all their efforts. It is a rare thing to purchase a basket of potatoes from them. . . ." [15]

And so the missionaries turned to the musket trade, and they

[10] Marsden, *Letters and Journals,* pp. 86–87, 102–103, 108; Nicholas, *Narrative,* I, 375, 377–78, and II, 46.

[11] Letter of Kendall to Marsden, July 6, 1815, vol. 54, no. 12.

[12] Letter of Hall, December 28, 1820, Ms vol. 67, no. 4; see also John Butler, *Earliest New Zealand. The Journals and Correspondence of the Rev. John Butler,* comp. R. J. Barton (Masterton, N.Z., 1927), entry for May 31, 1820, p. 80.

[13] Alexander McCrae, "Evidence Given before Commissioner Bigge . . . May, 1821," *HRNZ,* I, 548; see also pp. 542–43.

[14] Cruise, *Journal,* pp. 286–87.

[15] Letter of Williams, December 13, 1826, p. 162, typewritten copy of his letters, Hocken Library, Dunedin.

traded privately as well. Since these were things of which the Missionary Society obviously disapproved, references to them are not common. One reference to the musket trade can be found in a letter of Thomas Kendall, who mentioned the latter part of 1818 as "the time when the practice of parting with muskets and powder became general in the Settlement. . . ." [16]

Some of the settlers (Kendall, John King, Charles Gordon, and William Carlisle), evidently at Marsden's insistence, signed an agreement on March 30, 1819, that they would not engage in private trade again.[17] William Hall would not sign it because, he said, it "was merely drawn up for self-applause and calculated to blind the eyes of the Society and the public under a cloak of hypocrisy and deceit. . . ." [18] ("He is," wrote Marsden, "a very stubborn ass and never will be properly broken to the yoke.") [19] Only two months later, however, Hall joined those four in signing a document which stated: "respecting muskets and powder . . . it is our wish to abstain entirely from disposing of such articles to the natives of New Zealand. . . ." [20]

It is obviously impossible to discover exactly to what extent who did and who did not participate in the musket trade. When Marsden began to condemn the trade, it was, like any similar situation, a matter of accusing someone else of as much as possible. In 1822 Butler accused even Marsden himself of trading muskets and powder for flax and potatoes, and it is in fact not unlikely that as late as 1820 Marsden did occasionally utilize the trading power of European weapons.[21] Kendall was admittedly the most notorious trader. Hall, in 1820, denied ever having traded muskets and powder pri-

---

[16] Letter of Kendall to Marsden, September 27, 1821, Ms vol. 71, no. 9.
[17] Marsden, *Letters and Journals,* pp. 234–35.
[18] Letter of Hall, September 13, 1827, Ms vol. 67, no. 2.
[19] Marsden, *Letters and Journals,* p. 235.
[20] Marsden, *Letters and Journals,* p. 235.
[21] Butler, *Earliest New Zealand,* entries for 1821, 1822, pp. 163–65, 193–95; Alexander McCrae, *Journal Kept in New Zealand in 1820 . . . ,* ed. Sir F. R. Chapman (Wellington, 1928), p. 15; but see also the letter of Marsden, January 17, 1822, *Marsden's Lieutenants,* ed. J. R. Elder (Dunedin, 1934), p. 183.

vately.[22] But he wrote in 1822 that "I have long since left off the barter of muskets and powder. I have never done anything of the kind since the brethren in general agreed to the Society's instructions on that head." [23] John Butler's journal of February 12, 1820, records that he and Hall were "obliged" to do some musket trading.[24] The trade was resumed so quickly after the 1819 agreements, if it ceased at all, that in April 1820 Marsden, then in New Zealand, felt compelled to write Thomas Kendall as follows:

I found you had all fallen into that accursed traffic with muskets and powder again, notwithstanding all the resolutions that had been passed against it when I was with you in August last. . . . When I considered that the missionaries were furnishing the instruments of death to these poor savages by supplying them with muskets and powder, I could not but feel the greatest indignation at such a thought. . . . The argument generally urged has been that neither timber nor pork could be bought from the natives without muskets and powder. This I do not credit. . . . The Rev. J. Butler and all the settlers have once more promised to have nothing to do with this traffic in future.[25]

But the missionaries did not live up to their promises and the trade was not stopped until Henry Williams arrived, Kendall and Butler were removed from their positions, and large amounts of food were supplied from Sydney.

The number of muskets which the missionaries distributed will never be known, but it was probably not very large. The only way the missionaries could acquire muskets in ordinary circumstances was from the ships which came by. Not only were there few of these, at least until 1819 or 1820, but the captains themselves needed the muskets. In 1820 William Hall accused Kendall of taking for Maori

[22] Letter of Hall, September 13, 1820, Ms vol. 67, no. 2.

[23] Letter of Hall, April 6, 1822, Ms vol. 67, no. 10; see also his letter of January 19, 1822, Ms vol. 67, no. 8.

[24] Butler, *Earliest New Zealand,* p. 69; see also p. 72; see also letter of Marsden, Bay of Islands, April 24, 1820, *Marsden's Lieutenants,* pp. 157–59.

[25] *Letters and Journals,* pp. 333–34. See also pp. 331, 352; and *HRNZ,* I, 491.

trading eight blunderbusses and one hundred fifty pounds of pow-der from one ship,[26] but in 1820 these figures were not exceptional. At that time the spread of European weapons became very rapid and very noticeable.

If the musket trade was the only trade the missionaries thought immoral, it was nevertheless not the only one which helped the Maoris to make war and destroy each other. The sudden Maori craze for English hatchets, axes, hoes, knives, and other tools was due to no conversion to the sedentary life of farmers. Not only were these used to grow the things which could be traded for muskets and powder, but they were put to use directly in battle.

Metal tools represented an improvement over stone and wooden weapons, yet they were sufficiently similar to be readily understood. The Maoris responded to them immediately, and they were at first more popular than muskets. When the mission started, Marsden, who was flattered by and enthused at the Maoris' clamor for these badges of civilization, distributed them wholesale and always tried to have plenty on hand. Kendall wrote in 1815 that "all the natives who have come to our Settlement for Axes and other Iron tools have been supplied. We have suffered none to go away disap-pointed."[27] By 1820 hundreds and thousands had been distributed, but the missionaries could not seem to keep up with the demand. "September 17th [1819]—I remained the principal part of this day in the house," wrote Samuel Marsden, "in order to avoid the impor-tunities of those natives to whom we had not the means of giving an axe or a hoe. It was not possible to walk without being sur-rounded by them on all sides, some urging their requests with savage rudeness and others with pleasing civility. Their universal cry is: 'Give me a hoe, axe, or spade.' "[28]

The missionaries' demand for metal objects to use for exchange with the Maoris became feverish when the musket trade was stopped in 1823. For the supplying of schools and other public works in 1824, James Kemp requested "16 Dozen Broad Axes, 42 Dozen Falling

[26] Letter of Hall, September 13, 1820, Ms vol. 67, no. 2.
[27] Letter of Kendall to Marsden, July 6, 1815, Ms vol. 54, no. 12.
[28] Marsden, *Letters and Journals,* p. 176; see also pp. 169, 177.

Axes, 20 Dozen hatchets, 14 Dozen adzes, 30 Dozen hoes, 40 Dozen Plane Irons oncut, 25 Dozen assorted chisels, 18 Dozen pocket knives, [and] 25 Dozen pairs of scissors . . . ," as well as other assorted hardware.[29] This is a tidy little arsenal any way you look at it. And Kemp was not blind to the use Maoris were making of these tools. "Hatchets," he wrote, ". . . they use as an instrument of war, these are articles which they are always in want of, and whatever they bring for sale, they enquire for these articles generally."[30]

In 1818 thirty-five muskets, which the Bay of Islands chief Te Morenga, distributed among a force of six hundred warriors, were sufficient to rout a tribe from the Thames area.[31] It was indeed a great quantity of firearms for one tribe to possess at that time. In 1820, however, Richard Cruise estimated "some hundred stand of arms among the inhabitants of this bay . . . ,"[32] while his fellow voyager, Ensign McCrae, thought there were "not less than 500 stand of arms, with bullet moulds."[33] The number jumped even more rapidly with the increase in shipping and with the explosive manner in which the demand for European weapons spread. Thomas Kendall wrote in 1821, "I do not think there can be less than two thousand stands of Arms among the Natives,"[34] and in 1826 Richard Davis said, "They have at this time many thousand stands of arms among them, both in the Bay and at the River Thames."[35]

The demand for muskets did not become widespread in the south until the early 1820's, after the first musket-armed expeditions from

[29] Letter of Kemp to Marsden, April 1824, pp. 23–24, typewritten copy of his letters, Hocken Library.

[30] Letter of Kemp to Marsden, December 31, 1824, Ms vol. 70, no. 16; see also letter of Thomas Kendall to Marsden, September 27, 1821, *Marsden's Lieutenants*, p. 174.

[31] Marsden, *Letters and Journals*, pp. 265–66.

[32] Cruise, *Journal*, p. 36.

[33] McCrae, "Evidence before Bigge," *HRNZ*, I, 538–39.

[34] Letter of Kendall to Marsden, September 27, 1821, Ms vol. 71, no. 9.

[35] Letter of Davis, November 10, 1826, Ms vol. 66, no. 14.

the north into the interior had defeated the southern Maoris. But by 1826, in such a barren spot as Tolaga Bay, on the East Cape, the French explorer D'Urville found that muskets and powder were the most demanded articles of trade.[36] And in 1833, the whaler Knights was told that "muskets are now used altogeather as war instruments by the Natives on the North Island, & they are now as good judges & keep them in as good order as the Europeans." [37]

A new kind of war sprang up after 1815 with the new kinds of weapons. Subtribes and tribes combined, and the Maoris organized armies such as had never been seen before to fight against common enemies. The Ngapuhi began to fit out predatory expeditions every year. With firearms they defeated whatever tribes they met, and the fact that they were not attacked at home gave them freedom to travel where and when they wished. They terrorized the northern part of the island.

But these expeditions were small compared to those which Hongi, the Ngapuhi chief who protected the missionaries, organized in 1821. Less than two months after his return with three hundred muskets, from a visit to England, the missionaries could see that something entirely new was happening.

This day, about noon, Shunghee [Hongi], Rewah, and all their chiefs set off on a war expedition to the River Thames—indeed, the whole country for a hundred miles or more, are already on their way, and Shunghee and Rewah, and Wykato, and their men, are the last, in order to bring up the rear. The general place of assemblage is Wan-gahree. . . .

There has never been anything like such an arrangement in New Zealand before. Tooi, Teteree, and all their friends are in the general onset. Shunghee and Wykato have returned from England with a great quantity of guns, swords, powder, balls, daggers, etc., etc., etc., and thus they are fully armed to murder, kill and destroy, without reserve, which is the highest pitch of glory to a savage of New Zealand!!! [38]

[36] M. J. Dumont D'Urville, *Voyage de la corvette l'Astrolabe . . . 1826–29 . . . Histoire du voyage* (Paris, 1830–33), II, 105.

[37] "Journal of Brig 'Spy' of Salem. John B. Knights, Master," March–April 1833, Peabody Museum, Salem.

[38] Journal of Butler, September 5, 1821, *Earliest New Zealand,* p. 172.

The expedition lately fitted out against Mogoea with Shunghee at the Head, is very formidable, we think they will have at least 1000 Muskets and perhaps more than double that Number of Men.[39]

The expeditions which set out regularly from the Bay of Islands in the years that followed the return of Hongi consisted of armies of one thousand, fifteen hundred, or two thousand warriors. No tribes could afford to wait patiently for spring or autumn to campaign. The need of acquiring muskets and of using them before the other tribes did so, soon made chaos out of the old-time habits.

While it is impracticable to describe in detail all the expeditions of these years, some of their destructiveness can be seen in Hongi's famous campaigns. When Samuel Marsden, for example, visited the large Kaipara inlet in 1820, he found several villages and a thriving native population. Murupaenga, a local chief, said he wished Europeans would come and live there, because he felt they would bring peace and security. But if any Europeans did settle with those tribes, it was not for any length of time. Hongi had been hoping to revenge himself on the local tribes for twenty years. He attacked in 1825, and by 1830 the whole section of the peninsula had been depopulated, for the natives who had not been killed abandoned it.[40]

Hongi, to start at the beginning, had gone to England in 1820 with Thomas Kendall and a chief named Waikato to help Professor Lee of Cambridge write a Maori grammar. He returned to New Zealand on July 11, 1821, with his muskets and set off on the first of his great expeditions the following September. With him went between two and three thousand men, from all the tribes of the Bay and from as far away as Hokianga. Perhaps a thousand of them were armed with muskets. They went to attack the Ngatipaoa tribe (which lived in the environs of present-day Auckland) to avenge the death of Hongi's son-in-law probably, as well as many other past defeats and insults.

Hongi and his expedition sailed in their canoes up the Hauraki Gulf to the Ngatipaoa lands and assaulted the *pas* at Mokoia and

[39] Letter of Francis Hall, October 20, 1821, Ms vol. 53, no. 1.

[40] Marsden, *Letters and Journals,* p. 290; Edward Markham, "Transcript of New Zealand or Recollections of it," Ms vol. 85, p. 127, Hocken Library; and letter of Richard Davis, September 25, 1830, Ms vol. 66, no. 28.

Mau-inaina. At Mokoia, which was the *pa* of Te Hinaki, Hongi's special enemy, the Ngapuhi were victorious, supposedly after Hongi had formed a wedge with himself at the apex and charged the relatively unarmed Ngatipaoa army. Mau-inaina was taken easily. At least a thousand of the Ngatipaoa were killed in the two battles, or so the report goes, and the Ngapuhi indulged in an orgy of blood drinking and flesh eating for several days after the victory.

From Mau-inaina and Mokoia the war party moved on to the Thames and attacked Hongi's ancient enemies, the Ngatimaru, at Te Totara *pa*. After a siege of a few days, Hongi made a false peace, moved his army away, and then returned to surprise and take the *pa* at night. Perhaps a thousand of the Ngatimaru perished. The missionaries recorded that besides the people he had killed, Hongi brought back to the Bay of Islands two thousand prisoners of the Ngatipaoa and Ngatimaru tribes.[41]

Mrs. Felton Mathew visited Te Totara *pa* in 1840. It "was once the most important in this part of the country, and contained a very large number of people . . . ," she wrote. "Their bones lie scattered around in every direction, some in the enclosure, others down the sides of the hill, as if murdered in the attempt to escape; or hidden in some cleft or wooded recess, as if the poor wounded wretch had dragged himself there to die in peace. The greater number of bones are found scattered round the ovens where the horrid banquet was prepared and devoured."[42]

[41] Much information in Samuel Leigh, February–March 1822, *Report of the Wesleyan-Methodist Missionary Society,* 1822, p. xlviii; Francis Hall, December 21, 1821, *MR,* November 1823, p. 505; S. Percy Smith, *Maori Wars of the Nineteenth Century . . . ,* 2nd and enlarged ed. (Christchurch, 1910), pp. 185–99; René P. Lesson, *Voyage autour du monde . . . sur la corvette la Coquille* (Paris, 1839), II, 317–25. Marsden, *Letters and Journals,* pp. 356–59, gives a slightly different version. Reliance should not be placed on Maori statistics: see Nayti, *PP,* 1837–38, XXI, 114; and Edward Shortland, *Traditions and Superstitions of the New Zealanders: with Illustrations of their Manners and Customs,* 2nd ed. (London, 1856), p. 7.
[42] Sarah Mathew, *The Founding of New Zealand. The Journals of Felton Mathew, First Surveyor-General of New Zealand, and his Wife, 1840–1847,* ed. J. Rutherford (Dunedin, 1940), pp. 148–49.

According to the Missionary Leigh, over three thousand warriors left with Hongi on his next campaign, against the tribes of the Waikato. At the end of February 1822, Hongi's forces again sailed up the Hauraki Gulf, but this time crossed by a series of portages to the basin of the Waikato River. The terrified Waikato tribes had placed obstacles in the river and had collected together at the famous triple *pa,* Matakitaki, hoping, perhaps, that numbers alone might save them, for they had no muskets.

The Waikato is a rapid, shallow river, and difficult to ascend, but Hongi steadily advanced, patiently clearing the fallen trees, until he arrived in front of Matakitaki. The battle was as good as over when his muskets first went off. A number of the Waikato were killed by the musket fire, but most were smothered, frantically trying to escape across the large moat which surrounded the *pa,* pulling each other down into its bottom, crowding and stepping on their comrades, until a mass of human bodies formed a causeway to safety in the woods for those who had survived. When Hongi returned to the Bay of Islands he told the missionaries he had killed fifteen hundred Maoris on the banks of the Waikato.[43]

Early in 1823 Hongi's forces sailed to the Bay of Plenty and pushed their canoes up the small river which drains the lakes of the hot springs district. Te Arawa were famous warriors, and there were many of them, but they had few muskets. They collected on the island of Mokoia in the lake of Rotorua. Hongi, again crossing portages, and not without losses, finally launched his canoes on the lake itself. For three days his army circled the island, reconnoitering, yelling insults, and trying to capture any Te Arawa who attempted to swim to shore. Then Hongi landed on the north side of the island and drove Te Arawa into the lake. Many of them were killed outright, many were drowned, and many more were knocked on the head or captured from their helpless position in the

[43] Francis Hall, July 29, 1822, *MR,* November 1823, p. 507; George French Angas, *The New Zealanders (Illustrated)* (London, 1846–47), notes to plate 29; Smith, *Maori Wars,* pp. 225–34. According to Butler, *Earliest New Zealand,* entry for July 28, 1822, p. 238, the Maoris told him they had killed 2000 at Matakitaki.

water. The missionaries heard that three thousand Maoris had been killed.[44]

There is evidence that for a while the Ngapuhi thought they might stay in the Rotorua area, but if so the idea was soon abandoned and they returned home.[45] For a year they rested and made only small campaigns.

In 1825, Hongi finally struck at the Ngati-whatua, who lived around the Kaipara inlet. He left the Bay of Islands with five hundred warriors, a small army for him, in February. His specific object was evidently Te Ikaranganui, the large *pa* at the headwaters of the Otamatea River. The one thousand Ngati-whatua he opposed were said to have had only two muskets among them. There was an open battle, and, while seventy of Hongi's men were killed, the slaughter of the Ngati-whatua was nearly complete. Later Hongi pursued the remnants of the tribe to the Waikato district and, at the end of 1825, cornered them and defeated them again.[46]

After this campaign, Hongi returned to the Bay of Islands. He never moved far from it again. In five years he had killed upwards of five thousand Maoris in battle and had brought back countless prisoners to be killed at leisure. The Maoris believed that a branch of the pohutukawa tree at Te Reinga, the Maori spirits' final resting place, was weighed down by the spirits killed in Hongi's wars.[47]

But Hongi's campaigns represented only a fraction of the effect of European weapons, for Hongi, although the most famous, was only one of many chiefs engaged in the new kind of warfare. Te Rauparaha, Te Wherowhero, Pomare, Te Waharoa, and the other well-known chiefs also began to use muskets to satisfy their respective grievances. In 1833 Henry Williams visited the east coast of the Coromandel Peninsula. "How melancholy is the reflexion,"

---

[44] Smith, *Maori Wars*, pp. 243–63; John C. Bidwell, *Rambles in New Zealand, 1839*, 3rd ed. (Christchurch, 1952), p. 47; but see Thomas W. Gudgeon, *The History and Doings of the Maoris from the Year 1820 to the Signing of the Treaty of Waitangi in 1840* (Auckland, 1885), p. 51.

[45] Smith, *Maori Wars*, p. 254.

[46] Smith, *Maori Wars*, pp. 329–45, 369.

[47] Journal of William R. Wade, April 4, 1839, *CMR*, July 1840, p. 158.

he wrote in his journal, "that once these hills and valleys were peopled, though with savage hordes; but of late years, they have been hunted as the deer, until few remain, and they are driven into the interior!" [48] When warfare spread, the interior offered little protection. Reverend James Buller, late in 1838, visited some Maoris near Lake Taupo in the center of the island. He found that "in answer to the inquiry, 'Where are the people who formerly lived here?' you are informed, 'They have been killed and eaten, enslaved, or driven away.'" [49]

Now this may seem an inappropriate place to confess a certain admiration for Hongi, but one can hardly help it. With all his horrible deeds—which were actually perfectly acceptable to his contemporaries, who would have emulated them if they could—he was a magnificent individual. Hongi was a robust man, but unassuming and pleasant looking according to the Europeans, and his face was covered with whirls and spirals of tattooing from his forehead to his chin. His mannerisms were so colorful, his actions so remarkable and so unexpected, that a series of incidents have been attributed to him which may very well in some cases be apocryphal. But as is often the case in such matters, they give a better idea of his personality than many laborious explanations.

Picture Hongi at a palace during his trip to England in 1820, dressed uncomfortably in poorly fitting white man's clothes and about to be presented to King George IV. "Ho do you do, Mr. King George?" he said, in a famous, if undocumented, exchange. "How do you do, Mr. King Hongi?" replied King George, as befits the meeting of equals. It was the time of the famous divorce suit between King George and Queen Adelaide, and Hongi is supposed to have remarked on it, expressing surprise that such a great king as George could not handle one wife when he, Hongi, could control five at home with no trouble at all. Hongi was given a large num-

---

[48] Williams, February 24, 1833; *MR,* August 1834, p. 366; M. C. P. T. Laplace, *Voyage autour du monde . . . sur la corvette de l'état la Favorite . . .* (Paris, 1833–39), IV, 23.

[49] Letter of James Buller, February 11, 1839, *MR,* November 1840, p. 514.

ber of presents, among them a complete suit of chain armor which he had come across in the Tower of London and admired.[50]

Picture Hongi next in Sydney on the last leg of his journey home. There he converted all his gifts, except the armor, into muskets and powder. There he saw his enemy, Te Hinaki, about to depart for England and—according to one account, but not another—boasted of his power and warned Te Hinaki to return to New Zealand to prepare for battle before his people were destroyed.[51] "As soon as Shunghee and his army arrived within sight of Enakkee's settlement," wrote Marsden about the ensuing campaign, "he looked through his glass and saw Enakkee's colours flying. He called his officers and asked them if they saw Enakkee's colours. They answered that they did. Enakkee also blew his trumpet, and Shunghee observed him dressed in regimentals amongst his people. . . . Shunghee then put on his coat of mail, his sword, helmet, and red coat," [52] and after interminable preliminaries the battle began. It would seem ludicrous except that none of the Maoris thought it was, and hundreds of Maoris were killed.

Picture Hongi later, marching back and forth across New Zealand in his armor with a huge army at his heels. He evidently had five muskets of his own and had four men to carry and load them for him. He always wore his suit of chain which protected him, although his helmet was occasionally shot off his head. In personal relations Hongi was mild, loving, and gentle. His favorite wife, Turi, was blind, but was said to have accompanied him on all his expeditions and to have been one of his most esteemed advisors. (She was also believed to have been very cruel and was reputedly eaten alive by dogs on one of Hongi's last campaigns.) [53]

[50] He actually got the presents. The story of the wives is in Gudgeon, *History and Doings,* p. 44.

[51] See Charles Darwin, "Journal and Remarks," in Robert FitzRoy and others, *Narrative of the Surveying Voyages of His Majesty's Ships Adventure and Beagle . . . 1826–1836* (London, 1839), III, 500; and Alexander Strachan, *Remarkable Incidents in the Life of the Rev. Samuel Leigh . . .* (London, 1853), p. 155; *vs.* Marsden, *Letters and Journals,* p. 356.

[52] Marsden, *Letters and Journals,* pp. 356–57.

[53] Ernest Dieffenbach, *Travels in New Zealand; with Contributions to the*

In 1827, when Hongi was about to wipe out one more tribe before settling down in peace, a bullet struck him when he was without his armor and passed directly through his lungs and out the other side. For fourteen months he lingered on, tended by a wife and one of his daughters, receiving visitors in state. His wound never healed entirely, and he entertained the most favored of his guests by showing them how the wind, passing through it, made "a noise resembling in some degree that from the safety-valve of a steam engine. . . ." [54] This amused him very much.

As Hongi approached his death he called his family around him and gave to his sons his *meres,* battle-axes, muskets, and the coat of mail. Then, it is said, he exhorted them to be courageous against anyone who dared attack them on his death. He wished no slaves to be killed to accompany him, as was the custom, to Te Reinga. "His dying lips were employed in uttering, 'Kia toa, kia toa': 'Be courageous, be courageous.'" [55] And at his deathbed were "more men of rank than had ever before assembled to witness the dissolution of a warrior, and this is considered the greatest proof of attention and respect one chieftain can show towards another." [56]

The center of warfare was starting to move south by the time Hongi died, although the northern tribes had still a greater quantity of firearms. In the Bay of Islands muskets became less valuable and blankets superseded them in popularity. Yate said that in 1830 the Ngapuhi gave the Maoris of the south a thousand muskets "to show that they were not afraid of them." [57] But soon after, according to Henry Williams, the Ngapuhi began to fear the retaliation of southern tribes—which had also received many muskets from the spread-

---

Geography, Geology, Botany, and Natural History of that Country (London, 1843), II, 127.

[54] Peter Dillon, *Narrative and Successful Result of a Voyage in the South Seas . . . to Ascertain the Actual Fate of La Pérouse's Expedition . . .* (London, 1829), II, 332. This was evidently true. See letter of James Kemp, November 6, 1827, Ms vol. 70, no. 24.

[55] James Stack, March 12, 1828, *Report of the Wesleyan-Methodist Missionary Society,* 1828, p. 42.

[56] Earle, *Narrative,* pp. 208–209.

[57] William Yate, *PP,* 1836, VII, 190.

ing traders and whalers. Those Maoris in the south, said Williams, "are by far more numerous and within these last two years have possessed themselves with vast numbers of muskets and much powder. . . . The natives around us . . . are generally desirous of peace. . . . The accounts from the Southd. are distressing—many have been cut off within the last year. The trade with Port Jackson has considerably extended, consequently the importation of muskets and powder has been very great. . . ." [58] But the Ngapuhi need not have worried. The southern tribes were too busy fighting with each other to travel north to attack the well-armed Maoris of the Bay of Islands.

The Maoris of the whole northern peninsula, or what was left of them, were well armed at this time. In fact the very completeness of their acquisition of arms helped to bring peace among them. As Darwin noticed, in 1835, "When Europeans first traded here, muskets and ammunition far exceeded in value any other article: now they are in little request, and are indeed often offered for sale. Among some of the southern tribes, however, there is still much hostility." [59]

It is difficult to say exactly when the wars began to decline. Richard Davis wrote in 1832 that "The case and circumstances of the natives are truly lamentable. Many, very many, of them have died from sickness and disease while a greater number have been cut down on the field of battle, in fact they bid fair for annihilation for the Island is at this time in a very turbulent state." [60] Two years earlier, however, William Williams had stated that "Since the supply of firearms has been more equalized, the disposition to fight has been much on the decrease." [61] Williams was probably referring, in this judgment, to the north.

[58] Letter of Williams, Janaury 20, 1831, pp. 215–18, typewritten copy of his letters, Hocken Library.

[59] Darwin, "Journal," in FitzRoy, *Narrative,* III, 499; Polack, *New Zealand,* II, 35, 39–43; Ernest Dieffenbach, *New Zealand, and its Native Population* (London, 1841), p. 28.

[60] Letter of Davis, April 23, 1832, Ms vol. 66, no. 32.

[61] William Williams, November 29, 1830, *CMR,* December 1831, p. 206.

At any rate, by the late 1830's, the worst of the killing was over. The use of muskets against an unarmed tribe passed away fitfully as all the remaining Maoris gradually found the means to equip themselves; and New Zealand returned slowly to a balance of arms such as it had enjoyed before the European weapons were introduced.

In 1827 James Kemp wrote: "It is generally believed by the natives with whom we converse, that since the europeans came amongst them, very many more of them have died, than there were before europeans came amongst them. . . ." [62] In this manner he gave the first real indication that the Maoris themselves, at the Bay of Islands, recognized that their population was declining. In the years which followed they became increasingly affected by that fact. They conclude, wrote James Busby in 1837, "that the God of the English is removing the aboriginal inhabitants to make way for them, and it appears to me that this impression has produced amongst them a very general recklessness and indifference to life." [63]

While the Maoris in the interior were still relatively unaware of the European connection with their declining numbers, evidences of the change were everywhere. It could not be otherwise. The population of 200,000 which had existed fifty years before was withering away. The half-deserted villages, the burned and ravaged *pas,* the concentrations of skulls and bones at countless battlefields helped to remind these Maoris of the population that once had spread across New Zealand and but for, to them, the influence of the *atua,* might have been there still.

In 1840 there were about 125,000 Maoris, which was perhaps three fifths of the population in 1769. The causes of the depopulation are perfectly obvious. It undoubtedly had resulted almost entirely from the contagious diseases and the new methods of war, two

[62] Letter of Kemp, November 6, 1827, Ms vol. 70, no. 24.
[63] Letter of James Busby to the Colonial Secretary, June 8, 1837, Ms correspondence, Alexander Turnbull Library, Wellington. See also FitzRoy, *Narrative,* II, 569; and Journal of Richard Davis, June 16 [1835], Ms vol. 66, no. 147, Hocken Library.

instruments of destruction which could spread rapidly over New Zealand without white settlement. One can only guess to what extent each shared in the depopulation. The often quoted figure of sixty thousand deaths through war is probably too high. Thirty to forty thousand seems more reasonable, and then because these deaths were distributed over a number of years, their effect on the population as a whole was significantly less than that figure. In the north, wars came to an end shortly after 1830, but the population still declined. The diseases, first the sudden plagues and the early effects of venereal diseases, later the constant sapping of life through many minor illnesses, undoubtedly affected the Maori population more.

There was no one group of white people most responsible for the depopulation. The difference between the high aims of some and the indifference of others had little relevance to their effects. The muskets and diseases, and to a lesser extent, the liquor, harmful new foods, hatchets, and blankets which the explorers, missionaries, traders, whalers, and other visitors introduced, combined in a manner which it is both impossible and pointless to try to disentangle. It was the white people, as white people, who, by upsetting the Maori culture and introducing a variety of new elements, destroyed the balance of Maori health and warfare and caused the great depopulation.

PART THREE

Changing Patterns of Behavior

Chapter VI

The European View

Almost all the Europeans who visited New Zealand were interested in describing and explaining the behavior and activities of the
Maoris, both in their original state and as they were changing
through the influence of white contact. Like the earliest explorers
they made descriptive compendiums of all the different aspects of
Maori life. Some topics, such as *tapu,* polygamy, and cannibalism
were perennial favorites.

Cannibalism in particular, though it properly shocked, none the
less fascinated, the European travelers. They usually wrote about
it in detail. John Logan Campbell explained of the Maoris that
"when the craving to eat flesh overcame them, they could not help
themselves but by helping themselves—to themselves!" [1] Richard
Cruise concerned himself with anatomical details: "The limbs only
of a man are eatable, while, with the exception of the head, the
whole body of a female or a child is considered delicious." [2] Edward
Markham was more offhand and informative than most: They cut
the bodies up, he wrote, and "slash down the legs and take the
bones out, wash the Meat and roll it up like Beef Oliver. Then it
requires four Hours, before it is done. The palms of the Hands and
Feet are tit-bits for the Chiefs. Europeans are not considered so
good eating as the Mouries . . . but it is no protection to them, as
they delight in having a Hungry Dance round a fellow. Then the

---

[1] John Logan Campbell, *Poenamo. Sketches of the Early Days in New
Zealand . . . ,* "New Zealand" ed. (Wellington, 1953), p. 99.
[2] Richard A. Cruise, *Journal of a Ten Months' Residence in New Zealand,*
2nd ed. (London, 1824), pp. 271–72.

Chief with his Marré gives him a Clip on the Pipkin and he is speedily cut up, so ends the life and begins the feast." [3]

Writing colorfully about cannibalism was one thing; explaining the Maori personality was another. Several difficulties which the Europeans did not realize stood in the way of their proper comprehension of Maori behavior. One was that each European looked through his own peculiar frame of mind at only a limited set of experiences with the Maoris. The end result was a varied and often conflicting set of opinions reflecting, as well as different European points of view, the different facets of the complex Maori personality.

Furthermore, none of the contemporary Europeans, no matter what their predisposition, had sufficient experience with the problems involved in understanding and explaining the actions of people of another culture. They were unaware of the difficulty of getting outside one's own cultural framework in order to examine objectively the behavior of a different society and of then explaining that behavior in a way which is not misunderstood in the terms of one's own culture.

Even the most unprejudiced of them approached the Maoris with oversimplifications and crude analogies to European attitudes. In European terms they talked and disagreed about the Maori "form of government." "I believe the form of government of this part of New Zealand . . . ," wrote John Savage, "to be aristocratical, and hereditary." [4] John Nicholas thought the Maoris had a sort of feudal system, somewhat like "that which prevailed to a recent period in Scotland." [5] But Robert FitzRoy said: "Democratic, essentially democratic, is the present political state of the New Zealanders. . . ." [6]

[3] Edward Markham, "Transcript of New Zealand or Recollections of it," Ms vol. 85, p. 115, Hocken Library, Dunedin. This quotation contains an early European use of a variation of the word "Maori."

[4] John Savage, *Some Account of New Zealand; particularly the Bay of Islands, and Surrounding Country* . . . (London, 1807), p. 26.

[5] John L. Nicholas, *Narrative of a Voyage to New Zealand* . . . (London, 1817), I, 287.

[6] Robert FitzRoy and others, *Narrative of the Surveying Voyage of His Majesty's Ships Adventure and Beagle* . . . *1826–1836* (London, 1839), II, 609.

The visitors judged the character of the Maoris to the degree that it conformed or not to the "admirable" or "vulgar" traits of nineteenth-century Europeans, and they also disagreed. Savage saw signs of "undaunted courage, and a resolution not easily shaken. . . . The manners of these people are particularly kind and affectionate upon all occasions. . . ." [7] Nicholas and FitzRoy agreed with him.[8] But Peter Bays concluded that the Maoris were "a filthy, blood-thirsty, savage race: . . . being of a most revengeful, unforgiving, and ferocious disposition . . . ," [9] while Charles Wilkes, the American explorer, thought they seemed "destitute of any of the higher feelings, such as gratitude, tenderness, honor, delicacy, etc." [10]

It is curious, and significant, that two of the most persistent ideas today about the early period in New Zealand have developed in part from the unlikely coincidence of the reports of spokesmen for the missionaries, on the one hand, and the incoming settlers of 1840, on the other. In order to relieve prospective settlers of their fears about the Maoris and in order to dispel any association in people's minds between themselves and the well-known groups of Europeans at Kororareka, the new, self-styled "respectable" settlers were often eulogistic in their praises of the Maori character and ruthless in their condemnation of the white men in Kororareka. For obvious, if different, reasons, the missionaries propounded similar views. And, perhaps because of the vast amounts of literature which each group published on the subject, the exaggerations have become ingrained in casual thought about the period.

The proponents of organized settlement gave the Maoris recommendations of character which even the missionaries rarely surpassed. Supposed past barbarities were often explained as misunderstandings on the part of earlier observers. One had only to look at the Maoris from the proper point of view to see that their natural propensity was to be honest tradesmen or sober laborers. "We . . .

[7] Savage, *Account,* pp. 17, 36.

[8] Nicholas, *Narrative,* I, 13; FitzRoy, *Narrative,* II, 607.

[9] Peter Bays, *A Narrative of the Wreck of the Minerva Whaler of Port Jackson* . . . , (Cambridge, Eng., 1831), p. 154.

[10] Charles Wilkes, *Narrative of the United States Exploring Expedition during the Years 1838, 1839, 1840, 1841, 1842* (Philadelphia, 1845), II, 397.

find," affirmed William Brown, "that they are not naturally cunning, but open; while . . . they are a nation of traders, exhibiting the utmost eagerness to possess the good of others, they are scrupulous as to the means—using honest and even laborious industry, where others might not even hesitate to steal." [11] A phrenologist examined the preserved Maori heads in London museums and reported to the New Zealand Company that "the intellectual and moral region were decidedly above the British average. . . . In all, Benevolence, Veneration, Self-esteem, Conscientiousness, Imitation, Constructiveness, Wonder, and the perceptive faculties were very predominant." [12]

The unconscious habit of forcing explanations of the different Maori activities into European modes of thought pervaded every interpretation. The Maoris and the Europeans presumably thought very much alike. Similar activities, therefore, implied similar motives; dissimilar activities implied differences of individual character, not differences of culture. Even the artists who drew pictures of the Maoris from life unintentionally distorted the Maori physiognomies to look in a way like Europeans. It made visual sense to the European eye.

Undoubtedly the Europeans had certain things in common with the Maoris which simplified the cultural interchange between them and made relations easier than they might otherwise have been. Western domesticated plants and animals adapted readily to New Zealand soil, and the Maoris felt at home with Western foods. (It would, however, be stretching the point to say that the Europeans were at all enthusiastic about fern roots, grubs, lice, dogs, and human flesh.) The Maoris and the Europeans resembled each other physically in many ways, and no matter what each group thought of the behavior of the other as a whole, there was little racial explanation

[11] William Brown, *New Zealand and Its Aborigines* . . . (London, 1845), p. 106.

[12] *The New Zealand Journal,* London, vol. I, no. 7 (May 2, 1840), 73–74. See also E. G. Wakefield and John Ward, *The British Colonization of New Zealand; being an Account of the Principles, Objects, and Plans of the New Zealand Association* . . . (London, 1837), pp. 131–65 for denunciation of Kororareka and pp. 166–96 for praise of the Maoris.

or prejudice about it. The Maoris permitted great freedom of activity for individuals—except for slavery, which was still an easily understandable problem to the Europeans. There was no caste to speak of. In short, in many ways the Maoris were certainly more like the Europeans than the Bushmen of South Africa, the aborigines of Australia, or many of the West African tribes. But even this, in the last analysis, contributed to the general European misconception of the Maoris, and occasionally led, as will be seen, to further complicating, rather than simplifiying, the problems arising from the contact of the two societies.

The effect of Western contact on Maori behavior was, like the nature of the original Maori character, hotly debated by the European visitors. This was particularly the case so far as the missionary and nonmissionary groups were concerned. Here the enmity of two centers stood out clearly above all the rest. White traders and settlers at Kororareka and members of the Church Missionary Society at Paihia faced each other over scarcely three miles of water. One was the center of secular life in New Zealand; the other was the heart of the church.

Kororareka was an anathema to the missionaries. It seemed to symbolize everything they detested: sin, atheism, and the devil. Yet Maoris of all sorts went there because it provided, with no demands on souls, consciences, or imaginations, exactly what they most desired. Did they want muskets? The whalers would sell them if the missionaries would not. Did they wish for tobacco, axes . . . anything? The whalers did not demand conformity to a lot of strange beliefs before engaging in such trade.

Young girls who in the mission schools had been apparently well on the way to conversion would suddenly run down to the ships and for a gaudy dress give up both themselves and their slender hopes for Christian salvation. When liquor began to be popular at Kororareka, young mission students from as far away as Waimate came to sample it. If the Maoris wanted to meet before a war or have a cannibal feast, they could do so at Kororareka. "The great intercourse with the Shipping," wrote Henry Williams with a curious ambiguity of language, "is the curse of the land; the natives begin to see it but have not the power to resist those great temptations which are thus brought before them. . . ." [13] Kororareka was a living example of everything un-Christian in the white man's way of life. It was a terrible danger to the Maori people.

In opposition to this missionary criticism, the settlers and traders of Kororareka and others so inclined developed, though in haphazard fashion, a number of arguments.[14] The first was to maintain that the nonmissionary population was civilizing the Maoris as rapidly and thoroughly as the missionaries. Augustus Earle thought that the nonmission white men had turned "these once bloody-minded savages" to peaceful habits by treating them as equals when trading and by bringing them what they wanted.[15] ("The day is coming," wrote Richard Davis about Earle's followers, "when God will have these mockers in derision.") [16] Joel Polack believed that the Maoris became civilized by following Western occupations, and that this was accomplished primarily by means of commerce, not religion.[17] (The pious Mr. Tawell said he knew facts about Polack which would "make me disbelieve him on his Oath under any Circumstances.") [18]

[13] Letter of Williams, May 3, 1831, p. 232, typewritten copy of his letters, Hocken Library.

[14] Not all nonmissionary authors criticized the missionaries. Among those who favored them were (with the dates of their visits) Benjamin Morrell, an American sealer (1820), *A Narrative of Four Voyages to the South Sea . . . from 1822 to 1831 . . .* (New York, 1832), p. 371; Daniel Wheeler, an American Quaker (1836–37), *Extracts from the letters and journal of Daniel Wheeler . . .* (Philadelphia, 1840), pp. 303–304; Bays (1830), *Narrative,* pp. 34–37, 167–68, a balanced judgment; FitzRoy (1835), *Narrative,* II, 579ff.; and Charles Darwin, "Journal and Remarks," in FitzRoy, *Narrative,* III, 507–12.

[15] Augustus Earle, *A Narrative of a Nine Months' Residence in New Zealand, in 1827 . . .* (London, 1832), pp. 166–67; see also Charles Heaphy, *Narrative of a Residence in Various Parts of New Zealand* (London, 1842), pp. 51–63.

[16] Letter of Davis, April 17, 1833, quoted in R. A. A. Sherrin and J. H. Wallace, *Early History of New Zealand* (Auckland, 1890), p. 322.

[17] Joel S. Polack, *Manners and Customs of the New Zealanders . . .* (London, 1840), I, 188–90, and II, 236.

[18] J. Tawell, *PP,* 1837–38, XXI, 111.

A second line of argument elaborated the French claim that the Anglican missionaries were materialistic, uncharitable, and really more interested in themselves than in the Maoris. It maintained that the missionaries failed to make conversions because they set a bad example and were not primarily interested in trying to convert. There seemed to be no justification for the private purchase of land or the sale of Bibles.[19]

A number of people complained that the missionaries did not make any attempt to teach the Maoris English. This deprived the Maoris of the whole range of English literature and science, limiting them to whatever the missionaries chose to translate into the Maori language and print. Translation seemed foolish since the Maori tongue was so deficient in certain types of words, particularly abstract ones, that English terms had to be absorbed into it wholesale. And William Brown reported asking a missionary why English was not taught and being told that "the natives would only learn every species of vice through the medium of the English language." [20]

Critics also thought it was utterly useless to berate the poor savages for failing to follow theology they did not understand, to confuse them with *"pompous prayers"*, . . . formal lessons, and fanciful stories about the horrors and torments of a future state." [21] They thought the dissensions among the different societies on points of doctrine merely upset the Maoris. And of course they did not like the missionary habit of preaching against the nonmissionary white people, feeling (since they were, after all, the nonmissionary white people) that it was not a particularly charitable means of conversion. Edward J. Wakefield, who admittedly hated the mis-

[19] J. W. Cunningham, *MR*, November 1840, pp. 485–89; J. Beecham, *PP*, 1837–38, XXI, 256–59; "Journal of Brig 'Spy' of Salem. John B. Knights, Master," March–April 1833, Peabody Museum, Salem; Earle, *Narrative*, p. 40; and, for the sale of Bibles, Brown, *New Zealand*, pp. 84–85.
. . . (London, 1845), pp. 84–85.

[20] Brown, *New Zealand*, p. 101; Earle, *Narrative*, pp. 155–56; Polack, *Manners and Customs*, II, 147.

[21] Knights, "Journal," March–April 1833, Peabody Museum, Salem; see also Earle, *Narrative*, pp. 58–59.

sionaries, reported that he met one Maori who "asked us to explain what the missionaries meant by saying, 'that all the white men not missionaries were devils.'"[22]

Many whalers and settlers thought the missionaries were a failure because the converted Maoris were not always really Christian, were often faking. Joel Polack, for instance, said the Maoris joined whatever religion was most convenient at the time, and left it when it seemed more profitable to do so.[23] William Brown thought the missionaries had eliminated the old Maori beliefs in *tapu* and the *atua* without substituting adequately for them.[24] The result was a lack of any moral force over the Maoris, who no longer believed in the punishments of the Maori code and had no civil law to bolster the, in this case, ineffectual future judgments of the Christian.

The most depressing of the attacks on the missionaries argued that in Christianizing the Maoris the missionaries had somehow deprived them of their energy and independence, had in a sense made them less useful than they were before. The arguments as to whether the Maoris were hard workers or not began in 1769. In the mid-1830's the whalers and settlers said the Maoris had been so when heathen but no longer were. Most of the missionaries believed it was otherwise. Richard Davis, however, admitted that by making things easy for the Maoris the missionaries had indeed made them lazier. The Bishop of Australia thought so too.[25]

The naturalist Dieffenbach thought the Maoris had lost vitality through the ending of wars and the mission denunciation of dances,

---

[22] Edward J. Wakefield, *Adventure in New Zealand From 1839 to 1844. With some Account of the Beginning of the British Colonization of the Islands,* ed. R. Stout (Christchurch, 1908), p. 53. Wakefield was at Port Nicholson. For this issue see also Peter Dillon, *Narrative and Successful Result of a Voyage in the South Seas . . . to Ascertain the Actual Fate of La Pérouse's Expedition . . .* (London, 1829), I, 253–54 and II, 321; Knights, Journal, March–April 1833, Ms in Peabody Museum, Salem.

[23] Polack, *Manners and Customs,* II, 235.

[24] Brown, *New Zealand,* p. 88.

[25] Letters of Davis, December 14, 1835 and February 9, 1836, Ms vol. 66, no. 47 and no. 48, Hocken Library; Bishop of Australia, March 28, 1839, *CMR,* December 1839, p. 292.

songs, and games as forms of vice.[26] E. J. Wakefield wrote a long passage about the mission Maoris—their "miserable outward appearance," the dirt, sickliness, and abject attitudes—compared to some of the Maoris who were still heathen. "In a word," he concluded, "they appeared tamed without being civilized. Together with the ferocity they had lost the energy of the savage, without acquiring either the activity or the intelligence of a civilized man." [27]

The activities of the missionaries and the arguments between them and their nonmissionary critics reflect some of the problems which any examination of early New Zealand history should take into account: how to explain the failure of the missionaries before 1823; the Maori conversion to Christianity; the softening of "savage" Maori characteristics before 1840; the meaning of Christianity to the Maoris; the effect of the settlement at Kororareka on Maori life; and many of the other points on which, like modern scholars, contemporaries disagreed.

There are no definite or categorical answers to such problems. The ideal approach perhaps would be to try to view the period from the Maori point of view, to see it as the Maoris saw it. However, as the above passages suggest, it is hardly possible to do this. The difficulties the nineteenth-century Europeans had in describing the Maori character are not so much reflections of their shortcomings as examples of the problems which go with any attempt to discuss another society. It is easy to find their weaknesses, but this does not mean that all the efforts of present-day anthropologists to contrive apt terms and definitions devoid of preconceptions and emotional content have really satisfactorily solved the problem.

So much occurred between the Maori and European societies before 1840 that the following chapters must emphasize some aspects of the situation—the Maori "domination," the causes and effects of the Maori conversion to Christianity—at the expense of some of

[26] Ernest Dieffenbach, *Travels in New Zealand; with Contributions to the Geography, Geology, Botany, and Natural History of that Country* (London, 1843), II, 19.
[27] Wakefield, *Adventure in New Zealand*, p. 112.

the others. So far as the ticklish subject of generalizations is concerned it is only possible to hope, as the anthropologist Linton states, that while no two individuals behave alike, individual differences tend to cancel out where whole societies are concerned so that certain general statements can be made.[28]

[28] Ralph Linton, *Acculturation in Seven American Indian Tribes* (New York, 1940), p. 468. The concluding essay by Linton in this book is perhaps still the most fruitful theoretical essay on acculturation.

Chapter VII

The Maori Domination

After the first shock of the arrival of the white people in 1769 had subsided, the Maoris at the Bay of Islands quickly became used to, and in fact fascinated by, their unexpected visitors. In spite of the comparative rarity of ships, they became rapidly more sophisticated in their knowledge of the white men and Western ways of life. They curiously inspected every vessel that sailed into the harbor and adjusted their first estimations of the character and activities of the white men to embrace a growing set of experiences with different individuals. About the turn of the century some of them traveled abroad on merchant or whaling ships and brought back new concepts and ideas for their tribesmen to consider. These Maoris first dispelled the notion that the white men lived entirely on their ships, and they described cities, white women, and public ceremonies they had seen across the sea.

As the years passed, however, and as the Maori conception of the white people slowly took shape, the corresponding Westernization one might have expected did not take place. On the contrary, until well into the 1820's the Maoris at the Bay of Islands were singularly assertive about their own ways of life. They not only did not become Westernized to any degree, their behavior tended to force the Europeans to act in some ways like the Maoris. Most of the characteristics and events of this early period—the increasing Maori warfare, the activities of the missionaries and other Western visitors, the introduction of particular Western articles—show how the Maoris maintained their identity and grew in assertiveness not only in spite of, but to a certain extent because of, the pressure of the Europeans.

The first effect of the contact with white people was to make the Maoris self-conscious: They were faced with the problem of considering alternatives for action which they had always performed unconsciously before, and at the same time the many obvious differences between the two peoples emphasized what the various Maori groups had in common. One result was that the Maoris, who had had no occasion to find a collective name before 1769, gradually began to use the terms "Maori" and "pakeha" to distinguish themselves from the white people. Probably Maori originally meant "native" or "indigenous." There are variations of this word with similar meaning all over the Pacific islands. It has never been determined, however, whether "pakeha" originated in *pakehakeha,* a sea-god of reputedly pale complexion, or from the Maori transliteration of the English words "flea" or "pork" (*poaka*). John Nicholas wrote the terms down in 1815, but the Europeans rarely used them before 1840.[1]

Extended contact with white people also made the Maoris self-confident. They soon realized that the Europeans were not godlike, that they had all the human frailties, and that with a little care they could be killed like any Maori. The Europeans did not practice the Maori religion or observe Maori social customs. Since to the Maoris the Maori patterns of behavior were the only intelligible ones, the failure of the Europeans to conform to them constituted, one might say, a certain deficiency of character. And as the Maoris reflected on this their confidence in their own cultural explanations evidently grew.

They then behaved toward the Europeans as they did toward other Maoris, attacking European ships on minor provocation, for *utu,* and plundering the occasional wrecks, following the custom of

[1] A most careful study of the origin of these words has been made by Sydney J. Baker, "Origins of the Words Pakeha and Maori," *JPS,* LIV (1945), 223–31. There are other articles on the subject in the *JPS* as follows: I, 133–36; II, 60–63, 116–118; III, 27–35, 236; V, 128; VIII, 141.

muru, or raiding. The massacre of the *Boyd* and other slaughters were the natural consequences of this attitude. For a time the Maoris even killed Europeans rather indiscriminately, until they discovered this somehow diminished the Europeans' utility. After 1800, sensible captains approached New Zealand harbors cautiously. It was no accident that one of the most determined and successful attacks on the crew of a wrecked European ship took place in the Bay of Islands: the crew of the *Parramatta* was massacred at the Bay in 1812. The *Venus* may well have been cut off there a few years earlier.[2] Where the Maoris had the most contact with white people they were most arrogant and intractable in their behavior.

They stole everything they could from European ships. Any article lying loose on the decks was in the utmost danger of changing hands. On one occasion the Maoris on a ship in the Bay of Islands began to cut away the halyards and other lines and tried to disconnect the copper chain which ran from the wheel to the rudder. They then gathered in a body in the cabin of this unfortunate ship and refused to leave.[3] Ensign McCrae said that the "natives of the Bay of Islands . . . are more cunning in their dealings, and have a sort of forward independence which those in the interior have not."[4] D'Urville thought that of all the Maoris he had come across "the most vicious and least sociable appeared to me to be those of the Bay of Islands. . . ."[5]

Perhaps the most striking result before 1830 of the Maori contact with white people, however, was neither the Maori self-consciousness nor the Maori self-confidence with Europeans, but an increasing aggressiveness in the pursuit of traditional Maori goals. The

[2] Robert McNab, *From Tasman to Marsden. A History of Northern New Zealand from 1642 to 1818* (Dunedin, 1914), pp. 110ff.

[3] Journal of William Hall, February ?, 1825, Ms vol. 67, no. 27, Hocken Library, Dunedin.

[4] Alexander McCrae, "Evidence Given before Commissioner Bigge . . . May, 1821," *HRNZ,* I, 549.

[5] M. J. Dumont D'Urville, *Voyage de la corvette l'Astrolabe . . . 1826–29 . . . Histoire du voyage* (Paris, 1830–33), II, 408–409, my translation; see also Richard A. Cruise, *Journal of a Ten Months' Residence in New Zealand,* 2nd ed. (London, 1824), pp. 54–55, 88; J. Flatt, *PP,* 1837–38, XXI, 44.

Maoris used Western weapons and Western foods to attempt to restore the balance in the incredibly confused ledger of insults, arguments, and defeats in war which they had long been wanting to revenge. The great increase in the number of wars permitted the extension of associated practices and influenced the character of the entire period. This was especially so after Hongi's return from England. The larger numbers of captives made possible an indiscriminate slaughter of slaves. Cannibal orgies multiplied with the growing numbers of the dead. *Utu* became more practiced as it became more practicable.[6]

Cultural self-assertion is a reaction to foreign contact by no means unique with the Maoris, but it did display in New Zealand variations of its own. If there was a florescence in Maori art, such as occurred among the northwest American Indian tribes when they acquired metal tools and made their large and independent totem poles, or in social organization, such as occurred among the plains Indians when they acquired the horse, it was not noticed at the Bay of Islands. "From the length of time these people have been known to the Europeans," wrote Earle in 1827, "it might naturally be expected that great changes would have taken place in their habits, manners, arts, and manufactures; but this is not the case. . . . When they can obtain English tools, they use them in preference to their own; still their work is not better done. The only material change that has taken place is in their mode of warfare." [7] Thomas Kendall had summed up the situation in 1820: "The Native Spirit has been roused, by the long intercourse of the Natives with Europeans; but none of them having yet been converted to Christianity,

[6] For this period see William Williams, *Christianity Among the New Zealanders* (London, 1867), pp. 35ff., and the various publications of the Church Missionary Society during these years. Particularly useful is Thomas Kendall, *CMP,* January 1820, p. 204. A. Ngata and I. L. G. Sutherland, "Religious Influences," *The Maori People Today. A General Survey,* ed. Sutherland (London, 1940), pp. 337–38; and Thomas M. Hocken, *The Early History of New Zealand* (Wellington, 1914), p. 26, reach the same general conclusions about cannibalism and *utu.*

[7] Augustus Earle, *A Narrative of a Nine Months' Residence in New Zealand, in 1827 . . .* (London, 1832), p. 56.

the Native Heart with its blind attachment to its barbarous customs remains unchanged, and inclines its possessor to pursue them with additional vigour. . . . War is all their glory." [8]

A great deal has been written about the changes occurring in Maori culture in the years before 1830. It is easy to assume that the increased warfare was inspired by new, Western ideas introduced intentionally or unintentionally by the Europeans along with their muskets. The argument that ideas of conquest, or Napoleonism, dominated the minds of Hongi and his contemporaries is a common one. Different authors have written, for example, that there were "new ideas of conquest," that "a series of very affable ruffians set out to emulate Napoleon," and even that when in England Hongi suddenly realized: "One King George over all England—why not one King Hongi over all New Zealand?" [9] It is also easy to assume that an indifferent and sometimes hostile group of miscellaneous and immoral white men quickly demoralized the Maori character in the places that they visited. Statements implying that this had taken place by the 1820's—either at Kororareka or among the Maoris at large—are not hard to find. One reads that the settlers at Kororareka "debauched both themselves and the neighbouring Maori tribes" before 1816, or that "Before the missionaries came to set an example of honest work and decent living, large numbers of the Maori race had been demoralized by adding the rascalities of Kororareka to their own original weaknesses," and other similar remarks.[10] Neither of these assumptions of the effect of the infusion of Western ideas, however, adequately explains the information

[8] Thomas Kendall, *MR*, July 1820, p. 308.

[9] For these three statements in their contexts, see I. L. G. Sutherland, "Maori and Pakeha," *New Zealand*, ed. H. Belshaw (Berkeley, 1947), p. 55; J. C. Beaglehole, *New Zealand, A Short History* (London, 1936), pp. 16–17; and Harold Miller, *New Zealand* (London, 1950), p. 11. There are similar ideas in many of the other histories of New Zealand.

[10] For these two quotations see D. G. Ball, "Maori Education," *The Maori People Today*, ed. Sutherland, p. 270; and J. B. Condliffe, *A Short History of New Zealand*, 2nd ed. (Christchurch, 1927), p. 31. See also the passages of the authors mentioned in nn. 2 and 3 in Chapter II above.

which we have about that time. Changes in the Maori way of life were indeed taking place, as the next chapter will describe, but they still had not, by and large, even at the Bay of Islands, disturbed the confidence of the Maoris in Maori motives, activities, and cultural explanations.

The evidence of the early years points to traditional causes, for example, even for Hongi's wars. The first tribe Hongi fought on his return from England, the Ngatipaoa, had caused the death of his son-in-law a few months before. His next victim, the Ngatimaru of Te Totara *pa,* had defeated the Ngapuhi at Waiwhariki in 1793 and on other bitterly remembered occasions. Among other things, members of the Waikato tribes, whom Hongi attacked in 1822, had helped the Ngatimaru at Te Totara the year before—where another of Hongi's relatives had been killed. To compound this confusion, the victims of the following years, Te Arawa, had recently destroyed a Ngapuhi raiding party as revenge for the entirely accidental death one of their chiefs had suffered at the hands of Hongi's men in 1821. Hongi's campaign of 1825 was against the Ngati-whatua, who had killed two of his brothers and many other relatives in a battle in 1806, or 1807, at which Hongi himself had been present.[11]

One might argue that all these were ostensible causes, mere pretexts for conquest or to obtain goods for European trade. If so, a few questions immediately arise. If Hongi had really wanted to be a king or to emulate Napoleon, why did he not occupy the territory he had won and rule the beaten tribes? It is known that Samuel Marsden once urged Hongi to become a king and bring peace and a stable government to New Zealand, but the suggestion got nowhere. The Ngapuhi chiefs around the Bay of Islands, including Hongi, knew no chief would ever degrade himself to let another be his overseer. All knew Hongi's power to be only temporary. When Marsden mentioned his plan to one well-known chief,

---

[11] Williams, *Christianity,* p. 35; and Samuel Marsden, *The Letters and Journals of Samuel Marsden,* ed. J. R. Elder (Dunedin, 1932), p. 243. See also S. Percy Smith, *Maori Wars of the Nineteenth Century . . . ,* 2nd ed. (Christchurch, 1910), pp. 181, 198, 224, 242; and the references to Hongi's wars in Chapter V of this book.

Rewha, the chief replied that the Maoris "were in a very different state, and asked me if I intended to compare the chiefs in New Zealand with the chiefs in England." [12] If Hongi had wanted goods to trade to the Europeans, why did he not bring back from his victories some other things than slaves—perhaps the only Maori goods the Europeans would not buy? The fact is that Hongi fought for *utu* and for *mana*. He may have used insults as a pretext for war, but if so, it was to achieve more *mana,* a Maori, not a European concept. His muskets merely upset the balance of arms which would otherwise have limited his activities, and he was able to exploit a most unusual opportunity.

The battles of the other Maori warriors followed similar patterns. Their wars were based on motives which were generations old. A case has been made for Te Rauparaha as an embryonic Napoleon, because he did occasionally occupy territories which he had conquered.[13] But then there is no reason to suppose this occupation was motivated by new ideas rather than old ones: the acquisition of land had always been one of the many motives for war, and Te Rauparaha need not have had ideas of empire to behave as he did.

The contemporary Europeans noticed the increasing warfare and even in the late 1820's and the 1830's explained it in terms of traditional causes. Marsden said in 1830 that: "With respect to wars amongst the natives, they always originate in some crime committed, some injury done by the one party or the other." [14] William Williams analyzed the wars in the south in 1832 and concluded that: "The causes for their quarrels are only increased by their mode

[12] Marsden, *Letters and Journals,* p. 388; see also pp. 383, 386. This incident occurred in October 1823.

[13] Kenneth B. Cumberland, "A Land Despoiled: New Zealand about 1838," *New Zealand Geographer,* VI (April 1950), 20; A. Ngata, "Maori Land Settlement," *The Maori People Today,* ed. Sutherland, p. 104; T. Lindsay Buick, *An Old New Zealander, or Te Rauparaha, the Napoleon of the South* (London, 1911), pp. 110–15.

[14] Marsden, *Letters and Journals,* p. 465; see also pp. 154 (1819), 285 (1820). See also Earle, *Narrative,* p. 140; and Henry Williams, *MR,* August 1834, p. 367.

of obtaining satisfaction. . . ."[15] George Clarke wrote: "When we ask the Chiefs, when their wars with each other will terminate? they reply, never, because it is the custom of every tribe who loses a man never to be content without a Satisfaction and death of another."[16] There is no mention of Napoleonism or new ideas by these writers. One must conclude that the introduction of European weapons and of unrest through white contact merely aggravated and facilitated the manifestation of attitudes which were already there. The most famous warrior chiefs only did what every other Maori tried to do, and did it more successfully.

So far as the impact of Western vices on Maori morals is concerned, it must be admitted at once that the white settlers at Kororareka did extend themselves energetically in certain areas of loose living. There was plenty of elbowroom for the expression of European vices at the Bay of Islands. Virtually every male who did not bring his own wife found solace among the Maori women. Presumably, at least, the whalers and escaped convicts at Kororareka were no more continent than the employees of the mission. "I firmly believe," wrote the Reverend John Butler, in 1821, "that all the single men that have been employed by Mr. Marsden have committed fornication among the heathen!!"[17] Butler was "exceeding glad" that his own son, Samuel, was in Australia, safe from temptation, and hoped that "he will marry before he comes down to New Zealand."[18] Not only the European men behaved this way. James Busby, at a later date, claimed that even one of the few European women in New Zealand "lived with the chief's son . . . on payment

---

[15] Williams, November 2, 1832, *CMR,* November 1833, p. 248.

[16] Letter of Clarke, August 21, 1827, Ms vol. 60, no. 20. See also Peter Bays, *A Narrative of the Wreck of the Minerva Whaler of Port Jackson . . .* (Cambridge, Eng., 1831), p. 154; and Hugh Carleton, *The Life of Henry Williams. Archdeacon of Waimate,* ed. and rev. J. Elliott (Wellington, 1948), pp. 104–105, 247–48, on origins of 1830 and 1837 Ngapuhi wars.

[17] John Butler, *Earliest New Zealand. The Journals and Correspondence of the Rev. John Butler,* comp. R. J. Barton (Masterton, N.Z., 1927), entry for January 22, 1821, p. 113.

[18] Butler, *Earliest New Zealand,* entry for January 22, 1821, p. 113.

of six canisters of powder to her husband." [19] That the visitors at Kororareka drank, and that they blasphemed and cursed, sometimes stole and committed murder, as well as indulged themselves sexually, is not to be denied.

The question, however, is not the scope of European vices, but the degree to which those vices brought about a demoralization of the Maori way of life; and before 1830 it is quite obvious what the answer must be: to practically no extent. Confusion has arisen on this point undoubtedly because what was immoral to the Europeans was often perfectly moral to the Maoris; and so with different judgments the two peoples often behaved the same.

By Maori custom, as previously indicated, Maori girls were usually free before marriage to indulge in any kind of sexual attachment they desired, while slave girls were always subject to the demands of their masters. The only change before the 1830's in this extremely liberal moral code was that the Maoris soon discovered that sailors would give articles of trade for this particular service, and Maori promiscuity was put on an informal, commercial basis so far as the Europeans were concerned. Maori chiefs now had their slave girls behave for blankets and muskets in a way that formerly they forced them to behave for nothing. Nonslave Maori girls, who presumably could keep much of what they received, still did as they pleased.

All the young Maori women in the vicinity of the Bay of Islands were anxious to get out to the European ships. Even the daughters and sisters of the chiefs wanted to visit the sailors, and while the chiefs did not particularly like this, the daughters and sisters eventually got their way.[20] Dr. Fairfowl, in New Zealand in 1820, said that "the whole unmarried female population appeared to be at the service of the ship." [21] Young girls at the nearby mission stations ran to their canoes when they saw the ships sail in. Some of the

[19] Quoted in Eric Ramsden, *Busby of Waitangi. H. M.'s Resident in New Zealand, 1833–1840* (Wellington, 1942), p. 73.

[20] A. McCrae and Dr. Fairfowl, "Evidence before Bigge," *HRNZ*, I, pp. 541, 554; Cruise, *Journal*, p. 166.

[21] Fairfowl, "Evidence before Bigge," *HRNZ*, I, 554.

Maori girls supposedly had tattooed on their arms and throats the successive names of lovers, ships, and dates of passage, and thus, as Lesson said, by simply inspecting their bodies one could trace the itinerary of the ships which had passed that way.[22]

In the 1830's a correspondent for the *Sydney Herald* estimated that the food, clothing, and odds and ends given to the Maori girls amounted in value to at least a third of all that the Europeans had acquired from the Maoris while in port. When to this was added the value of the articles stolen and dropped overboard into waiting canoes, the sum reached about £7000 a year.[23] This estimate was based on 150 ships. Du Petit Thouars, in 1838, was more extravagant. He put the figure at 200,000 francs (or £8000) for 120 ships.[24] Both estimates are probably and, for the sake of the European business reputation, fortunately, exaggerations, and both pertain to the 1830's when the ships at the Bay had become a great deal more numerous than they had been earlier. At any rate, both are, also, a little beside the question of Maori demoralization.

In the 1820's there was really little more prostitution at the Bay of Islands than there was premarital intercourse elsewhere. Venereal diseases existed, but these have nothing to do with the issue of corrupting Maori morals. While the single Maori women were perhaps excessive in their desire to visit the Europeans, they evidently broke no Maori standards in doing so—at least at this time. Contrary to popular opinion, the married women apparently did not go on board the ships until the 1830's.[25]

The other European vices had no greater effect on the Maori morals. Testimony has already been presented to show that in the 1820's the vast majority of the Maoris would have nothing to do with European liquor. They did not adopt insulting language or

[22] René P. Lesson, *Voyage autour du monde . . . sur la corvette la Coquille* (Paris, 1839), II, 339.

[23] Quoted in [E. G. Wakefield and John Ward], *The British Colonization of New Zealand; being an Account of the Principles, Objects, and Plans of the New Zealand Association . . .* (London, 1837), pp. 146–51.

[24] Abel Du Petit-Thouars, *Voyage autour du monde sur la frégate la Vénus . . .* (Paris, 1839–41), III, 104.

[25] D'Urville, *Voyage*, II, 406, 432–33, for example.

the habit of swearing. Idle European references to "breaking" one's head or "boxing" one's ears were too much of an insult to the Maoris—always sensitive about their heads—to be picked up lightly.[26] And although there are occasional reports of Maoris swearing, irreverent references to God meant little to the Maoris and were rarely made. There was nothing immoral for the Maoris in stealing from the Europeans, and the morality of killing another person depended on who he was.

The Maoris, in short, were not demoralized in the 1820's by copying Western vices. They behaved only in a manner to which they were already accustomed and with motives of their own. What was forced prostitution to the more righteous Europeans was merely enlightened self-interest to the Maori chiefs: the sexual aspect meant nothing, but trade helped in war and in creating *mana*. Both wars and sexual promiscuity undoubtedly increased in degree in the 1820's, but the ideas behind them were the Maoris'.

Until late in the 1820's at the Bay of Islands, and until later elsewhere, the Maoris made no attempt to copy the Europeans (or their suggestions) indiscriminately, but were, as is commonly the case with generally well-satisfied societies, selective in their attitude toward the culture which confronted them.[27]

The Europeans brought to New Zealand—intentionally and unintentionally—a confused assortment of the elements of their culture. The traders brought what they thought the Maoris would want, a variety of articles based on a cumulative experience with native tastes around the world. They carried beads, baubles, and the like to attract the native love of novelties. Their trading chests were filled with items of a red color—red worsted ties, red flannel shirts, red bunting. The holds of their ships bulged with metal articles

---

[26] Edward Shortland, *The Southern Districts of New Zealand; A Journal, with Passing Notices of the Customs of the Aborigines* . . . (London, 1851), p. 28; see also Carleton, *Williams,* pp. 72–79; and Marsden, *Letters and Journals,* p. 478.

[27] See Ralph Linton, *Acculturation in Seven American Indian Tribes* (New York, 1940), pp. 483–500, for a theoretical discussion.

and tools as well as flat iron, hoop iron, and tons of steel. Their supply rooms had stores of fishhooks and muskets and liquor.

The missionaries brought to New Zealand articles designed to "civilize" the Maoris as well as to amuse them. In one of the first requisitions for goods which Marsden sent to London for the benefit of the New Zealand mission he asked, besides metal tools and clothes, for: a few hundred pairs of scissors, 72 frying pans, over 850 small-toothed and common combs, the same number of knives and forks, 144 pewter plates "for the chiefs," and half a ton of common yellow soap.[28] And the missionaries did not intend to exchange everything they brought to New Zealand; they wished to give many things away. They hoped to put young Maori neophytes in navy blue jackets and heavy dresses, to plant English fruit trees and grains, and to show the Maoris how to tend such crops. Christianity must not be forgotten: it was the most important element of Western culture which the missionaries hoped the Maoris would accept.

Besides the things they brought intentionally, the missionaries, traders, and whalers also brought to New Zealand the cultural odds and ends incidental to any white man's presence. There was the person of the trader or missionary himself, his diseases, and the characteristically Western habits and manners of cooking (the Maoris did not boil or fry), eating, and dressing. There were ships, and in some cases, European houses, European languages, and, always, new ideas. It made an impressive, if distorted, conglomeration of potential choices for the Maoris.

The value of the European importations to the Maori depended on the particular angle of mental vision from which the Maoris looked. The only importations the Maoris had to accept were diseases. They rejected many others. Most of these were either incompatible with their purposes or not sufficiently attractive alternatives to the usual way of doing things. They turned down baubles, not because of any antipathy to baubles, but because they soon discovered how easy it was to get more useful articles. While the Maoris at the Bay of Islands were perfectly aware of the way in which

[28] Marsden, *Letters and Journals,* pp. 137–38.

Europeans talked, ate, and dressed, they were in general indifferent to this at first because of the Europeans' low prestige. To the Maoris the European was nothing more than a vehicle for the acquisition of certain European goods, and his habits and suggestions were largely left alone. Not only were alcohol and swearing rejected, for example, but such things as putting manure on crops violated the Maori sense of propriety, and for decades the Maoris could not be induced to perform this useful task.[29] The attempts of Marsden and later missionaries to interest Ruatara and other chiefs in raising wheat were pronounced a failure by Richard Davis in 1827.[30] William Colenso thought the early reluctance of some Maoris to take red clothing was because red was a *tapu* color.[31] The endeavors and prayers of the missionaries failed to gain a single convert in the first ten years of missionary labor.

In one highly personal way the missionaries and other Europeans were fortunate. Although those who wandered through New Zealand were helpless, they generally remained uneaten. There were two practical Maori reasons for this. Not only were the Europeans usually too valuable as agents of trade to be so inhospitably treated, but the Maoris agreed that "the flesh of New Zealanders was much sweeter than that of an European in consequence of the white people eating so much salt."[32] When the Maoris did eat Europeans it was either from a necessity for revenge and *mana* or from culinary inexperience.

In rather apathetic fashion the Maoris absorbed a few other Western elements. Handshaking was a novelty which had a certain vogue wherever it was introduced. Tobacco—readily assimilated through-

[29] William Colenso, "On the Vegetable Food of the Ancient New Zealanders . . . ," *TPNZI,* XIII (1880), 11.

[30] Davis, *MR,* December 1827, p. 623.

[31] William Colenso, "On the fine Perception of Colours . . . ," *TPNZI,* XIV (1881), 64–65.

[32] Marsden, *Letters and Journals,* p. 214. See also Cruise, *Journal,* p. 272; Edward Markham, "Transcript of New Zealand or Recollections of it," Ms vol. 85, p. 115, Hocken Library; and John Logan Campbell, *Poenamo. Sketches of the Early Days in New Zealand . . . ,* "New Zealand" ed. (Wellington, 1953), p. 31.

out the world—became increasingly popular. Around the Bay after 1820, a few Maoris took to Western blankets and Western mannerisms, while many took up Western foods. But muskets and iron tools were the only articles of almost universal demand, as the missionaries discovered.

When the Maoris did accept Western articles, they altered them in form and function to fit their Maori purposes. Crozet noticed in 1772 that it took the Maoris only a short time to reject nails two or three inches long in favor of ones four inches or more. This was strange, since they had nothing to hammer anyway. But as Crozet said: "Their object . . . was to make small wood chisels . . . [and] as soon as they had obtained a piece of iron, they took it to one of the sailors and by signs engaged him to sharpen it on the millstone. . . ." [33]

The Maoris used countless metal tools for purposes of war. Tobacco was smoked, but the Maoris also enjoyed decorating themselves by putting small pipes when not in use through the holes in their ears. Tobacco later had wide circulation as a medium of exchange. The Maoris accepted red ties, according to Colenso, because they discovered they could unravel the material and weave the threads into the borders of their fine flax mats.[34] They used red sealing wax to decorate the white sharks' teeth which chiefs and others often hung from their ears.[35] The Maoris who took to Western clothing were not accustomed to the restrictions it imposed and wore the garments in a most outlandish fashion. Blankets became more popular as clothes than clothes themselves. When the Maoris were induced to take money instead of goods for their services, white traders were occasionally startled to find that shillings were preferred to sovereigns. The shiny silver coins were more suitable for decoration.[36]

---

[33] M. Crozet, *Crozet's Voyage to Tasmania, New Zealand, the Ladrone Islands, and the Philippines in the Years 1771-1772,* ed. and trans. H. Ling Roth (London, 1891), p. 27.

[34] Colenso, "On Colours," *TPNZI,* XIV (1881), 65.

[35] Colenso, "On Colours," *TPNZI,* XIV (1881), 65.

[36] John L. Nicholas, *Narrative of a Voyage to New Zealand* . . . (London, 1817), I, 132; F. E. Maning, *Old New Zealand* (Wellington, 1948), p. 6.

There was in fact no Western article which the Maoris thought of or used exactly as the Europeans did. The traditional Maori ideas of novelty, material benefit, and prestige were those which largely determined which Western articles penetrated into New Zealand. And so in spite of European offerings, the Maoris were neither corrupted nor converted at this time.

The most interesting characteristic of Maori-white relations in the years before 1830 resulted from the fact that at that time the Maoris' feeling of self-confidence and of superiority toward the Europeans was perfectly justified. The Maoris could have destroyed all the Europeans in New Zealand at any time with little difficulty. And as they controlled, they therefore affected, the existence of every white or Westernized person who came to live among them. No matter how convinced the Europeans were that their relations with the Maoris should be otherwise, they were all forced, in varying degrees, to adjust their behavior when in New Zealand to the New Zealand environment and to the wishes of the Maoris.

The pakeha Maoris, as their name implies, made a great many adjustments of this sort. They might think, but they could not act, like Westerners. They usually lived alone in a sea of Maoris. This meant that they had to speak Maori, to take Maori girls, and to learn and observe the Maori *tapus* and other customs. Many also got themselves tattooed, began to wear Maori clothing, and joined Maori war parties, even though their skin color and knowledge often brought them a special status in their tribe. Polack met a European who said he was beginning to believe in the power of the Maori *tohungas* to divine the future in supernatural ways. There is nothing unusual in what happened to the pakeha Maoris, however. They were temporarily molded by their geographic and social environment as the *coureurs de bois* were in America and the bushrangers in Tasmania. Those who did not adapt their behavior to their environment did not survive for very long.[37]

---

[37] Joel S. Polack, *Manners and Customs of the New Zealanders* . . . (London, 1840), I, 44–45, 55–57; Ernest Dieffenbach, *Travels in New Zealand;*

To a lesser degree, the Maoris dominated the lives of the other white people in New Zealand. Even the traders and whalers who stopped by the Bay of Islands only briefly and had the sanctuary of their ships in time of danger, had, after 1816, to bring muskets if they wanted refreshments, because the Maoris would not trade for anything else. When on shore, they had to be rigorous in their observance of local *tapus* or, as Peter Bays said of the Maoris, "satisfaction they will have, or cut off your communication for water, wood, or trade of any kind, as they know ships come here for refreshment, and for one ship to resist by force, would make it worse for all others, till a recompense be made." [38]

Those white settlers who lived permanently or semipermanently at the Bay of Islands, the same ones who were supposedly ruining the Maori spirit with their wicked living, though they gathered together at Kororareka and other places, still behaved in many ways like the lone pakeha Maoris in the interior. The Europeans did have some special privileges and a considerable amount of independence, but as Earle incidentally remarked, the Maoris' "taboo'd grounds would not be so respected by us, if we were not quite certain they possessed the power instantly to revenge any affront offered to their sacred places." [39]

The activities of these Europeans were inconceivable to those at home. "Nothing can be more lawless than the Europeans who are there;" said John Watkins, as a respectable Englishman: "they frequently lay aside the English Dress, and take up the native Mats, and have promiscuous Intercourse with the Native Women." [40] But, however immoral to the Englishmen at home, these activities were the normal mode of procedure for the Maoris; and at this time, anyway, the Maoris drew the lines of behavior in New Zealand.

White people were not the only ones affected by the Maori way

---

with Contributions to the Geography, Geology, Botany, and Natural History of that Country (London, 1843), I, 191; Maning, Old New Zealand, pp. 121–29; Campbell, Poenamo, p. 36.

[38] Bays, *Narrative*, p. 156.

[39] Earle, *Narrative*, p. 147.

[40] J. Watkins, *PP*, 1837–38, XXI, 19.

of life. All the Maoris who had been Westernized abroad quickly reverted to Maori habits on their return to New Zealand in spite of the sanguine expectations of the missionaries and others who had schooled them in the Western ways. The best known of the Ngapuhi travelers were Moehanga (Moyanger), Ruatara, Titore, Tuhi, Hongi, and Waikato. Although Hongi was in England for only four months, he had also visited Australia in 1814. His behavior on his return to New Zealand is described on preceding pages. Waikato tended to follow Hongi's lead. Moehanga, the first Maori to visit England (1805), was there for only a few weeks, and by 1815, when John Nicholas saw him in New Zealand, he had only a jargon of English terms and a few memories to differentiate him from any other Maori.[41] Ruatara spent from 1805 to 1815 aboard English whalers and sealers, visiting Australia and England. Within three months of his return to the Bay of Islands, however, he died, faithfully observing the harmful and superstitious *tapus* connected with his illness.[42]

Tuhi and Titore, both men of high rank, were perhaps the two Maoris most likely to be able to retain their Western ways upon return to New Zealand. Both spent about two years in Australia under Marsden's supervision. At Marsden's request, both went from Australia to England in 1818, returning in 1819, with the Reverend John Butler, to their homes near the missionary stations. The letter Tuhi sent to the Church Missionary Society on his departure from England, though probably well-edited by his missionary friends, is a poignant expression of the converted savage:

DEAR REVEREND BROTHER—

I am just told I going to leave you, day after tomorrow. I will therefore write you,
Dear Sir.

I go home tell my countrymen, that Jesus is the true God. Atua is false—no God, all nonsense.

[41] Nicholas, *Narrative*, I, 426–31.
[42] Marsden, *Letters and Journals*, p. 121; Journal of Thomas Kendall, March 11, 1815, *Marsden's Lieutenants*, ed. J. R. Elder (Dunedin, 1934), pp. 78–79.

I tell my countrymen, Englishman no hang his self—not eat a man—no tattoing—no fall cutting his self. My countrymen will say to me, "Why Englishman no cut himself?" I tell them Book of Books say, "No cut—no hang—no tattoo." I tell them "Jesus say all they that do so go to Hell." I tell them they sin—they do wrong. I know that Jesus Christ's blood cleanseth all sin. I tell my poor country man so. He no find out the way to Heaven—poor fellow! Jesus our Lord, He found a way to Heaven for all who know Him. . . .

I get home to New Zealand, and I go tell my countrymen, "Come, Countrymen, into the House of Worship, where true God is worshipped!"

I hope you farewell. Good bye.

Your affectionate Friend.
THOMAS TOOI [43]

In July 1819, Tuhi and Titore landed at the Bay of Islands for the first time in four years. Within a matter of months, both of them had left their Western teaching behind and gone off to war.[44] Tuhi actually had not been at his home a week before he realized that he could not long keep his veneer of Western civilization without Europeans around him—or so he said.[45] Seven months after his return from England he was still affecting a blue coat, trousers, and cocked hat on occasion. He spoke English and remembered his table manners when he visited Lieutenant Cruise. But Cruise said that in his general behavior Tuhi "scrupulously adhered to the barbarous prejudices of his country . . . ," and later, that he was "without exception the greatest savage, and one of the most worthless and profligate men in the Bay of Islands." [46]

Between 1820 and 1822 Tuhi was away fighting almost continuously and, as Francis Hall said, war seemed to be his delight.[47] By the end of that time he had reverted almost entirely to his native

---

[43] Letter of Tooi, December 14, 1818, *MR,* July 1820, p. 309; see William R. Wade, *A Journey in the Northern Island of New Zealand: Interspersed with Various Information Relative to the Country and People* (Hobart Town, 1842), pp. 184–88, for comments on the sincerity of Maori writing.

[44] See *CMP,* 1821–22, pp. 202–203, on general failure; also Cruise, *Journal,* pp. 36–37.

[45] Marsden, *Letters and Journals,* p. 149.

[46] Cruise, *Journal,* pp. 36, 145; see also p. 34.

[47] Journal of Hall, June 8, 1822, *MR,* November 1823, p. 507.

clothing.⁴⁸ He had also evidently lost the last vestiges of Christian teaching. In 1824 two different Frenchmen paid him visits. To one he boastingly insinuated he had had intercourse with a missionary's daughter while he was in Australia; to the other he offered to exchange a tattooed head for a pound of powder.⁴⁹

Titore lived thirteen years longer than Tuhi, who died in 1826, and after a while he began to aid the missionaries occasionally when the missionaries could help satisfy his Maori aims. But like all the other Maoris who had been abroad, he had only a few superficial mannerisms to remind the Europeans that he had once been "civilized."

Of all the groups whose aims and activities were modified by the Maori environment, the missionaries were the most disheartened, for their intent was to change the Maori way of life, and they had seemed at first well organized to do this. They brought their entire culture, so far as it was possible, to New Zealand with them. With its English cottages, English crops, healthy English families, books, domesticated animals, and religious enthusiasm, the mission station represented a small island of Western culture in New Zealand.

However, even a clear definition of aims and a methodical approach made no headway with the Maoris. The missionaries had to make difficult adjustments immediately. They were forced to cling to Hongi, who wanted white settlers, because they needed protection. They were largely dependent on Maori foods because at first they could not grow crops at the place set aside for them, Rangihoua, for it was infertile. They learned Maori quickly, since they had to converse to convert and the Maoris had no desire to speak English. They submitted to constant thefts and insults by the Maoris as gracefully as they could, because there was no way to control them. And they entered the musket trade because the Maoris wanted muskets and there was nothing else to do.

The missionaries found they even had to observe many of the

⁴⁸ Letter of Henry Williams, November 21, 1823, p. 49, typewritten copy of his letters, Hocken Library.
⁴⁹ Lesson, *Voyage*, II, 213; D'Urville, *Voyage*, III, 691. See also the letter of Thomas Kendall to Marsden, c. 1819, in Butler, *Earliest New Zealand*, p. 31, which probably bears on the missionary's daughter.

heathen *tapus* and superstitutions they had come so far to eradicate. In September 1815, William Hall moved from Rangihoua to Waitangi, a more fertile section of the Bay. Four months later he was attacked and almost killed by a gang of Maoris because he, or some of his Maori friends, had violated a Maori custom there, and he was driven back to the *tapu* district of the missionaries.[50] Cruise said that the white people in New Zealand found that the best way to keep Maoris from molesting them was to hang a dead pigeon or a piece of pork above their doors.[51]

The missionaries certainly could not proselyte successfully when they were so completely on the defensive. They might induce occasional Maoris to conform to a few superficialities, but to gain active adherents they had to make the Maoris actually change their minds. The only way it was possible for anyone to influence the Maoris at the time, however, was to become as "Maorified" as possible. Then, however, one was in no position to preach Christianity. This has always been an insoluble predicament for missionaries; it is the key to the enigma of Thomas Kendall.

Kendall clearly saw that to gain influence over the Maoris he had first to conform to their patterns of living and win them to his side. There was no point lecturing the Maoris on their wars and cannibalism, let alone the fine points of Christian doctrine, if they would not listen. "Let the circumstances of our situation be duly weighed," he wrote Marsden, defending the mission musket trade. "Reflect for a moment that we are not only connected with, but we are the subjects of, a heathen government. Consider the absolute control which the natives have over us directly and over our property and proceedings indirectly. . . ."[52] Kendall thought the missionaries could only gain the confidence of the Maoris by conforming to their

[50] Alexander McCrae, *Journal Kept in New Zealand in 1820 . . .* , ed. F. R. Chapman (Wellington, 1928), p. 13; letter of Thomas Kendall to Marsden, July 25, 1817, *Marsden's Lieutenants,* p. 140.

[51] Cruise, *Journal,* p. 180. A good example of general Maori insults to the missionaries is in Butler, *Earliest New Zealand,* entry for August 18, 1821, pp. 149–51.

[52] Letter of Kendall to Marsden, September 27, 1821, Ms vol. 71, no. 9.

habits. He therefore learned Maori thoroughly, helped Hongi with his schemes, traded in muskets, and lived with the Maoris until they accepted him as one of them and he finally achieved the influence he had thought necessary. This was fine.

But the difficulty was that Kendall became so completely "Maorified" in the process that eventually he lost sight of his ends. Marsden found that Kendall had acquired a great knowledge of Maori customs, manners, religion, and language, but that he was so involved with Maori habits of thought that he could not communicate this knowledge to the other missionaries. He was unable to express the obscure reasoning in English terms.[53] When he was discredited for living with a Maori girl and removed from his post, he was unfit for any other place, so he and his family lived on in the Bay of Islands for several years afterwards. Kendall had gained tremendous influence with the Maoris. In several ways he had saved the mission from destruction. But he was no longer of any use for preaching Christianity.[54]

The dependence of the missionaries on the protection of Hongi is another example of the predicament in which they found themselves. As Kendall said, "he would be an enemy to us if we opposed his interests."[55] The missionaries were terrified by any action of Hongi's which might be construed as relaxation of his support, but were helpless to do anything about it. When Hongi set off with Kendall for England in 1820, the missionaries were convinced that jealous tribes would attack them in his absence. "By taking away Shunghee, you take from us all our protection . . ." wrote John Butler to Kendall, "I greatly question whether we shall be able to live among them when he is gone. . . ."[56] Ensign McCrae said that even Marsden resorted to offering Hongi a double-barreled gun, one of Hongi's stated objectives, if he would remain.[57] Hongi, how-

---

[53] Marsden, *Letters and Journals*, p. 347.

[54] A good description of Kendall in 1824 is in D'Urville, *Voyage*, III, 677.

[55] Letter of Kendall to Marsden, September 27, 1821, Ms vol. 71, no. 9.

[56] Butler, *Earliest New Zealand*, p. 73; see also Cruise, *Journal*, p. 20.

[57] McCrae, *Journal*, p. 15; note Marsden's endorsement of McCrae in *Letters and Journals*, p. 239n.

ever, insisted. He and Kendall needed each other. One wanted help in acquiring all the muskets possible; the other required support for his own questionable missionary status. The two of them went off with few good wishes from the missionary group.

When Hongi returned from England he was temporarily hostile toward the missionaries, and their fears revived. Marsden and Butler had evidently advised the Church Missionary Society not to favor him too much because of their dissatisfaction with Kendall. Also, as Francis Hall reported it, Hongi discovered "that King George knew nothing about us nor Mr. Marsden either." [58] He remained surlily in his hut at Kerikeri for a few days, and, "In consequence of this we have had many hard speeches and cruel mockings. . . . The Native Sawyers immediately struck work. . . ." [59]

In short, Hongi protected the missionaries, but treated them as he pleased. Once, when a sailor gave Hongi a musket and asked for a Maori girl, Hongi chose for him one of the best of the missionary girls, well-clothed, well-taught, and freshly scrubbed. The missionaries knew better than to interfere between Hongi and a musket. They did nothing. [60]

When Hongi's death seemed imminent, the missionaries' fears increased. Shortly after he was wounded they loaded twenty tons of goods on a ship and buried as much as they could of the rest of their possessions in preparation for a flight to Sydney. But the missionaries escaped the plundering they expected because of their association with a famous chief: Hongi lived for fourteen months more; during that time he stayed near Whangaroa, not Kerikeri; and coincidentally with his death a crisis at Hokianga engaged the attention of all the local Maoris. [61]

---

[58] Letter of Francis Hall, October 20, 1821, Ms vol. 53, no. 1.

[59] Letter of Hall, October 20, 1821, Ms. vol. 53, no. 1. See also letter of James Kemp, November 13, 1821, Ms vol. 70, no. 3; and Journal of John Butler, *Earliest New Zealand,* entry for August 21, 1821, pp. 152–53 for Marsden and Butler in opposition to Hongi.

[60] Journal of William Hall, January 2, 1823, Ms vol. 67, no. 26, Hocken Library.

[61] Hongi died March 5, 1828. For the missionary situation see Williams,

In 1827 George Clarke summarized the relations between Hongi and the missionaries: "It has been hitherto understood by the great body of Natives around us, that we are in New Zealand solely for Shunghee's purposes, and under his entire protection: while, on the one hand, such a supposition on the part of the Natives kept them in awe and afforded us a measure of peace; on the other, the body of Natives could take but little interest in us, for fear of exciting the jealousy of Shunghee." [62] Like Thomas Kendall, Hongi was a valuable, if not entirely satisfactory, link between the Europeans and the Maoris.

In spite of the difficulties of the missionaries, Marsden and many of the interested well-wishers in England were optimistic about the progress of the Maoris in English ways. Superficially, at least, this seemed justified. Schools were usually in operation for the Maori children. By the early 1820's proper clothing was being distributed among the Ngapuhi, and English tools were eagerly asked for by all the Maori tribes. Missionaries were wanted everywhere. Many of the Maoris at the Bay would shake hands, repeat prayers and catechisms, and refrain from work on Sundays near the mission stations. When Marsden induced fourteen Maoris to help him cut timber on a beach, it was to him "a scene of happiness and busy civilization . . . the dawn of civil and religious liberty to this land of superstition, darkness, and cruelty." [63]

But it was a form of self-deception. Marsden lived twelve hundred miles from New Zealand, rarely visited it, and generally believed implicitly what the Maoris told him. When he did come to see the Maoris and the mission stations, as Henry Williams said, "dispensing his presents on every side, he always had workers at command, yet learned but little of the real state of things." [64] To Marsden, the New Zealand missionaries were always to blame for

---

Christianity, p. 88; Carleton, *Williams,* pp. 96–104, 107; and William Williams, March 11, 1828, *MR,* August 1828, pp. 411–12.

[62] Clarke, *MR,* December 1827, p. 625; see also Cruise, *Journal,* pp. 54–55.

[63] Marsden, *Letters and Journals,* pp. 150–51.

[64] Letter of Williams, May 13, 1826, pp. 136–47, typewritten copy of his letters, Hocken Library.

the persistent heathenism of the Maoris, who seemed to him so anxious to be Westernized.

The missionaries, however, were perfectly aware of the real state of things. They understood as well as the Maoris themselves that the Maoris' assumption of civilized appearances was merely to get what they wanted—muskets, hatchets, blankets—more easily. John King wrote in 1819 that the Maoris "are very desireous for missions —one Chief says come and live with me—another says come and live with me—and one almost angry there is so few—and are very impatient to wait untill more comes—they see—clearly see the temporal benefit arising from the mission. . . ." [65]

The new policies and new personnel of Henry Williams were at first no more effective than the earlier missionaries' efforts had been. The Maori attitude did not change. Williams said in 1823 that the reason the Maories wanted the missionaries was for "the influence their tribe may obtain over that of another, and also the Axes, Blankets, etc., etc., which may fall into their hands." [66] James Kemp came to a similar conclusion late in 1824: "Their object in letting us live amonst them, is to get all they can from us, self interest is the motive by which they are actuated." [67] Three years later George Clarke reported that "The Natives in general are very candid when conversing with us on religious topicks and do not hesitate to tell us, that it is worldly good they seek and want; if we can assist them, they tell us, in the acquisition of that, they will listen to us." [68] At the end of 1827 Richard Davis wrote that "they know Missionaries possess property and it raises a chief in the eyes of his countrymen if he has a Missionary living with him. . . . If a New Zealander or any other heathen wished to have a Missionary on Missionary principles it would be a miracle. . . ." [69]

[65] Letter of King, November 4, 1819, Ms vol. 73, no. 1.
[66] Letter of Williams, November 21, 1823, p. 50, typewritten copy of his letters, Hocken Library.
[67] Letter of Kemp, December 31, 1824, p. 42, typewritten copy of his letters, Hocken Library.
[68] Letter of Clarke, August 21, 1827, Ms vol. 60, no. 20.
[69] Letter of Davis, November 14, 1827, Ms. vol. 66, no. 19.

When the Maoris who gathered at the missionary stations had gotten what they wanted, they departed. There were always some useless, lazy Maoris hanging around the English settlements expecting favors. "Those natives who have received the most of the society's Property do not always beheave the best," wrote John King, "but often the reverse." [70] In 1829 as in 1819, the attendance at the schools was determined by the amounts of food on hand.[71] Mrs. Henry Williams was concerned about the Maori girls, because "as soon as you have cleaned them, clothed them, and they are beginning to do something, they will go." [72]

It is a tribute to the missionaries that they labored on in spite of the disillusionment and the apparent futility of their work. Assuming that if they could not make Christians of the Maoris, they could at least soften some of their savagery, they continued teaching, clothing, praying, and healing. Whoever came to their schools, they accepted in good faith. Whoever was ill, they tried to heal. They saw the first baptism of a Maori in 1825 and the next in 1827 as signs that sooner or later their endeavors would be abundantly rewarded by the total Christianization of New Zealand. They did not let the difficulties in their way discourage them. "If we had all come to New Zealand only to effect, with God's blessing, this one conversion," one of them wrote about a later convert, "—to save this one soul—it was worth all that we have done or all that we can ever do." [73]

Those people who say that Henry Williams had a stronger character than the earlier New Zealand missionaries are undoubtedly correct. Those who say that it was this character which brought about a change in the Maoris, however, are both unfair to the earlier missionaries and inaccurate. While Williams may have acquired a certain amount of *mana* through his personality, this is hardly

[70] Journal of King, July 29, 1823, Ms vol. 73, no. 13, Hocken Library.

[71] See Thomas Kendall, *MR*, November 1819, p. 464; and William Williams, *MR*, February 1830, p. 113.

[72] Letter of Mrs. Williams, February 11, 1824, Ms extracts, 1822–24, Alexander Turnbull Library, Wellington.

[73] William Yate, May 14, 1832, *MR*, May 1833, p. 212.

indicative of Maori change. Throughout the 1820's the Maoris would generally listen patiently and with occasional curiosity to what the different missionaries had to say. At other times, however, they would break out into noise-making disturbances, bang on the walls with their fists and kick the benches, jeopardizing the safety of the missionaries themselves.

As long as the Maoris were confident and satisfied that what was happening to them was a matter of their own choice, as long as their culture could satisfactorily explain their experiences to them, they could scarcely be expected to change their habits of thought or ways of life. They knew that if they wished they could destroy the English settlements. They welcomed the missionaries and traders only as long as these white people provided useful articles and did not violate important customs or *tapus*.

Chapter VIII

The Maori Conversion

In 1845, George Clarke, who then held the government office of Chief Protector of the Aborigines, compiled some rough statistics on the religious beliefs of the Maoris. He estimated that out of a total population of about 110,000 there were 42,700 Maoris who regularly attended the services of the Church of England, 16,000 who attended Methodist services, and 5,100 who were associated with the Roman Catholics. If these statistics are accurate, there were then about 64,000 nominally Christian Maoris compared to 46,000 pagans.[1] Only ten years before, in 1835, there had been but a handful of Maoris interested in Christianity. A few years before that there had been none. How did these remarkable changes come about?

By 1830, in spite of the Maori domination, the Maoris at the Bay of Islands were outwardly undergoing a marked and rapid change. The canoeloads of red-ochred warriors which had only recently kept the surface of the Bay in continual disturbance were by this time rarely seen. Many Maoris were wearing European shirts and pants in whatever grotesque fashion pleased them. Some of them worked up the creeks and shallow inlets with saws and hatchets to cut out timber, while others labored in gardens with hoes and spades—all engaged in the increasingly difficult task of earning the price of a musket or a blanket. A number of English

---

[1] George Clarke, April 1, 1845, *PP,* 1846, XXX, 47. Clarke may be a little hard on the Catholics (for a Catholic estimate see n. 66 in this chapter). Clarke remarks in general: "I find it impracticable to obtain sufficiently accurate data . . . on account of the daily diminishing number of the Pagans."

words had crept into their vocabularies as the chiefs discussed the
flax and timber markets with visiting captains and traders.

Many old customs and habits were dropped. The Europeans who
had returned to the Bay after an absence of several years could
scarcely help noticing how much easier it was to get along with
the Maoris and how much more trustworthy they had become.
There was not so much theft, and the irritating abuses which the
missionaries and traders had become accustomed to suffering had
begun to abate. In 1820, King George, the chief at Kororareka, had
joined with some friends of his to bully white traders in order, he
said, " 'to get as much as they could from the white man.' " [2] By
1827 King George was pleased to be known as the protector of
white traders in the Bay.[3] Not only did the Maoris at the Bay of
Islands now rarely practice *utu* and *muru* on the Europeans, but
they did so less among themselves. There was not so much osten-
tatious cannibalism around the European settlements. The Maoris
were less careful of the hair on their highly *tapu* heads. Some of
them were sleeping in the same houses in which they ate. They
did not call upon *tohungas* to officiate at as many activities as had
been common only a short while before.[4]

Symptoms of white influence had crept into many Maori ceremonies and amalgamated with the old. Francis Hall noticed a
change in a *hahunga,* or exhumation, ceremony as early as 1822.
"Many guns were fired this morning," he wrote, "Shunghee has been
having the bones of his son-in-law removed, and the firing was to
drive away the Attua." [5] Burial symbolized a growing mixture of
the two cultures. James Stack described a burial late in 1829: "The

[2] Richard A. Cruise, *Journal of a Ten Months' Residence in New Zealand,*
2nd ed. (London, 1824), p. 121; see also pp. 54–55, 60, 119–21.

[3] Augustus Earle, *A Narrative of a Nine Months' Residence in New Zealand,
in 1827* . . . (London, 1832), p. 87. The contrast between Earle and Cruise
shows best the changes of a few years. These changes, however, can be
overemphasized. Earle does give examples of cannibalism, *muru,* and other
Maori practices imposed on the Europeans in 1827. See pp. 91–107, 183–90.

[4] *MR,* December 1826, pp. 612–13. Several missionaries, particularly George
Clarke, discuss these changes.

[5] Hall, August 7, 1822, *MR,* November 1823, p. 507. Hongi was as westernized as any Maori at the time.

body, as is usual, was in a sitting posture, clothed in a blanket; the head richly dressed with feathers, having been previously well soaked in oil. His face was covered. On his knee rested a powder-horn. Close to him were placed his guns, and a whale-bone, a native weapon: close by his side sat his youngest wife, dead; having, in her first paroxysm of grief, last night, hung herself: her body was clothed with a blanket, and her head dressed with feathers." [6]

Changes came from two different sources. The Maoris still made many of them deliberately, simply as concessions to get more articles of trade, just as they superficially conformed to missionary requests. The Maori youths who went on European whaling voyages evidently suspended their *tapus* while they were away from home. Individual Maoris at the Bay of Islands often complied with Western ideas of behavior when missionaries or regular traders threatened to withhold their blankets and muskets. "They have seen the detestation that theft is held in by Europeans," wrote Earle, "and the injury it does to trade, and have, in consequence, nearly left it off." [7] King George said he had given up cannibalism " 'out of compliment to you white men.' " [8]

The Maoris were under no illusions about these changes. When out of view of Europeans they reverted to their customary habits in the same way that Europeans leaving New Zealand dropped matter-of-factly the mannerisms they had had to adopt in order to get along with the Maoris. In the immediate vicinity of the Bay of Islands before 1840 and, after British settlement elsewhere, changes of this sort did help to some extent in creating an appropriate context for the ferment of Western ideas, but this is the most one can say about their influence on conversion.

For the Maoris to turn to Christianity there had to be things

[6] Stack, *MR*, August 1830, p. 379 (at Hokianga River); see also William Williams, *MR*, December 1828, pp. 613–14.

[7] Earle, *Narrative*, p. 16. See also pp. 49, 78–80, 261–64; M. J. Dumont D'Urville, *Voyage de la corvette l'Astrolabe . . . 1826–29 . . . Histoire du voyage* (Paris, 1830–33), II, 224; John Logan Campbell, *Poenamo. Sketches of the Early Days in New Zealand . . . ,* "New Zealand" ed. (Wellington, 1953), p. 23; and Samuel Marsden, *The Letters and Journals of Samuel Marsden,* ed. J. R. Elder (Dunedin, 1932), p. 214.

[8] Earle, *Narrative*, p. 121.

happening which they could not explain in terms of their own culture and could not control by traditional means. In order to explain the cultural confusion which did undeniably spread among some of the Maoris at the Bay of Islands before 1830, one must turn to the other type of changes which were going on.

The fact is that the Maori self-confidence and domination of white visitors were only the most prominent characteristics of the early period of Maori-white relations and by no means explain everything that was taking place. Even as the Maoris were carelessly selecting and adapting the Western articles which seemed best to serve their Maori purposes and were using the Europeans as means of trade, they were unwittingly helping to create the forces which would finally destroy their own self-confidence. Starting insignificantly, but then gradually increasing in complexity and compulsion, these unknown disturbances acted and reacted in a multiplicity of ways which eventually culminated in the partial dislocation of the Maori culture. At first the Maoris were unaware of what was happening; later they only aggravated the situation by trying to use traditional means to rectify it.

One of the most important ways in which the Maoris contributed to their own mental disorganization was by applying traditional beliefs to Western diseases. Since Maori diseases were thought to originate with some evil-doing on the part of the sufferer, the fact that whole tribes of perfectly upright Maoris became ill was virtually inexplicable. Confusion increased with the growing evidence that traditional Maori methods could not cure the illnesses. The *tohunga* who spent all the hours of the night determinedly arguing with the *atua* yet failed to make his patient better obviously lost prestige. Maori faith in Maori remedies rapidly declined. The accepted formulas of behavior seemed particularly ineffective when the Maoris could see the contrast with the relatively good health of the white people.

The Maoris also became confused because they could not control by Maori means the Western articles they took so much trouble to acquire. There was a long chain of cause and effect which followed the introduction of any Western articles and led inevitably to cultural disturbances. The first link was the simple replacement of Maori artifacts by their Western counterparts. Iron tools replaced greenstone adzes. The musket replaced the spear and the club. Then, for the proper utilization of the new Western articles, the Maoris looked for a steady stream of additional ones. Maoris who used muskets wanted balls, cartridges, wadding, rags to keep the locks dry, and belts in which to keep all this extra paraphernalia. They also had to find a steady source of powder.

The Western articles also forced alterations in cultural elements which the Maoris retained. Muskets, to continue the example, made many of the old hilltop *pas* untenable, and the Maoris began to build their *pas* at more practicable sites in the broad river valleys. Warriors, used to hand-to-hand combat, had to learn to keep their distance in battle and to find cover behind trees and rocks. New means of defense demanded new methods of attack: towers to permit firing down into *pas,* and so on.[9]

Even more serious, however, was the way in which the increasing changes jumbled the traditional sense of values. Muskets and iron weakened the *mana* of greenstone and, ultimately, most of the religious symbolisms connected with it. The Western articles, as Stack and others noticed, even began to intrude into the highly mystical procedure of burial. Muskets made the traditional ways of catching birds obsolete and eventually destroyed the previously important hunting rites and mysteries. The inevitable decline of hand-to-hand fighting was disturbing. It meant that even a slave, if he had a musket, could kill a chief, and that no one could really

[9] Marsden, *Letters and Journals,* pp. 261, 272, 295. See also D'Urville, *Voyage,* II, 463, for a good summary of Cook, Nicholas, and Cruise on the subject of *pas;* Edward Shortland. *Traditions and Superstitions of the New Zealanders: with Illustrations of their Manners and Customs,* 2nd ed (London, 1856), pp. 251–52; Elsdon Best, *The Pa Maori . . .* (Wellington, 1927), pp. 272–83; and Charles Darwin, "Journal and Remarks," in R. FitzRoy and others, *Narrative of the Surveying Voyages of His Majesty's Ships Adventure and Beagle . . . 1826–1836* (London, 1839), III, 498. William Yate, *An Account of New Zealand; and of the Formation and Progress of the Church Missionary Society's Mission in the Northern Island* (London, 1835), pp. 122–26, seems to be discussing both hill-top and river *pas* together.

tell by what means a chief had died.[10] The efforts to acquire muskets also led to a series of indirect consequences. The fact that tattooed heads could be traded for muskets had confusing implications. Maoris stopped preserving the heads of their friends who had been killed in battle. Strict notions of *mana* were disturbed when slaves were tattooed before being killed and their heads sold.[11]

When to the disturbing introduction of muskets is added that of iron tools, new foods, blankets, and all the other Western articles the Maoris wanted, one begins to see how the ramifications of using these Western articles eventually helped to undermine the Maori culture. While this happened only by degrees, and while in fact the old Maori standards of behavior are by no means entirely gone today, the disruption was sufficient to confuse the Maoris. The Maoris were short-sighted and could see only that each Western article that they wanted seemed immediately useful for traditional ends. They could not realize there was no easily reached equilibrium once European articles had been introduced, no way the influence of Western elements could be kept within traditional bounds.

A third source of Maori confusion grew out of the application of traditional attitudes to the new means of making war. The increased pace of warfare and the staggering numbers of deaths which resulted were not unnoticed by the Maoris. Before the advent of the Europeans, peace had sometimes been brought about by outside arbitration, which saved the *mana* of both contending sides.[12] For a time after 1820 this became impossible. The Maoris were in too much of a frenzy to repay old grudges. The Ngapuhi especially lost all sense of proportion.

By 1830, however, the Ngapuhi had discovered that other tribes had muskets and became slightly apprehensive of new campaigns. Several successive defeats and the loss of life disheartened them.

[10] F. E. Maning, *Old New Zealand* (Wellington, 1948), p. 240; FitzRoy, *Narrative*, II, 608; Herbert W. Williams, "The Reaction of the Maori to the Impact of Civilization," *JPS*, XLIV (1935), 226.

[11] Yate, *Account*, p. 131; letter of Henry Williams, April 24, 1834, p. 291 of typewritten copy of his letters, Hocken Library, Dunedin.

[12] viz, Earle, *Narrative*, pp. 140–41.

Insults which would formerly have demanded revenge aroused only indifferent response. In 1828 a Ngapuhi tribe went to Hokianga to fight and returned without having done so. The local Ngapuhi had a battle at Kororareka in 1830 about the insults made by two girls jealous over the same white man, but there was more anxiety to make peace than to prosecute the fighting. The occasional comments in Henry Williams' journal of 1832, when he accompanied a Ngapuhi war party to Tauranga, indicate how upset the Ngapuhi were that warfare had gotten out of their control. Only four hundred fighting men were gathered in the first place, said Williams. "This is termed an army. . . . Their speeches were poor. . . . All were now tired of the expedition . . . ," and so on.[13] The Ngapuhi at first, and the other tribes later, no longer wanted to keep fighting wars, but knew of no obvious formula for stopping them. Traditional Maori ideas, as usual, when applied to Western importations, resulted in eventual confusion.

As a result of the sudden sicknesses and death, the constant threats of war, and the dawning realization of their inability to regulate their own lives, many of the Ngapuhi around the Bay of Islands in the late 1820's were ready to admit their increasing bewilderment. The confusion led to various reactions, which were later typical of other Maori groups, and which ultimately prepared the way for the first conversions.

One reaction was the temptation to run away. "For some time past," wrote Richard Davis in 1827 about some of the Ngapuhi, "many of the natives have expressed a strong desire to emigrate to some distant Island where they may be delivered from the oppression of their countrymen and live in peace."[14] By the early 1830's all the northern Maoris had withdrawn from the area south of

---

[13] Journal of Williams in Hugh Carleton, *The Life of Henry Williams. Archdeacon of Waimate,* ed. and rev. J. Elliott (Wellington, 1948), pp. 161, 162, *passim.* For 1830 see also Peter Bays, *A Narrative of the Wreck of the Minerva Whaler of Port Jackson* . . . (Cambridge, Eng., 1831), pp. 148–50; and letter of Richard Davis, March 5, 1830, Ms vol. 66, no. 25.

[14] Letter of Davis, July 13, 1827, Ms vol. 66, no. 16. See also Journal of William Williams, April 10, 1827, N.Z. Ms Copybook, 1826–28, p. 146, library of Church Missionary Society, London.

Bream Head in fear of retaliation on the part of southern tribes.[15]

Another reaction was to conclude that the white man's God was responsible for the Maori's troubles, since there seemed to be no other explanation. If Maoris were sick, it was because "the european God enters into their inside, and so causes them to die a lingering death, by eating their inside out. . . ."[16] Until the Europeans came, "young people did not die, but they say all lived to be so old as to be obliged to creep on their hands and knees. Our God they say is cruel, therefore they do not want to know him."[17] In war as in sickness: when the Maoris of Waimate came back from an unsuccessful campaign in 1832, they said "that it was our God which took away their fighting heart so that they had no desire thereto; in short, some of them speak surely and say that we have bewitched them by our prayers. . . ."[18]

The most common reaction to the growing depopulation and bewilderment, however, was simply an increasing depression of spirit. Every year around the Bay of Islands the inadequacies of the traditional systems of guidance became more apparent. Finally, indifference overcame those Maoris who could no longer contend with the complex realities of their lives. George Clarke wrote: "they very often with the most unaccountable apathy . . . tell us they shall leave their country to us and our children, so true is it that in every sense of the word they are without 'natural affection' either for their country or for their families."[19]

[15] William Williams, *Christianity Among the New Zealanders* (London, 1867), pp. 38, 181; John Butler, *Earliest New Zealand. The Journals and Correspondence of the Rev. John Butler,* comp. R. J. Barton (Masterton, N.Z., 1927), entry for June 2, 1823, p. 276.

[16] Letter of James Kemp, November 6, 1827, Ms vol. 70, no. 24; see also Journal of John King, August 4, 1815, Ms vol. 55, no. 27, Hocken Library.

[17] Letter of George Clarke, March 6, 1827, Ms vol. 60, no. 18. See also Butler, *Earliest New Zealand,* entry for February 17, 1821, p. 114; Joel S. Polack, *Manners and Customs of the New Zealanders . . .* (London, 1840), II, 235; Journal of John King, July 2, 1815, *Marsden's Lieutenants,* ed. J. R. Elder (Dunedin, 1934), p. 111; and C. Leigh, August 20, 1822, quoted in *PP,* 1837–38, XXI, 208.

[18] Letter of Richard Davis, July 9, 1832, Ms vol. 66, no. 33. Yate, *Account,* pp. 238–39, disagrees slightly.

[19] Letter of Clarke, September 13, 1833, Ms vol. 60, no. 43.

Eventually the white people took on a new stature. They seemed, once again, imbued with superior powers. The white people were practically exempt from disease at the same time that their God was destroying the Maoris. They increased in numbers and did not go to war with each other. They could violate the most sacred Maori *tapus* and receive no retribution from the Maori *atua*. They could read and heal. They could also repair muskets. This was important, because while the Maoris had the appropriate cultural background and adaptability to use certain Western tools, they were not always able to do much more. They needed the Europeans to supply powder and more muskets, and when a musket was taken "sick" they turned to any sailor or trader at hand. "They cannot be made to comprehend," wrote Earle, "that every white man does not know how to make a musket, or, at least, to repair it." [20] The fact was that the Europeans seemed to be the masters of the very things which were so upsetting to the Maoris.

Like the members of any comparable society in such a situation, many of the confused Ngapuhi—still a small minority—who lived near the European centers at the Bay of Islands began to ape the Europeans. A rage for European clothing began in the 1820's. Some Maoris began to cut their hair short; all took up tobacco. European table habits and conversational postures were adopted. Some of the Maoris affected wine drinking. But taking on the outward aspects of Western culture and adopting European social mannerisms made no difference. The Maoris were Maoris still with no understanding of the European mind. The fact that posturing as white men did not give the corresponding *mana* of the whites served only to confuse them further and to give the white men even more prestige.

At this critical time, one group of white people at the Bay of Islands came to the rescue with specific suggestions of behavior for the Maoris to follow. The missionaries, who had long been laboring to catch the ears of the Ngapuhi, finally found willing listeners. It is now necessary to turn to the missionaries to see exactly what it was they offered the bewildered Maoris.

The misionary methods and techniques for inducing the Maoris

---

[20] Earle, *Narrative*, p. 73; for anthropological theory see A. L. Kroeber, *Anthropology*, new and rev. ed. (New York, 1948), pp. 418–19.

to turn to Christianity had been developing for fifteen years. They consisted of whatever seemed to be effective in any given situation. Some followed the age-old technique of adapting Christianity to the environment of the heathen. In New Zealand, among other things, this meant using familiar Maori words. For "God" the missionaries used *atua*—the Maori word for "god." For "worship" they used *karakia,* the Maori word for "rite." "Baptism" became *iriiri,* a Maori word used in the *tohi* rite connected with the removal of a child's natal *tapus. Tapu* itself was substituted for "Holy." [21]

The missionaries found that the Maoris liked religious services in which they could participate. Church of England services at Paihia adopted more chants and responses, and emphasized singing. When the missionaries discovered that the Maoris valued something more highly when they had paid for it than when it was given to them, they decided to sell copies of the New Testament at four shillings apiece. And, finally, realizing that in no society do the members of high position welcome social dislocations, the missionaries directed their efforts at first primarily toward the slaves and children. They approached the chiefs and *tohungas* with more circumspection.[22]

The missionaries also appealed to the material interests of the Maoris. This was both normal and necessary. Native peoples have always been willing to listen to missionaries in exchange for an axe or a blanket. Even in 1829 the missionaries were still giving away articles of trade just to restrain the Maoris at the mission from going elsewhere. As late as 1833 every chief who visited the missionaries received portions of sugar and flour.[23] This is not to imply that the missionaries bribed Maori conversions wholesale with

[21] William Colenso, "On the Maori Races of New Zealand," *TPNZI,* I (1868), 18, on "iriiri"; see also the instructions to Pompallier in *Fishers of Men,* ed. Peter McKeefry (New Zealand, 1938), pp. 1–20.

[22] For this paragraph see William Brown, *New Zealand and its Aborigines* . . . (London, 1845), pp. 85–86; Yate, *Account,* p. 289; C.M.S. Report in *Marsden's Lieutenants,* p. 19; Robert Maunsell, *MR,* August 1840, p. 380; William Colenso, *Fifty Years Ago in New Zealand* . . . (Napier, N.Z., 1888), p. 20; and R. FitzRoy, *PP,* 1837–38, XXI, 166.

[23] Letter of James Busby to the Colonial Secretary, June 18, 1833, Ms correspondence, Alexander Turnbull Library, Wellington.

articles of trade, for they could not and did not try. They were simply aware of the need for material items to maintain Maori interest and utilized them freely. "What I mean, Sir," wrote John King about the Maoris, "is this: they want now and then a small present to lead them on." [24]

The missionaries also added the pressure of fear to the appeal of material interests. They informed the Maoris not only that Christianity was directly responsible for all the scientific miracles, the peaceful habits, and the intelligence of the white people, but that continued observance of the Maori paganism would bring disastrous consequences. [25] They held the acts of a few short years of mortal life responsible for one's eternal state. When Christian Rangi, the first Maori convert, was on his deathbed and presumably already considering his somewhat uncertain future, the missionaries preached to him in the following manner: "Those, who do not believe in it [Christianity], are the Devil's servants here, and will be his slaves in the Rainga, where they will dwell in fire for ever and ever; and it is impossible for the tongue to describe the pain and torment which they will endure. Those, who believe in the Great God, will be taken to heaven; and it is impossible for the tongue to describe the happiness which they will there enjoy for ever." [26] Who would not consider Christianity under such conditions?

Some of the missionary methods pertained especially to the increasing bewilderment about illnesses and war. When some Maoris told William Williams that they thought not observing the Sabbath had caused their sickness, he "endeavoured to correct their views telling them the origin of sickness through sin." [27] George Clarke thought that visiting sick people was "generally a seasonable oppor-

---

[24] Letter of King, July 6, 1815, *Marsden's Lieutenants,* p. 99.

[25] Journal of George Clarke, April 16, 1826, Ms vol. 60, no. 96, Hocken Library; Henry Williams, March 31, 1825; *MR,* March 1826, p. 162; J. Anderson, "Maori Religion," *JPS,* XLIX (1940), 543.

[26] Henry Williams, *MR,* April 1826, p. 186.

[27] Journal of Williams, December 9, 1828, p. 165, copied extracts of his correspondence, Alexander Turnbull Library.

tunity of speaking to the Natives to seek their souls health." [28]
Samuel Marsden told some Maoris that the *tapu* could "neither
heal their wounds, preserve them from danger, restore them to
health when sick, nor save them from death; but that our God,
though they knew Him not, could do all these things for them." [29]
And when the Maoris became willing to have white people inter-
cede in their quarrels, the missionaries had another "seasonable
opportunity" of talking to them about the benefits of Christianity.

About 1830 the combination of the Maori desire for leadership
and the missionary desire to lead began to show effects in the increased numbers of baptisms, among them the first full-grown and
healthy Maoris, and the preparation of the new mission station
at Waimate. In that year some of the Maoris began to ask, wrote
George Clarke, "how, to use their own words, they may please the
Father in heaven." [30] Christian Maoris began to place some of their
problems in the hands of the missionaries: how should they act
toward their heathen families? In what cases should they go to
war? Some of the heathen Maoris wondered how to dispose of
Christian offspring who had died, and asked the missionaries what
to do.[31] Although over half the Maoris, even at the Bay of Islands,
were still heathen in 1840, and although only a small number of
those baptized ever became communicants, each year after 1830
found both increasing numbers of Christian Ngapuhi and of those
whose behavior was influenced by Christian teaching.

While the specific elements of the Maori confusion and of the
missionary methods are quite clear, it is difficult to say in what
particular ways they combined to produce conversions among particular Maori groups. The material wealth of the missionaries, for

[28] Journal of Clarke, July 5, 1834, Ms vol. 60, no. 97, Hocken Library.
[29] Marsden, *Letters and Journals,* p. 274. Marsden was in the Thames area
at this time. See also William Williams, December 25, 1831, *CMR,* September
1832, p. 208.
[30] Letter of Clarke, March 6, 1830, Ms vol. 60, no. 30; see also *MR,* January
1831, pp. 60–67, for comments by H. Williams, W. Williams, W. Yate, J.
Kemp, C. Baker, J. King, etc. to the same effect.
[31] Journal of John King, June 6, 1834, Ms vol. 73, no. 16, Hocken Library;
and FitzRoy, *Narrative,* II, 584, give examples.

example, had an indeterminable effect. It created interest and kept Maoris at the missionary stations, but brought about very few genuine conversions by itself. The missionaries realized this. While they used blankets and hatchets to arouse enthusiasm, they always guarded against conversions brought about in this manner because the conversions represented either hypocrisy or confusion on the part of the Maoris. Still, the material attractions of the missionaries did provide a context within which other forces might induce conversions, and this was at first a necessary, if not by itself sufficient, element. "I do not know a case," wrote Richard Davis in 1830, "in which saving faith hath showed itself in a saving way out of the Settlements save the case of Christian Rangi."[32]

Christian services and other ceremonies also kept the Maoris interested, but did not generally bring about conversion in themselves. The gift of mimicry, the fascination with strange rites, the interest in group participation, and the love of singing kept many Maoris in the Christian churches who would otherwise have not been there. The Maori could enjoy all this without discarding any of his own attitudes and beliefs. But once he was confused, the semimystical proceedings did take on a new and important significance. The Maoris found the Catholic ceremonies, as Indians had in North America, particularly impressive.[33]

The first important pressure toward conversion on the Maoris resulted from the increasing sicknesses. It is not remarkable that most of the early converts were, or had been, seriously ill. The missionaries were successful doctors. They raised blisters, fed the sick, and stopped them from using streams to cool their fevers. Thomas Kendall noticed even in 1815 that the Maoris would make a few exceptions in their *tapus* if he would visit them when they

[32] Letter of Davis, September 1, 1830, Ms vol. 66, no. 26. For more cynical attitudes see Brown, *New Zealand,* p. 85; Polack, *Manners and Customs,* II, 237 *passim.*

[33] Letter of R. P. Servant, May 1838, *Annales de la propagation de la foi,* XI (1838–39), 145–46; letter of Servant, Hokianga, 1838, *Fishers of Men,* p. 23; Jean B. F. Pompallier, *Early History of the Catholic Church in Oceania* (Auckland, 1888), pp. 51–52.

were sick.[34] By the 1820's the missionaries were secure enough in their reputations as healers to refuse to help sick Maoris unless the *tapus* were omitted entirely.[35]

As the prestige of the missionaries increased through healing, that of the *tohungas* declined. Incidents such as the following one impressed the Maoris: Christianity had become popular in an area near Waimate in 1831. A *tohunga* took the opportunity of the illness of a member of his tribe to try to crush this change, arguing that the disease was a just sign of the anger of the *atua* because of the acceptance of Christianity by some members of the tribe. By all Maori thinking this was reasonable. It was the way the *atua* worked, and there was almost conclusive Maori proof—the man was unquestionably sick. But it backfired. Defying the *atua* and all the threats of the *tohunga,* Richard Davis came by and cured the dying man.[36] The more the natives had believed in the *tohunga* and the power of the *atua,* the more this disillusioned them, and the more impressive seemed the power of the missionaries.

The peacemaking ability of the missionaries had its main effectiveness after 1830, especially with the warrior class. The first peace in which the missionaries were involved was that between the tribes of Hokianga and the Bay of Islands in 1828. In this affair, however, they were tolerated, rather than requested. The battle on the beach at Kororareka in 1830, on the other hand, brought the Maoris to the missionaries for advice. When the Europeans tired of their efforts, the Maoris "replied that we must not be tired, but we must act with firmness and continue to go backward and forward until the difference was settled, for they could not make peace themselves." [37] After several more fruitless battles the Ngapuhi

---

[34] Journal of Kendall, July, 1815, *MR,* August 1817, pp. 348–49.

[35] Letter of Henry Williams, 1824, *MR,* March 1826, p. 161; see also letter of George Clarke, November 22, 1828, Ms vol. 60, no. 25. Carleton, *Williams,* p. 180, shows an instance of heathenism returning as the sickness becomes desperate.

[36] Letter of Davis, September 5, 1831, Ms vol. 66, no. 30.

[37] Marsden, *Letters and Journals,* p. 463. See also Williams, *Christianity,* p. 112; and Journal of Henry Williams, March 1828, *MR,* September 1828,

were always anxious to have missionary intercessions. When Williams went with the tribe to Tauranga in 1832 and 1833, he noticed that: "There is much pleading for missionaries to be sent among them to preserve the peace." [38] This was particularly the case among the young men, who became Christian in increasing numbers.[39]

The status of the different Maori groups was, as the missionaries rightly judged, important in determining their attitude toward Christianity. It was sensible to direct the principal efforts at first toward the slaves and children. William Williams once said that, "It was among persons of little note, principally slaves living at the mission stations, that the power of the Gospel began to appear." [40] And he was right. In New Zealand as elsewhere, Christianity has always been a very attractive religion to the underdog.

The great numbers of slaves Hongi brought back from his wars, when added to those already around the Bay of Islands, created a pool of miserable persons out of which many of the first converts were drawn. Betty, who was taken into the Davis home about 1825, was a slave girl from Kaipara. Dudidudi was a captive cared for by Francis Hall and later John King. He was finally converted (partly through King's description of Hell), but died in 1827 just before he could be baptized. Ann Waiapu was an ex-captive who lived with the Kemps. She was baptized in 1830 and shortly thereafter died. ("A more pleasing death-bed scene, than here presented," wrote William Yate, "cannot well be imagined. . . .")[41] Huka was a slave who ran to the missionaries when his master threatened to kill him.[42] Children were more pliable than adults; and old Maoris

---

pp. 466–69. W. Yate, February 1830, *PP,* 1836, VII, 189–90, does say they asked for the missionaries in 1828.

[38] Journal of Henry Williams, February 27, 1833, in Carleton, *Williams,* p. 176; for general information see Shortland, *Traditions and Superstitions,* p. 238.

[39] J. Flatt and T. Chapman, quoted in *PP,* 1837–38, XXI, 44, 204; *CMR,* October 1833, p. 225, July and December 1836, pp. 156, 296.

[40] Williams, *Christianity,* p. 126.

[41] Yate, *Account,* p. 174.

[42] Accounts of the four Maoris mentioned above may be found in *MR,*

who wished to continue their old ways often had no objection to their children's acceptance of Christianity.[43] Theoretically the perfect prospect for conversion was a sick, youthful Maori slave, and there were many of them.

The reaction of the chiefs and *tohungas* to Christianity changed with the years, but it was always determined by whatever seemed most likely to maintain their own high status. The attitude of the chiefs was complicated by the fact that their authority was not particularly strong in the first place, except during times of war, but that having missionaries (who preached peace) reside near a tribe, like having any white man, gave both muskets and prestige. At first the chiefs and *tohungas* liked the missionaries, but as soon as the missionaries began to convert members of the tribe, the possibility of losing important prerogatives and of slaves becoming equals was too much. The missionaries first noticed active opposition on the part of the chiefs and *tohungas* during the early 1830's when Christianity was beginning to become popular around the Bay. The *Missionary Register* reported in 1834 that "the Chiefs of one district have forbid the Missionaries from going among their people again on a 'teaching errand.'" [44] One important chief and *tohunga*, who went by the name of Campbell, followed the curious practice of "firing a number of muskets, in order, as he said, to drive away Jesus Christ." [45] Visits to Owaiawai, a village of two or three hundred Maoris near Waimate, were discontinued in 1835 because of the opposition of the chiefs.[46]

The chiefs and *tohungas*, however, soon began to reverse their attitudes. The *tohungas* found themselves losing prestige in every encounter with the Christian God and began to realize that they had better join what they could not defeat. One priestess conceded

---

respectively: August 1831, p. 339; March 1828, pp. 149–52; October 1834, pp. 425–27; October 1834, pp. 427–28.

[43] Pompallier, *Early History*, p. 51; Kendall, *MR*, July 1820, p. 308.

[44] Report, *MR*, February 1834, p. 106; see also November 1834, pp. 513–15.

[45] Richard Davis, April 5, 1835, *MR*, July 1836, p. 337.

[46] William Williams, Waimate, July 5, 1835, *MR*, December 1836, p. 557.

early and turned to Christianity in 1832, since "her god had lost his power on account of the Missionaries having come among them."[47] The chiefs began to consider their fading prestige as warfare declined. When it became apparent that their slaves were not only Christian in spite of efforts to stop them, but that they could read, write, and perform other Western skills, it was time to accept the inevitable. From 1835 on, increasing numbers of young chiefs (also impelled by the dislike of war) became Christian. Their actions in turn influenced Maoris who had a lower status, and the numbers of conversions spiraled.[48]

The conversion of the Maoris at the Bay of Islands greatly facilitated the conversion of the rest of the North Island; for once Christianity had penetrated the shell of Maori resistance it spread rapidly. While the missionaries had struggled for two decades at the Bay of Islands to convert four or five hundred Maoris, the south turned Christian almost overnight. In 1833 there were no Christian Maoris south of the Bay of Islands and very few who could be called interested. By 1840 there were over a thousand baptized Maoris in the southern parts of the North Island and over ten thousand others who attended churches regularly. Throughout the 1830's Maoris had come from the south to ask for missionaries and had even founded churches of their own. To the missionaries this rapid transformation seemed to be something of a miracle.

The Maoris of the south, particularly the interior, were much less Westernized than the Ngapuhi in the 1830's. For years they had been virtually unaffected by the events which were taking place in the harbors to the north. Western diseases killed many of them, and pigs and potatoes spread across New Zealand by 1820, causing a temporary disorder of their eating habits. Incidental disruptions must have occurred, such as *tohungas* losing prestige by failing to stop a plague, or pigs causing wars by trespassing on *tapu* areas.

---

[47] Richard Davis, June 25, 1832, *MR*, May 1833, p. 241.
[48] Rev. J. Orton in Eric Ramsden, *Marsden and the Missions. Prelude to Waitangi* (Sydney, 1936), pp. 125–26; William Fairburn, April 30, 1838, *MR*, July 1839, p. 348.

But without the constant pressure and consciousness of white contact, these changes caused no great ferment or confusion. Every
culture, even the most isolated, is continually faced with natural
accidents and unexpected occurrences for which explanations must
be made. Diseases, without the constant reminder created by the
actual presence of white people, could—like earthquakes and floods
—be explained in simple Maori terms as the punishment of the *atua*.
Pigs and potatoes fit so easily into everyday patterns of living that
they were soon an integral part of Maori life. Before 1820 very few
of the Maoris who lived even a few miles back from the ocean had
ever seen a white man. The changes which occurred among them
had little more effect on their minds than if they had originated
within the Maori culture itself.

Around 1820 the first muskets began to spread among the interior
tribes, as the victories of the Ngapuhi made obvious to Maoris in
all parts of the North Island the fact that the greenstone weapons
were obsolete. Shortly after, the Maoris in the interior saw occasional
white men pushing their way up rivers looking for flax or trying to
escape from whaling ships or the Australian convict settlements.
With the increasing introduction of Western artifacts and the
presence of white men, the first serious stages of acculturative ferment in the interior began. Cultural self-consciousness and the other
obvious manifestations of Western contact, which had begun at the
Bay of Islands decades before, slowly started to take their characteristic shape.

"In the formation of new Stations," wrote John Morgan from
Tauranga in 1835, "the main object of the poor Natives is temporal
advantage." [49] Maoris of Otawao, near Mangapouri, in 1838, "honestly avowed that it was by the blankets and other articles of trade
their hearts would be turned." [50] After Europeans had made their

[49] Morgan, October 2, 1835, *CMR*, December 1836, p. 292.

[50] William R. Wade, *A Journey in the Northern Island of New Zealand:
Interspersed with Various Information Relative to the Country and People*
(Hobart Town, 1842), p. 115. See also J. Hamlin, October 1835, *CMR*, October 1836, pp. 238–39; Williams, *Christianity*, pp. 220–21 (for Waikato);
and Shortland, *Traditions and Superstitions*, pp. 121–23 (for Rotorua).

appearance and had finally been associated with the increasing sick-
nesses, the southern Maori tribes felt the same distrust of the white
God that the Maoris of the Bay of Islands had. A tribe of the Thames
River migrated north in the belief that that powerful *tohunga,*
Samuel Marsden, with his *atua,* had brought an epidemic among
them.[51]

There were several factors which hastened the conversions in the
interior, compared to those in the north. One of them was the more
rapid disillusionment with warfare. This came about partly through
the influence of the Ngapuhi, whose muskets almost invariably
beat the southern tribes during the 1820's. At Mokoia, old Ngapuhi
enemies asked for missionaries because: "They are at present afraid
of the Ngapuhi, but then they would not be so. . . ."[52] The Maoris
of Puriri asked William Fairburn: but " 'why did you all remain at
the Bay of Islands so many years? was your love only to them, that
you put them in possession of muskets and powder, through which
means, so many hundreds of our fathers, wives, children, etc., have
been murdered or made slaves?' "[53] Muskets were soon fairly
evenly distributed among the southern tribes. When they fought
among themselves, there were few easy conquests. This also made
them realize the pointlessness of war more quickly than had the
northern Maoris. "They are tired of their wars . . . ," wrote Fairburn
about the Thames River tribes in 1833.[54] And later a missionary
described other southern Maoris who said "that they were quite
willing to attend to the things of God; but they were like ships
without an anchor, driven about by the wind."[55]

Another factor which contributed to, in fact, which made possible,
the wholesale conversions of the late 1830's was the distribution of
Christian ideas through the agency of Maori teachers. There were
various sorts of Maori teachers. The first ones were apparently a

[51] D'Urville, *Voyage,* II, 168.

[52] William Fairburn, January 27, 1832, *MR,* December 1833, p. 546.

[53] Fairburn, June 24, 1834, *MR,* August 1835, p. 382.

[54] Fairburn, May 31, 1833, *CMR,* November 1833, p. 256.

[55] Missionary is not named; October 26, 1837, *MR,* July 1839, p. 349; for
general confusion see Waterhouse (a Methodist), *MR,* December 1841, p. 547.

few local Ngapuhi converts who went out from Paihia, Waimate, and Mangungu (the Methodist station at Hokianga) on Sundays, when there was good weather, to preach in their own villages and among their friends. This activity began late in 1830 or early in 1831, and by the next year was quite common.[56] Another class of teachers, with a less defined function, was composed of school-children who had been educated at the mission stations. They left the stations for various reasons and helped to stir up the minds of their families and home communities.[57] Both the local Ngapuhi converts and the schoolchildren were, however, on the whole limited in their influence to the areas immediately around the Bay of Islands.

The most widely effective Maori teachers were those drawn from the pool of slaves who had been captured by the Ngapuhi in battles at distant parts of the North Island. These slaves came to the missionaries through escape or rescue and were returned to their homes as opportunity offered. The missionaries had no particular intention of using them as itinerant preachers and did not train them for the work. The slaves nevertheless became enthusiastic exponents of the missionary cause. Maoris who had become slaves lost their *mana,* and the fact that they were freed or returned home was not evi-dently in itself sufficient to restore them to their former status.[58] Maoris who could read, however, whatever their previous status, were so evidently imbued with special qualities that prestige came to them immediately. An ex-slave, for example, one dropped off by the mission schooner at his home on the East Cape or the Bay of Plenty, was likely to be able to read, to repair broken tools, and to

---

[56] Letter of Richard Davis, April 28, 1831, Ms vol. 66, no. 29. Various accounts are in *MR,* November 1833, pp. 497–99; and Henry Williams, *CMR,* September 1831, p. 196. For Methodists see letter of W. White to W.M.S., December 26, 1831, *Wesleyan Missionary Notices,* no. 204 (December 1832).

[57] Thomas Chapman, *MR,* October 1834, p. 459.

[58] This disagrees with Sir A. Ngata and I. L. G. Sutherland, "Religious Influences," *The Maori People Today. A General Survey,* ed. I. L. G. Suther-land (London, 1940), p. 338; it agrees in part with Peter H. Buck, *The Coming of the Maori* (Wellington, 1949), pp. 401–402.

cultivate Western crops with some efficiency. It was only natural
for him to wish to lead and for the rest of his tribe to follow.

The missionaries were undoubtedly surprised to find Christian
worship in unexpected places and to see the demand for printed
religious matter sky-rocketing. Near Te Totara *pa,* in 1833, Henry
Williams went through an evening service before the local Maoris
and found that these Maoris sang a hymn and responded in unison
to the prayers. He discovered there were "three boys here from the
Mission, who had lived in our families for some time, and had acted
as Teachers." [59] The Methodist, Whiteley, went to Kaipara, where
no missionary had been before, and "yet they have erected a Chapel,
and have obtained books; and, to the best of their knowledge, have,
for sometime past, regularly attended to the ordinances of religion. . . ." [60] Ripahu was a slave who was dropped off at his home
in the Cook's Straits region, with "no reason to think that he had
become a Christian," [61] but who turned his tribe toward Christianity.

The East Cape was at first Christianized entirely by Maori teachers, most of whom were left there by William Williams on an
exploratory visit in 1834. Williams dropped off twelve Maoris who
had been taken to the Bay of Islands by a whaler eight months before
and about thirty others who had been captured years earlier by
Hongi on one of his campaigns. The East Cape had suffered from
Hongi's wars, but was quite isolated from white contact. No European missionaries could be spared to go there, but six more Maori
Christians were returned in 1838.[62] By the time Williams and Richard Taylor stopped by in 1839, the Maoris at the East Cape were
well on the way to conversion. The inhabitants of Whakawhitira
had built a sixty by twenty-eight foot chapel, had started several
schools, and enjoyed congregations of about five hundred interested
Maoris every week. In January 1840, Williams established at Turanga (not to be confused with Tauranga), the first European
mission station in the area. In 1841 he estimated that there were

[59] Williams, November 11, 1833, *MR,* September 1834, p. 420.
[60] John Whiteley, February 22, 1834, *MR,* August 1835, p. 383.
[61] Williams, *Christianity,* p. 269.
[62] Williams, *Christianity,* pp. 162–63, 172–73.

already about 8600 church-goers and 2115 candidates for baptism on the East Cape: Maoris who had been converted almost entirely by each other.[63]

In 1839 and 1840 both Henry Williams and James Buller made extended journeys through the interior of New Zealand. Both found interest in Christianity wherever they went. "In my recent long journey," wrote Henry Williams, "every party of the natives I came to I saw a congregation worshipping God in much simplicity, and their books bore evidence of earnest examination—but it was extremely pleasing to observe in these wild settlements, where no Europeans had ever been before, that harmony of voice in giving the responses in their services. . . . Every part of the country is now waiting for the gospel. . . ." [64] By 1844, the effects of Maori teaching had been felt at the southernmost tip of the South Island.[65]

The statistical habits of the missionaries in New Zealand were fairly hit and miss. Nevertheless, the annual figures of the *Church Missionary Record* reveal the mushrooming appeal of Christianity in the years just before and after 1840. The rough estimates listed in the table of Anglican Maori churchgoers, scholars, and communicants are given for the North Island as a whole since the missionaries did not subdivide such figures for smaller areas.

ANGLICAN MAORI CHURCHGOERS, SCHOLARS, AND
COMMUNICANTS, NORTH ISLAND

Year	Attendants on public worship	Scholars	Communicants
1836	1530	1019	31
1837	2300	1555	160
1838	2176	1431	178
1839	2203	1351	202
1840	8760	1796	233
1841	29320	7236	584
1842	35000	13736	

[63] Williams, *Christianity,* pp. 267, 283–90.

[64] Letter of Williams, January 23, 1840, p. 405 of the typewritten copy of his letters, Hocken Library; J. Buller, February 11, 1840, *MR,* November 1840, pp. 513–16.

[65] J. F. H. Wohlers, "On the Conversion and Civilization of the Maoris in the South of New Zealand," *TPNZI,* XIV (1881), 124–25.

In one year, 1839 to 1840, the number of Maoris regularly attending Anglican churches almost quadrupled, and during the next year it almost quadrupled again, although for the two previous years it had been relatively stable. Figures are not available for the Methodist and Catholic missionary bodies, but from their incidental reports it is clear that the Maoris joined these two church organizations in similar fashion.[66]

The number of Maori baptisms was even more haphazardly recorded by the missionaries than were the attendants on public worship, the scholars, and the communicants. A few figures are available. In 1835, William Yate wrote that the missionaries had baptized 300 Maoris since the founding of the mission—presumably all at the Bay of Islands or Waimate.[67] In August 1838, the missionaries reported that the figure was 533 adult Maoris and 305 children.[68] This represented a gain of 538 baptisms, or 175 per cent, in three years. Only two years later Henry Williams estimated the number of living, baptized Maoris at "not fewer than 2000." [69] This was a gain of almost 250 per cent in two years. The year 1839 was important. Evidently, from June 1837 to June 1838, there were 89 baptisms at Waimate; but from June 1839 to June 1840, there were 765.[70] In the south, Robert Maunsell said he personally baptized 426 Maoris in the two years before 1840.[71]

Christianity was becoming fashionable in the late 1830's. The first

[66] For the Methodists see the annual *Report of the Wesleyan-Methodist Missionary School* for scattered statistics which become a little more organized with the 1842 issue; for the Catholics see Pompallier in almost any report. In *Early History,* pp. 66, 78, he said there were 15,000 tentative Catholics in the spring of 1840 and 46,000 catechumens and neophytes late in 1841. These statistics were not certified by the Protestants.

[67] Yate, *MR,* March 1836, p. 157.

[68] Missionary Committee Report, August 1838, *CMP* (1839–40), Appendix V, p. 166.

[69] Letter of Williams, July 25, 1840, p. 418, typewritten copy of his letters, Hocken Library.

[70] William Williams, *MR,* May 1839, p. 267; R. Taylor, *MR,* November 1841, p. 515.

[71] Maunsell, July 22, 1840, *MR,* April 1841, p. 219; see also Williams, *Christianity,* pp. 248ff. for general increase.

signs of this were evident at the Bay of Islands about the middle of the decade when many Maoris became unusually devoted followers of the missionary precepts and exceptionally eager candidates for baptism. "Before my heart began to listen to the words of Jehovah," wrote one enthusiastic convert, "I was a liar, a murderer, an adulterer, a fornicator, a thief, a troublesome man. . . ."[72] The missionaries soon recovered from a shock of pleasant surprise at what had at first seemed divinely inspired. They began to fear that the new converts "may often proceed from a desire to conform to the views of their neighbours, now that an avowal of their principles ceases to draw upon them shame or reproach."[73] This movement occurred about the same time that the young chiefs around the Bay began to give up their opposition to Christianity.

At first the missionaries curbed over-eagerness by being more strict in the requirements for baptism. However, they were unable to restrict churchgoing and other manifestations of enthusiasm everywhere. And it was hard to tell at what point a line should be drawn. The Maoris became so interested in Christianity that rival parties vied in getting missionaries to visit their tribal areas first. Sometimes the tribal divisions became divisions of sects. According to Edward Shortland, Octavius Hadfield might have converted the whole Cook's Straits area to the Church of England had it not been for a Maori intertribal jealousy. The Ngati-toa tribes were envious because a relation of Te Rauparaha had received credit for bringing Mr. Hadfield to the south. They therefore went north and persuaded the Methodists to send one of their number to live with them.[74] In the interior, Reverend William Wade found the Maoris demanding a European missionary for every subtribe of fifty or so members. Each group of Maoris wanted a missionary for itself.[75]

While by 1840 certainly not even half the Maoris were nominal churchgoers, the movement toward Christianity was in such full

[72] Letter of Kupa to William Yate, *MR*, October 1834, p. 464.
[73] Report of William Williams, June 1835, *MR*, October 1836, 471.
[74] Shortland, *Traditions and Superstitions*, pp. 124–25.
[75] Wade, *Journey*, p. 163; see also T. Gudgeon, "The Maori People," *JPS*, XIII (1904), 177–78.

swing that, as Clarke later reported, almost two thirds of them were attending Christian services by 1845. The combination of spontaneous Maori confusion and missionary effort, which took so long to produce the first results in New Zealand, had suddenly taken hold and made Christianity, for good or ill, a part of the Maori way of life.

Chapter IX

The Christian Maori

The extraordinary popularity of Christianity about 1840 led many contemporaries, including the missionaries, to suspect the sincerity of the conversions. The missionaries were not concerned about the factors that brought individual Maoris to the point of conversion. The means through which the Divine Will chose to act were not for them to question. They felt that it was neither immoral to try to induce conversions with well-designed techniques, nor that it mattered if the first Christian Maoris were confused and sick. The only requirement was that Christian Maoris act and think as Christians should.

Whether the Maoris did actually think as Christians should has been a matter of debate ever since the first conversions and will form the subject for most of this chapter. There has been no denying, however, that by and large the converted Maoris acted according to Christian precepts; and even the most convinced critics of the missionaries have always had to admit that this represented a considerable disturbance to the Maoris.

The religious observances of the converted Maoris were for the most part irreproachable. They attended church services regularly; they sang hymns and answered the responses with enthusiasm. Most of them learned to read and write; and all knew the Bible well, many having memorized long passages. They observed the Sabbath regularly. Many proselyted and taught among those tribes which were still heathen.

Still more significant was the fact that the Christian Maoris gradually abandoned most of the customs which were inconsistent with Christian behavior. They also induced many heathen Maoris to do so. Some of the customs had constituted important parts of the Maori social fabric, and giving them up entailed genuine sacrifices. Others, while less upsetting, contributed nonetheless to the general difficulty of behaving according to Christian principles.

Most of the changes started in the Bay of Islands and spread, either rapidly or slowly, to the south and to the interior. Some were simply the result of missionary requirements for all Christian Maoris. The missionaries forbade tattooing. By the early 1840's the effects of this injunction became visible as large numbers of Maoris who were old enough to be tattooed remained with unmarked faces.[1] Baptized Maoris automatically gave up their native (heathen, to the missionaries) names in exchange for Mohi (Moses), Hoani (John), Hare (Henry), Wetere (Wesley), or others. The missionaries forbade polygamy. Chiefs with several wives upon conversion were faced with the decision of choosing which one they wished to keep. The other unfortunate wives had little alternative but to wait patiently for the first one to die, in the hope that they might be the next one chosen.[2] As a result of missionary insistence, the Maoris also gave up the customary drubbing given to newly joined couples: it did not harmonize with the Christian marriage service.

Missionary disapproval was enough to speed the decline of other Maori practices. Children's games became more Westernized. According to a recent writer the missionaries were more tolerant of the Maori games which were consistent with those played by "civilized" children.[3] Vigorous wrestling and the traditional singing and dancing fell into disuse. The missionary disapproval of the sculp-

---

[1] William Yate, *An Account of New Zealand; and of the Formation and Progress of the Church Missionary Society's Mission in the Northern Island* (London, 1835), p. 150; Charles Darwin, "Journal and Remarks," in R. FitzRoy and others, *Narrative of the Surveying Voyages of His Majesty's Ships Adventure and Beagle . . . 1826–1836* (London, 1839), III, 509. Generally speaking, specific instances of the trends described in the next few pages can be found in the appropriate issues of *MR*.

[2] See George French Angas, *The New Zealanders (Illustrated)* (London, 1846–47), "General Remarks" and notes to plate 37.

[3] Brian Sutton-Smith, "The Meeting of Maori and European Cultures and its Effects Upon the Unorganized Games of Maori Children," *JPS*, LX (1951), 93–107.

tures and designs which decorated every Maori structure meant that at every mission station these visible signs of the former sway of the Devil were removed. Elsewhere they went out of fashion. The *hakari,* a kind of harvest feast, ended, with appropriate ceremonies, at the Bay of Islands in 1835.[4]

The disappearance of the traditional Maori religious customs under Christian influence was nowhere more remarkable than in dealing with the dead. The extravagant ceremonies at the burial of a chief gradually became of less importance among Christian Maoris. The missionaries openly attacked the *hahunga* rite, or exhumation of the bones of long-buried individuals, at Waimate in May 1835, when a large non-Christian gathering met near the missionary station. In spite of the fact that "some of Satan's more faithful ones endeavored to make a stir . . . ,"[5] the majority of the chiefs agreed to have no more such feasts. *Hahungas* became virtually nonexistent in that area, since Christian Maoris had already abandoned them. The usual suicides of favorite wives on the death of a chief were also given up around the Bay of Islands about the middle of the 1830's. The custom of killing slaves at a burial died out a little more slowly.[6]

[4] William R. Wade, *A Journey in the Northern Island of New Zealand: Interspersed with Various Information Relative to the Country and People* (Hobart Town, 1842), pp. 118–19. For wrestling and dancing see William Brown, *New Zealand and its Aborigines* . . . (London, 1845), p. 94; and Edward Shortland, *Traditions and Superstitions of the New Zealanders: with Illustrations of their Manners and Customs,* 2nd ed. (London, 1856), p. 158. For Maori sculptures see Abel Du Petit-Thouars, *Voyage autour du monde sur la frégate la Vénus* . . . (Paris, 1839–41), III, 24.

[5] Letter of Richard Davis, May 30, 1835, Ms vol. 66, no. 44; see also William Williams, *Christianity Among the New Zealanders* (London, 1867), pp. 214–16.

[6] For suicides of wives see Joel S. Polack, *Manners and Customs of the New Zealanders* . . . (London, 1840), I, 66; and Ernest Dieffenbach, *Travels in New Zealand; with Contributions to the Geography, Geology, Botany, and Natural History of that Country* (London, 1843), II, 40. See also Henry Williams, *MR,* August 1834, p. 368; Joel S. Polack, *New Zealand: Being a Narrative of Travels and Adventures* . . . , new ed. (London, 1839), II, 356; and W. Brodie, *PP,* 1844, XIII, 41.

The whole tenor of life became less violent under the aegis of Christianity. Francis Fenton said that infanticide ceased to exist about 1835, but his date was evidently a little too optimistic.[7] According to George Clarke, Jr., infanticide was "more than usually prevalent" among three tribes of the Cook's Straits area as late as 1840.[8] At any rate, the practice soon subsided.[9]

More significant was the decline of war and cannibalism.[10] Unconnected Maori skirmishes continued until toward the end of the century, but the large-scale, intertribal wars died out even in the south before 1840. The last known case of cannibalism before the exceptional circumstances of the 1860's was in 1842. Taraia, a chief of the Thames district, attacked some Maoris at Tauranga in that year. He enslaved some, killed others, and ate a few, because, as he said, "I was angry about my land, and the bones of my fathers."[11] Taraia's action excited the minds of many Maoris for a while, but the agitation soon subsided. About the time that wars ended, slavery itself was given up.

The *Missionary Register* described the differences between the Maoris of the north and those of the south in the mid-1830's, so far as war was concerned. In 1836, there was a war in the south; in 1837, there was one in the north.

In the Northern District, where the Missionaries have longest dwelt and laboured, there were no CHRISTIAN Chiefs found to participate in the war; and even some of the Heathen Chiefs refused to join. Natives themselves cooperated to put a stop to the war. . . . Not more

[7] Francis D. Fenton, *Observations on the State of the Aboriginal Inhabitants of New Zealand* (Auckland, 1859), p. 36. Yate, *Account*, p. 99, says infanticide is "almost banished" from the Bay of Islands (1835).

[8] Report of G. Clarke, Jr., June 14, 1843, *PP*, 1844, XIII, Appendix, p. 351.

[9] "The Polynesians: and New Zealand (by a N.Z. colonist)," *Edinburgh Review*, XCI (1850), 461.

[10] Edward Markham, "Transcript of New Zealand or Recollections of it," Ms vol. 85, p. 136, Hocken Library, Dunedin; "Journal of Brig 'Spy' of Salem. John B. Knights, Master," March–April 1833, Peabody Museum, Salem.

[11] Quoted in G. W. Rusden, *History of New Zealand* (London, 1883), I, 313–14; for reports on Taraia see *PP*, 1844, XIII, Appendix, pp. 162–65, 189–96.

than fifty perished, during a warfare of several months. . . . [There was no cannibalism.]

Whereas in the Southern . . . as soon as war burst out, it was universal and indiscriminating: none of the leading Natives interposed to arrest its progress: the carnage amounted to not fewer than 500; and was succeeded by horrific scenes of cannibalism, such as have never before been narrated by the Missionaries.[12]

Actually, all the things the Christian Maoris did constituted rather impressive evidence that they fully understood the implications of their conversion. The missionaries were most enthusiastic over the numbers of Maoris who wanted to become Christian and over the abandonment of savage practices. It is strange, therefore, that many of them worried seriously about the attitudes of their converted Maoris.

Richard Davis, in 1834, while admitting that professing Maoris threw over their old practices and attended Christian services, wrote "there is not that increase in vital godliness which we so much wish to see." [13] Similarly, Joseph Matthews at Kaitaia, in 1835, said the "Natives are outwardly civil, yet the savage heart lies hidden under the civilized face." [14] The missionaries became increasingly suspicious as the number of conversions multiplied. In 1839, John King wrote: "The number of Natives under Christian Instruction, and favoured with the means of grace, is very large; but the number of those only who are, in my opinion, decidedly Christian, is small." [15] A. N. Brown, who was at Matamata in 1839, said that eight hundred Maoris regularly attended the missionaries' Sunday services in the Tauranga district. "We speak not of this number as sincere converts: of the majority of them, perhaps, it may be said, they worship they know not what. . . ." [16] And in the botanical metaphor common to all missionaries, James Shepherd added that, "Many can talk

[12] Report, *MR*, April, 1839, pp. 197–98.

[13] Davis, October 27, 1834, *CMR*, June 1836, p. 144.

[14] Matthews, January 24, 1835, *CMR*, July 1836, p. 156; see also letter of George Clarke, September 6, 1831, Ms vol. 60, no. 37.

[15] King, March 5, 1839, *CMR*, October 1839, p. 262.

[16] Brown, Spring 1839, *MR*, August 1840, p. 382.

well of their thoughts, as they say, and yet have not one grain of sincerity in their hearts. . . . I trust that there is wheat among much tares." [17]

The difficulty was that the Maoris thought of the Christian religion in terms of their own. One reason they did this was because of the apparent similarities of the two religions. The missionaries often thought of the Maori religion in European terms; the Maoris thought of the Christian religion in Maori terms. There was a mutual misunderstanding which affected the assumptions of both converter and converted.

The missionary use of Maori words has been mentioned before in connection with the conversion of the Maoris. To the missionaries, *atua* and *tapu* were rough approximations of the corresponding English terms and were used confidently as such, because the missionaries really did not fully understand what the Maoris meant by *atua* and *tapu*. By the same token, one could not blame the Maoris for thinking of the Christian "God" and "Holy"—particularly since the Maori words were used—in terms of the Maori meanings. The result was that religious phrases, such as *Tapu, tapu, tapu, rawa E Ihowa te Atua o nga mano tuariuri waioio* ("Holy, Holy, Holy, Lord God of Sabbaoth"), which were used by both the missionaries and the Maoris in common, had entirely different connotations for each group.[18]

The same sort of mutual misunderstanding was everywhere. The missionaries tended to think the Maori *tohi* rite was more like baptism than it actually was, for example, and the Maoris thought of baptism in terms of the *tohi*. Furthermore, the missionaries thought the Maoris must have been associated with the Jews at some early period of their history or even have had a Jewish origin, because the Maoris were much like Old Testament Jews in many aspects of their behavior. Samuel Marsden quoted scripture and

[17] Shepherd, 1838–39, *MR*, January 1840, p. 53. Shepherd was at Whangaroa at this time.

[18] See James Stack, "Notes on Maori Christianity (1874)," quoted in *JPS*, XLIX (1940), 539; see also Charles Terry, *New Zealand, its Advantages and Prospects, as a British Colony* . . . (London, 1842), pp. 180–82. For example given see *MR*, February 1834, p. 119.

pointed to the Maori love of trading to support his statement that the Maoris had descended from some dispersed Jews.[19] "Do not Maui and Kina," wrote Bishop Pompallier about an old Maori tradition, "stand for Adam and Eve?"[20] And, as the missionaries found signs of the Jews in the Maoris, the Maoris, turning to the Old Testament, found that the missionaries' religion affirmed, in large part, their traditional ways of life.

Certain aspects of the Christianity of the missionaries fitted well even with the superstitious Maori world of gods and supernatural wonders, for the missionaries had their own spirits and angels and miracles. In the missionary mind the Devil, the "Prince of Darkness," waged his ceaseless struggle against the "Lord of Glory, Him Who Keepeth Israel," and like the Maori *atua,* the implicit assumption of the Devil's existence was based on the things he made some people do. "I have met with no New Zealanders," Marsden wrote in 1820, "even the most enlightened amongst them, but who do firmly believe that their priests have communication with their god. . . . This is a subject of such a mysterious nature that I cannot make up my own mind either to believe or disbelieve. . . . I do not pretend to know how far the agency of Satan may extend in a barbarous and uncivilized nation. . . ."[21] Christians avoided harm from the Devil in much the same ways that the Maoris avoided harm from the *atua:* by the observance of certain rules. One religion had a variety of ordinances embodied in the Decalogue and the Sermon on the Mount; the other had *tapu.* For the Maoris to confuse one of these systems with the other was only natural.

[19] Samuel Marsden, *The Letters and Journals of Samuel Marsden,* ed. J. R. Elder (Dunedin, 1932), p. 219. See also the letter of T. Kendall, England, to secretary of C.M.S., July 3, 1820, *Marsden's Lieutenants,* ed. J. R. Elder (Dunedin, 1934), p. 162; Alexander Strachan, *Remarkable Incidents in the Life of the Rev. Samuel Leigh* . . . (London, 1853), p. 197; and Shortland, *Traditions and Superstitions,* pp. 77–78. Some comparable traits are listed in A. Ngata and I. L. G. Sutherland, "Religious Influences," *The Maori People Today. A General Survey,* ed. I. L. G. Sutherland (London, 1940), pp. 342–43.
[20] Jean B. F. Pompallier, *Early History of the Catholic Church in Oceania* (Auckland, 1888), p. 49.
[21] Marsden, *Letters and Journals,* p. 287.

One reflection of all this was that Sunday became sacred to converted Maoris not essentially for Christian reasons, but because, like any *tapu,* it had to be observed. Even the Maoris who were not Christian believed the Christian *tapu* might help them in dealing with the Christian *atua.* It has been mentioned before that some thought the heavy sickness of 1828 was "a visitation from our God in anger to them for not observing the Sabbath day." [22] Earle said the Maoris called Sunday the " 'white taboo'd day.' " [23] And later, in the interior, A. N. Brown came across some heathen Maoris, on a Sunday in 1838, at Matamata, who "remained quiet during the day, from a superstitious dread of breaking the Lord's Day. . . ." [24]

The Maoris also thought of prayer in Maori terms. William Wade, near the Coromandel Peninsula in 1838, was besieged by Maoris wanting his assistance. "Their most urgent request was for a form of prayer and thanksgiving before and after meat; but I discovered, from the manner of their asking, that their own superstitious notions mainly prompted the request; for they called prayer before a meal, 'He wakatapu kai,' or the making of food sacred: and the thanksgiving afterwards, 'He wakanoa kai,' or the setting of consecrated food free from the tapu." [25] Even in 1874, James Stack, the missionary's son, said that "prayer and worship appear to them more in the light of potent charms and incantations than of communion and fellowship with God. . . ." [26]

Large numbers of Maoris imbued the Christian world of one God with their own world of many. To them the Christian God was merely another *atua,* and professing Maori Christians put Him

[22] Journal of William Williams, December 9, 1828, p. 165, copied extracts, Alexander Turnbull Library, Wellington; see also Journal of George Clarke, October 26, 1828, Ms vol. 60, no. 96, Hocken Library.

[23] Augustus Earle, *A Narrative of a Nine Months' Residence in New Zealand, in 1827 . . .* (London, 1832), p. 146.

[24] Brown, October 21, 1838, *MR,* January 1840, p. 58.

[25] Wade, *Journey,* p. 184.

[26] Stack, "Notes," *JPS,* XLIX (1940), 538. See also F. E. Maning, "History of the War in the North . . . ," *Old New Zealand* (Wellington, 1948), p. 233; and John Logan Campbell, *Poenamo. Sketches of the Early Days in New Zealand . . . ,* "New Zealand" ed. (Wellington, 1953), pp. 166–72.

at the head of their already existing pantheon.[27] Once baptized, the Maori was presumably free of the wrath of that powerful *atua*. The missionaries became alarmed at the number of Maoris who progressed enthusiastically until they were baptized and then stopped, satisfied.[28] There was a degree of *mana* in a baptism; it gave the Maori who had it a certain self-esteem. " 'When you enter a wood,' " said one of them, " 'you see a great many inferior trees; but a very few good ones. I am like a fine Kauri-tree, surrounded by the Pa Natives, who represent the stunted useless timber!' " [29]

The Maoris, like the American Indians and other non-European peoples, ascribed supernatural qualities to the Western articles they could not understand. A ship's compass, windmills, watches, even muskets at first, were all thought sacred. A Maori once handed a sextant to a white captive of his and asked the captive to tell him whether or not an enemy tribe was about to attack. The only reason we know this story—for what it is worth—is because the captive said it would, but that it would be beaten, and was, fortunately, correct. This feat, said the ex-captive later, made him an *atua* in his own right.[30] And perhaps one of the reasons the Maoris never killed any missionary until the 1860's was because the missionaries, having the closest connection to the awesome Christian God, were themselves sacred and inviolable to some extent in Maori terms.

The Maoris took to the Bible with remarkable enthusiasm. Once the missionaries had taught the first Maoris to read, late in the 1820's, the knowledge spread extraordinarily rapidly. It far outdistanced conversion to Christianity. In 1833, William Yate estimated that five hundred Maoris could read—presumably all in the

---

[27] Shortland, *Traditions and Superstitions*, p. 85. M. J. Dumont D'Urville, *Voyage de la corvette l'Astrolabe . . . 1826–29 . . . Histoire du voyage* (Paris, 1830–33), II, 518–19, uses information of Marsden and Leigh.

[28] W. Williams (quoted), June 1835, *PP*, 1837–38, XXI, 194; H. Williams, February 28, 1834, *MR*, August 1835, p. 426; J. Hamlin, November 6, 1832, *CMR*, November 1833, p. 259.

[29] Quoted by A. N. Brown, July 23, 1837, *MR*, May 1838, p. 262.

[30] [John F. Atkins], "New Zealand in 1829," *United Service Journal*, no. 18 (June 1830), p. 655.

area around Hokianga and the Bay of Islands.[31] Many of these Maoris had never seen a missionary settlement. Others came from long distances to induce the missionaries to visit the south and teach their tribes to read, or at least to send them books. When James Buller traveled through the interior late in 1839, he found that wherever he went—Rotorua, Taupo, Wanganui—the Maoris pleaded for Bibles.[32] The Catholic missionaries became worried because many Maoris "even become Protestants, preferring to be in the false Church with books, rather than in the True one without them."[33]

The missionaries did not often reflect on the reasons the Maoris were so eager to have Bibles. One reason was simply that the Maoris desired to read. To do so was a remarkable accomplishment, and they would have read anything. It happened that the only texts printed in the Maori language before 1840, besides grammars, were religious ones. Even the heathen read Bibles. When some Maoris of the Thames area saw the mission boys of Henry Williams reading letters from the Bay of Islands, they were "struck with wonder at hearing, as they described it, 'a book speak:' for though they expect that a European can perform any extraordinary thing, yet they cannot understand how it is that a New-Zealand youth can possess the same power."[34] At Hokianga in 1833, the Methodist missionary, John Hobbs, wrote that "For this long Time past it has become fashionable for the young People to try to learn to read . . . no doubt there is a great deal of Pride and Vanity among them in their Teaching and Learning. . . ."[35] According to William Fairburn, in 1838, reading and writing had become a form of amusement

---

[31] Eric Ramsden, *Marsden and the Missions. Prelude to Waitangi* (Sydney, 1936), p. 28. For general spread of reading see also Marsden, *Letters and Journals,* p. 474; letter of James Kemp, April 15, 1833, Ms vol. 70, no. 44; and *MR,* March 1836, p. 157, and August 1840, p. 379.

[32] Buller, *MR,* November 1840, pp. 513–16.

[33] Letter of Antoin Garin, Kororareka, 1843, *Fishers of Men,* ed. Peter McKeefry (New Zealand, 1938), p. 41.

[34] Williams, November 8, 1833, *MR,* September 1834, p. 419.

[35] Hobbs, quoted in *PP,* 1837–38, XXI, 227.

which "superseded their once favourite game of Draughts." [36] It was partly this spirit which paid for the 60,000 New Testaments which the British and Foreign Bible Society distributed in the six years after 1840.

Still, the Bible was not just any book: it was the holy book of the mysterious Christian God. For supernatural purposes reading it was not always even necessary. "Alass!," Richard Davis wrote, "Satan is ever on the alert. . . . Many people who know not a letter wish to possess themselves of a Copy of the translated scriptures because they consider it possesses a peculiar virtue of protecting them from the power of evil spirits." [37] Some Maoris believed that Bibles could be used to foretell the future. After Bibles had become fashionable, the Maoris often buried worn-out ones, rather than throwing them away, not so much "from their respect for the Scriptures, as from a superstitious dread of the anger of God. . . ." [38]

Bibles had other attractions: They were useful in warfare for two different reasons. In the first place the paper from any book made good cartridges. Henry Williams remarked on this in 1824, when some as yet illiterate Maoris took an unaccountable fancy to two volumes of Milner's *Church History*.[39] William Colenso stooped to pick up a cartridge during the Maori battle at the Bay of Islands in 1837 and discovered the paper came from II Samuel, 13: 34 ("How long have I to live?").[40] So the Europeans suffered from the theft of books for the sake of Maori military science.

Bibles, in the second place, were occasionally reputed capable of warding off bullets. Taumatakura was a famous Maori preacher of Christianity—one of those dropped off at the East Cape by William Williams in 1834. Several years after his return home,

[36] Fairburn, April 30, 1838, *MR*, July 1839, p. 348.

[37] Letter of Davis, November 10, 1832, Ms vol. 66, no. 34; see also W. G. Puckey, January 21, 1835, *CMR*, July 1836, p. 155.

[38] William Fairburn, April 30, 1838, *MR*, July 1839, p. 348; for foretelling see Williams, *Christianity*, p. 191.

[39] Hugh Carleton, *The Life of Henry Williams. Archdeacon of Waimate*, ed. and rev. J. Elliott (Wellington, 1948), p. 60.

[40] William Colenso, *Fifty Years Ago in New Zealand . . .* (Napier, N.Z., 1888), p. 42. The phrase Colenso quoted is actually in II Sam. 19:34.

Taumatakura led an attack on an enemy *pa*. "When the Pa was at length assaulted, Taumatakura led the attack, with his book in one hand and his musket in the other; and though the balls flew thickly around him, he was not hit. The natives at once ascribed this circumstance to the protection of the God of Taumatakura. . . ."[41] And both Taumatakura and his God enjoyed a considerable rise in prestige.

Those Maoris who itinerated and preached Christianity among their tribes usually also added to the general Maori misconception. Although the ones who had lived at the missionary stations were eager and not infrequently well-taught, they occasionally relapsed; and even the most disciplined of them could not keep services absolutely pure when they were isolated among heathen tribes. And when the Maoris they had taught, who may never have seen a white man, began in their turn to preach, some strange aberrations occasionally cropped up.[42]

The Maoris evidently had an amazing ability to memorize, but did not always understand the things which they had memorized.[43] The feeling was common that the mere repetition of the Christian rites and ceremonies would be sufficient to keep the Christian God's favor. "The whole of the native population of this place profess the Christian religion," wrote one early settler at Port Nicholson, "and though there are no Missionaries among them, they are strict in the performance of their religious exercise. As is to be expected, however, they are imperfectly acquainted with the doctrines of Christianity, and are superstitious in many of their observances."[44]

Papahurihia ("one who relates wonders") was a prophet cult

[41] Williams, *Christianity,* p. 256. Pompallier, *Early History,* p. 69, says the Protestants *told* the Maoris that Bibles would so serve them.

[42] Various relapses and aberrations are recounted in Wade, *Journey,* pp. 114–15; Edward Shortland, *The Southern Districts of New Zealand; A Journal with Passing Notices of the Customs of the Aborigines* (London, 1851), pp. 267n–68n; *MR,* January 1840, pp. 59–60, and July 1848, p. 322; and the letter from Richard Davis, April 23, 1832, Ms vol. 66, no. 32.

[43] Wade, *Journey,* pp. 81–82; R. Maunsell, July 27 and September 21, 1839, *CMR,* 1840, pp. 165–67; Elsdon Best, *The Maori,* (Wellington, 1924), I, 12.

[44] Mr. Hanson, *MR,* January 1841, p. 57.

which originated right on the missionaries' doorstep, near the Bay of Islands, and which had quite a vogue for the short time it existed. It was a curious amalgam of Christianity and the old religious beliefs. Missionary reports indicate it probably began early in 1834 and lasted for a few years, particularly in the area between the Bay of Islands and Hokianga. A native youth, who was supposed to have caused a tree, and then a stone, to speak, was its messiah. Sailors may have taught him ventriloquism. At any rate, he later became a well-known Maori priest under the name of Te Atua Wera ("The Red God"). This new messiah proclaimed Saturday, not Sunday, to be the holy day. Generous to Christianity, however, Papahurihia admitted the Christian God to be supreme; and the religion had baptisms and a scripture. The rites centered about a flagpole; and in the night the priests performed a variety of nameless ceremonies. The cult had aspects of a nativistic revival. It was generally more hostile to the Christians than to the heathen. Several small wars developed between Christians and the adherents of Papahurihia.[45]

Whether Papahurihia was the result of members of the old religion trying to find added strength in Christianity, or whether it came from Christian Maoris confusing and perverting Christianity so as to embrace their former practices, no one could tell. It was an example, however, of what the missionaries most dreaded: the confused intermingling of two systems of thought.

However much the missionaries were disturbed by the fact that most Maoris professing Christianity misunderstood it in one way or another and that religious aberrations occasionally occurred, they were delighted in the meantime at the steady Maori abandonment of war, slavery, tattooing, cannibalism, infanticide, and other non-Christian practices. Yet while Maori desire to conform to the Christian *tapus* must have promoted this abandonment to some extent, there was another important factor, which has only been hinted at

[45] For best accounts of Papahurihia see Yate, *Account*, pp. 220–21; Ramsden, *Marsden and the Missions*, pp. 160–74; Polack, *Manners and Customs*, II, 237; and *MR*, July 1835, p. 309, September 1835, p. 428, and July 1836, pp. 336–37.

previously, that helped to bring it about and that further complicated the cultural mixing.

No culture is entirely satisfactory to all its members. Every aspect
of life is constantly undergoing some modification. Some aspects
are especially irritating and tolerated only because there seem to be
no other alternatives to them. There are many historical examples
of this. In 1819 the Hawaiians, who had had only slight contact
with Europeans, threw over their religion. The mother of the chief
of the islands and the high priest helped to bring the overthrow
about, and although Christianity was in the offing, apparently none
of the prime movers had particular interest in it. The network of
taboo and other religious restrictions had, presumably, just become
too obviously cumbersome to bear.[46] Scientists in New Guinea
have discovered that some of the native tribes like Western roads
built through their tribal lands because this helps them give up
their headhunting and wars.[47] Though Thomas Kendall undoubtedly wished the Maoris had some inclination to give up their un-
Christian practices, he was too outspoken to let his wishes serve for
facts. Yet in 1814 he wrote: "I have been told that there are usages
of a barbarous nature amongst the people of New Zealand which
are not approved by them all, and others followed by some to which
others are averse and which they hold in detestation. . . ."[48]

While the ultimate Maori source of this information may well
have been only trying to tell his Christian audience what he thought
it wanted to hear, there is no doubt that war, slavery, and cannibalism were onerous to large numbers of Maoris. The customs were
maintained and justified unconsciously because of their function in
the total scheme of Maori life. While accepted in ordinary circumstances, however, and entrenched by centuries of practice and tra-

---

[46] A. L. Kroeber, *Anthropology,* new and rev. ed. (New York, 1948), pp.
403–405; but see also R. Redfield, *The Primitive World and its Transforma-
tions* (Ithaca, 1957), pp. 128–30.

[47] This information transmitted verbally by Prof. F. M. Keesing of Stanford
University, Summer 1956.

[48] Letter of Kendall, Parramatta, September 6, 1814, *Marsden's Lieutenants,*
p. 67.

dition, they represented tensions which serious disturbances might suddenly release. They were potential sources of drastic change. Moreover, they were so involved with one another that change in one was bound to result in change in all.

The early years of Western contact had at first accentuated these practices. But when the Maori culture lost its power to explain all the new situations which the Maoris were experiencing, the whole network of practices began to collapse of its own weight. The Maoris saw war, slavery, and cannibalism in a new perspective, and they found that many tiresome religious conventions no longer had meaning.

While the Maoris undeniably followed the Christian *tapus* according to the desires of the missionaries, it does not necessarily follow, therefore, that they did so entirely because of them. In their cultural confusion the Maoris turned to Christianity in several stages. At first they recognized the power of the Christian God but hesitated to give up their old beliefs "lest they die through the anger of their Atua." [49] When they did put some of their trust in missionary leadership, they discovered the missionaries advocated giving up many of those customs which were most burdensome. In their misunderstanding, and groping for leadership, they assumed Christianity to be something it was not—a Maori panacea—and turned to it in great numbers. Then, under the influence of the missionaries, they abandoned more customs more thoroughly than they would have otherwise done because they assumed that Christianity would replace their old customs in a Maori way and satisfy their serious needs.

This was the case with the abandonment of war. The previous chapter argued that the excesses of increasing and uncontrollable warfare constituted one of the reasons that the Maoris turned to Christianity. It was not Christianity which began the decline of war. This is quite clear. The unprecedented slaughters, the abnormal numbers of slaves, and the unrestrained cannibalism had produced

[49] Letter of William Fairburn, June 24, 1834, *MR,* August 1835, p. 381; see also R. Davis, April 21, 1833, *MR,* October 1834, p. 457.

a serious reaction among the Maoris of the north by the 1830's. The widening distribution of muskets which made easy conquests impossible emphasized the futility of it all. Internecine war was already declining when the large-scale interest in Christianity began.

One of the reasons for Maori interest in the missionaries, it has been mentioned, was that they provided a vehicle for salving tribal *mana* by justifying peace and acting as peacemakers. In 1828, 1830, and other times, the missionaries were neutral arbiters as the Maoris desired; Christianity and the end of war were thereafter always closely associated, thus, perhaps, confusing cause and effect in the missionary mind. Still, the influence of the missionaries was important later in that they provided a disorganized, negative movement with positive direction. For as the Maoris increasingly accepted the power of the Christian God and believed in the necessity of adhering to His *tapus,* the end of war took on the aspects of a Divine injunction, a gigantic *tapu,* and peace spread more rapidly across the North Island than it would otherwise have done.

With the decline of war, most of the customs and practices associated with it necessarily declined also. The arbitrary power of the chiefs was damaged. Slavery became a thing of the past, because there were no more enemies to be taken captive. The Maori reaction against cannibalism, with the assistance of pork and other Western foods, led to its gradual disappearance. Tattooing lost much of its function when there was no need for warriors. The Maoris gave up infanticide, apparently in part because of the increasing Maori fear of depopulation, but also because female children were no longer any less desirable than male ones.

Maoris gave up old religious customs as their value and meaning declined in the face of new experiences. The missionaries again assisted. The acquiescence of the non-Christian chiefs when in 1835 the missionaries asked for an end to the *hahunga* ceremonies is a case in point. Was this action a result of missionary influence, or was it merely something which the Maoris wanted to do anyway and for which they found the missionaries provided the excuse? William Williams himself said that the heathen chiefs were "weary of the practice, because it was attended with much trouble and expense; and they were glad to avail themselves of the missionaries to get them out of the difficulty." [50]

The *tapu* itself was burdensome to some. A highly *tapued* Maori chief, according to Thomas Gudgeon, gave the following reason for turning to Christianity: " 'I was quite tapu, and could do nothing for myself. I found it very irksome, and when the missionaries came and preached I made up my mind to break my tapu and accept their God, which I soon afterwards did by carrying a kit of potatoes on my back. . . .' " [51] Maoris stopped committing suicide on the death of a chief about the same time that the chiefs' prestige began to decline. Feminine lacerations of the arms and face at funerals became less frequent as the ritual lost meaning and because the cuts were painful. Young Maori women, in particular, began to substitute similar, but less rigorous, actions. When a specific religious practice had lost some of its meaning and sanctity, the Maoris usually kept it if it had other compensating aspects and dropped or changed it if the sheer inconvenience of continuing was too much without every traditional religious sanction.

The missionaries indeed had some ameliorative influence. They persuaded many Christian Maoris to free their slaves, and from this the practice of manumission became widespread. Their abhorrence of infanticide and cannibalism was important in the abandonment of those practices. Without the missionaries, very few Maoris would have given up polygamy. But two things should be remembered. The first is that in most cases Christian teaching supported, rather than brought about, the changes which were going on. Christianity was either an excuse or an incentive, not a cause. The second is that the influence of Christianity was not Christianity as the missionaries understood it, but as the Maoris misunderstood it. To the Maoris Christianity provided the *tapus* for the security they so badly needed.

---

[50] Williams, *Christianity*, p. 215.

[51] Thomas W. Gudgeon, *The History and Doings of the Maoris from the Year 1820 to the Signing of the Treaty of Waitangi in 1840* (Auckland, 1885), p. 32.

As more and more Maoris began to believe in the efficacy of missionary *tapus,* they accepted the advice of the missionaries with increasing obedience. A Maori chief wrote a letter to Samuel Marsden. "Will you give us a law?" [52] The chief was concerned about women, pigs, and Christians fighting one another. Maoris wished to adopt every possible Christian characteristic. Some complained at Hokianga when the missionaries suggested that the baptized ones retain their old surnames.[53] Even some of the non-believers began to see the inevitability of Christianity. " 'It is of no use to argue any longer against the Religion of the Missionaries,' " they said, " 'for every other will be walked over by it.' " [54]

In the last analysis the Maoris turned to Christianity and abandoned certain non-Christian practices essentially for traditional Maori reasons. The missionaries did not really induce conversions nor did they make the Maori give up their non-Christian practices. For the most part the Maoris converted themselves, one might say, and gave up their non-Christian practices in the attempt to restore their shaken self-confidence.

They were still Maoris thinking as Maoris and trying to solve what they thought were traditional Maori problems: the inadequacy of their *atua,* the loss of *mana* they had suffered, the dislocation of the desirable aspects of their social system. The application of Maori patterns of thought to the problems which Western culture had introduced resulted in both the acceptance of Christianity as a means of deliverance and the misunderstanding of it, once accepted. The degree to which Christianity was effective for Maori purposes became fully apparent only in the next decade, and to this we now turn briefly.

[52] "Letter of a New Zealand Chief to the Rev. Samuel Marsden," *Waimate,* May 14, 1837, *CMR,* April 1838, p. 119.
[53] Journal of Nathaniel Turner in J. G. Turner, *The Pioneer Missionary: Life of the Rev. Nathaniel Turner* . . . (Melbourne, 1872), p. 168.
[54] Quoted by W. G. Puckey, Kaitaia, *MR,* May 1839, p. 268.

CONCLUSION

New Zealand in 1840, and After

New Zealand in 1840, and After

When Governor Hobson proclaimed the sovereignty of Great
Britain over the whole of New Zealand on May 21, 1840, he marked
the beginning of a new period for both the Maoris and the white
people. Planned colonization of the country had already begun.
Government officials and settlers had been arriving for six months.
As a large and active stream of white immigrants arrived and spread
over the North Island, determined to lay the foundations of a new
Britain in the South Seas, they increased the Western pressure on
the Maoris and forced changes of a sort the Maoris had not experienced before.

Almost everybody already in New Zealand, both Maori and
white, welcomed the British annexation when it came. The settlers
and traders looked forward enthusiastically to an increase of business as the middlemen between the Maoris and the government.
Several hundred merchants, land-sharks, and settlers from Australia
had already descended upon the New Zealand ports in the last
months of 1839. By early 1840, as previously mentioned, they had
transformed Kororareka. "At the period of my arrival," wrote R. G.
Jameson, who waxed a trifle poetic in his description, "it contained
little more than fifty European dwellings,—white painted and
verandahed cottages of wood;—a church of the same materials, but
of larger dimensions; and a native pa-a. . . . Kororadika, at the
beginning of 1840, contained about three hundred European inhabitants, of all ages and sexes, exclusive of the numerous sailors
whose nightly revels constituted the only interruption of the peace

and harmony which usually prevailed. . . . crimes, misdemeanours, and larcenies, were of remarkably rare occurrence. . . ." [1]

Missionaries of all denominations accepted the Treaty of Waitangi because it meant the establishment of law and order. Roman Catholics were disappointed that France had not made the annexation, but they did nothing to hinder the British activities. [2] Both Protestant denominations were sorry that any large white population had had to come to disturb their work in New Zealand in the first place, but fear of Catholicism and of the large numbers of ungoverned white people who were already there made the British annexation seem desirable. Both Anglican and Methodist missionaries assisted in the circulation and promotion of the Treaty of Waitangi.

The Maoris on their part looked forward to the British settlement because it promised increasing opportunities for the acquisition of British goods. The new settlers would give quantities of valuable merchandise for Maori foods and the use of Maori lands. Some tribes, particularly heathen ones, opposed the Treaty of Waitangi, but on the whole the Maoris signed it willingly.

New Zealand was still unquestionably the Maoris' country in 1840, although this condition would not continue for long. The Maoris dominated all the British thinking because their friendly attitude was still a prerequisite for British settlement. The increasing

[1] R. G. Jameson, *New Zealand, South Australia, and New South Wales . . .* (London, 1842), pp. 188–89. Jameson's description of Kororareka, while the most detailed, is also much the most favorable of several made about the same time. See, for example, Journal of F. Mathew, January 30, 1840, in Felton and Sarah Mathew, *The Founding of New Zealand. The Journals of Felton Mathew, First Surveyor-General of New Zealand, and his Wife, 1840–1847*, ed. J. Rutherford (Dunedin, 1940), p. 26; and Charles Wilkes, *Narrative of the United States Exploring Expedition during the Years 1838, 1839, 1840, 1841, and 1842* (Philadelphia, 1845), II, 374. Wilkes, as the representative of a foreign government (see II, 375–76), and Mathew, as a British official (see p. 77), were in no better position than Jameson to be objective about Kororareka.

[2] The most comprehensive discussion of the attitudes of the Catholics at this time is in T. Lindsay Buick, *The Treaty of Waitangi. How New Zealand Became a British Colony,* 3rd ed. (New Plymouth, N.Z., 1936), pp. 192–207.

British population would not equal the Maori population, in its decline, until after 1855, not until later if the North Island is considered by itself. Meanwhile the Maoris were for the most part better armed and more skillful warriors than the ordinary British colonists.

To describe the state of the Maoris at this time is difficult because, as usual, it was changing, and because in many ways the Ngapuhi were far more Westernized than the Maoris to the south. New Zealand in 1840 was, however, a peaceful country throughout. The previous section described the religious condition of the Maoris and the decline of the more violent customs. Although there were sporadic intertribal raids, large-scale wars had ceased entirely. White men traveled alone across New Zealand without fear. Many of them did not carry weapons, finding that tobacco was a sufficient means of persuasion and protection. The Maoris applied themselves to the tasks of reading, writing, and acquiring British goods. Jameson reported that the Maoris used up a hundred thousand pounds worth of English manufactured goods annually, besides the money they spent on fowling-pieces, powder, shot, and tobacco.[3] The *hahunga* and the more violent aspects of the burial ceremonies had almost disappeared. Tattooing was less common. Cannibalism and slavery were quickly losing ground.

The economic condition of the Maoris was not seriously disturbed except around the Bay of Islands and Hokianga, where Western contact had been most extensive. Although since the Western contact had begun the Maoris had put excessive emphasis on dressing flax and cutting timber, they still organized their economic activities along the traditional lines of an extended family group under the leadership of a head man and, except for the use of metal tools, worked according to their usual methods.[4]

The principal economic dislocation (except for the effects of this type of labor on their health) came in the neglect of other, once important activities. The Maoris worked harder with a specific goal

[3] Jameson, *New Zealand*, p. 248.
[4] Raymond Firth, *Primitive Economics of the New Zealand Maori* (London, 1929), pp. 454-55.

in mind, and the decline of war gave them more time to work. But for the most part they recruited the labor needed to acquire Western articles from occupations which were fast becoming obsolete. The musket and potato obviated the necessity of looking for food every day. The efforts of the fowlers and fishermen became less important and were gradually abandoned. There was no longer need for the craftsmen who had spent long hours fashioning stone tools and weapons.[5]

While the repercussions of these changes had begun to affect most of the North Island, they had advanced markedly only among the Ngapuhi. There the Maori sea canoes had already begun to vanish as the need for them declined along with war and the desire for fish, and also because Western sailing vessels were so superior when it was necessary to go to sea. Canoes were infrequently built in the north; and the art of decoration declined with that of canoe-building, for without a function there was no need of its existence.[6] Perhaps the Ngapuhi were always behind the interior tribes in art work and crafts. By the 1820's, in any case, they had ceased to provide many of the more ornamental products which they needed for themselves. "All their fine mats and carvings," wrote Samuel Marsden in 1823, "are made at the southward, which as yet remains unknown to the Europeans." [7] Both Lesson in 1824 and Laplace in 1831 remarked on how noticeably the standards of decoration had deteriorated in the north, where the Maoris had metal tools which should have made their carving easier.[8] The knowledge of weaving

[5] Elsdon Best, "Maori Agriculture," *JPS*, XL (1931), 19.

[6] I am indebted to A. Ngata, "Maori Arts and Crafts," *The Maori People Today. A General Survey*, ed. I. L. G. Sutherland (London, 1940), pp. 311, 334. See also Wilkes, *Narrative*, II, 389.

[7] Samuel Marsden, *The Letters and Journals of Samuel Marsden*, ed. J. R. Elder (Dunedin, 1932), p. 351. See also Richard A. Cruise, *Journal of a Ten Months' Residence in New Zealand*, 2nd ed. (London, 1824), p. 25; F. E. Maning, *Old New Zealand* (Wellington, 1948), p. 51; and Joel S. Polack, *Manners and Customs of the New Zealanders* . . . (London, 1840), I, 228.

[8] René P. Lesson, *Voyage autour du monde* . . . *sur la corvette la Coquille* (Paris, 1839), II, 361–62; and M. C. P. T. Laplace, *Voyage autour du monde* . . . *sur la corvette de l'état la Favorite* . . . (Paris, 1833–39), IV, 38. See also Wilkes, *Narrative*, II, 388–89.

faded as European clothing became common, but though rarely worn in the north, the old mats still had prestige and were exchanged as gifts.[9]

While the content of economic activity had changed in the north, its structure was, as in the south, as it had always been. The systems of exchange and distribution, the ownership of property, the bases for evaluating the worth of goods was still the same. In economic affairs as in others, the Maoris were exposed to many European ways of doing things which they had no inclination to adopt.

The social system of the Maoris remained secure. Although the chiefs, especially in the north, had lost prestige, they were in 1840 still the focus around which tribal organization revolved. Tribal loyalties had primary importance, and even today sporting events take place between the old tribal groups. Family and extended kinship loyalties were scarcely touched by the white contact. Much of the Maori world was uncontrollably changing, and the Maoris clung to what they knew.

Of particular Maori beliefs it is more difficult to speak. The section on religion has already tried to indicate the general character of Maori thinking. Although the Maoris had broken the shackles of certain inhibiting *tapus,* their over-all belief in the efficacy of *tapu* generally persisted. At odd times throughout the rest of the century the *tapu* cropped up in districts long considered to be thoroughly Westernized. After the wreck of the steamer *Wairarapa* in 1894, in which over 120 lives were lost, the Maoris of the Great Barrier Island, where the wreck occurred, *tapued* all fish in the surrounding waters and would eat no sea food for a long time afterwards.[10] The *tapu* still survives in a series of miscellaneous prohibitions today, particularly those concerned with birth, sickness, and death. The belief in *maketu,* or witchcraft, also survived in spite of Christianity. Since the Maoris saw in Christianity only what they wanted to see, there is nothing remarkably inconsistent in this fact. Recourse is had in the present day to *tohungas*—of an admittedly inferior breed

---

[9] Peter H. Buck, *The Coming of the Maori* (Wellington, 1949), p. 177.
[10] James Cowan, *The Maoris of New Zealand* (Christchurch, 1910), p. 117.

—when Western medicine fails to effect a cure or when it is believed
that further and more reliable assistance will be required.[11]

The Ngapuhi had experienced the most disconcerting collapse of
traditional values and confidence and were further Westernized
than any other tribal group. Nevertheless they still considered most
of the changes which had taken place in Maori terms. Those who
professed Christianity did so only to the extent that it could be
incorporated into the rest of their lives. The missionaries, for example, in 1840 were still embarrassed at the un-Christianlike dirtiness of their Maori converts, but could do nothing about it.[12]

The northern Maoris accepted the Treaty of Waitangi and the
other treaties preceding annexation for reasons similar to their conversion. The Maoris thought the government would assist the
missionaries in telling the Maoris what to do. "We have now," said
Nopera, in a famous speech at the Kaitaia meeting on April 28, "a
helmsman for our canoe." [13] Some of the Maoris were willing to
abide by whatever the missionaries recommended. According to
William Colenso, Hone Heke at Waitangi said, "But we Natives
are children—yes, mere children. Yes; it is not for us, but for you,
our fathers—you missionaries—it is for you to say, to decide, what
it shall be. It is for you to choose. For we are only Natives." [14]

---

[11] For detailed and careful studies of Maori survivals in two small localities
see Ernest and Pearl Beaglehole, *Some Modern Maoris* (Christchurch, 1946),
passim; and Harry B. Hawthorn, *The Maori: A Study in Acculturation*
(Menasha, Wis., 1944). A more general treatment is in I. L. G. Sutherland,
"Maori and European," *JPS,* LXI (1952), 154.

[12] See, for example, letter of Henry Williams, October 3, 1840, p. 438, typewritten copy of his letters, Hocken Library, Dunedin.

[13] Nopera, April 28, 1840, quoted in Buick, *Treaty of Waitangi,* p. 186.
While the quoted speeches of the Maoris which the missionaries and others
supposedly translated cannot be accepted verbatim (the quotations disagree),
they nevertheless represent what the contemporary observers conceived to be
typical of the Maoris' thought. See also Puhipi Ripi, quoted in Buick, *Treaty
of Waitangi,* pp. 184–85.

[14] H. Heke, quoted in William Colenso, *The Authentic and Genuine History of the Signing of the Treaty of Waitangi, New Zealand, February 5 and
6, 1840* . . . (Wellington, 1890), p. 26. See also the purported conversation
between Busby, Hobson, and Colenso, pp. 32–33.

Maoris also signed the treaty to get blankets and tobacco. Neither Hobson nor the British government intended to buy signatures, and they withheld presents until after the decision to sign had been made. The presents were given as tokens of friendship. Nevertheless, when the word spread about them, the Maoris came to expect and looked forward to the bright red blankets, which soon became tokens of prestige.[15]

Prestige was also an element of importance for those chiefs who opposed the Treaty of Waitangi. The fear of losing land was to some a decisive factor, but around the Bay of Islands most of the tribes had already parted with large sections of their land to members of the Church Missionary Society and other settlers. Besides, land was not in 1840 as important as it later became. *Mana,* however, was crucial. " 'Governor high up, up, up, and Te Kemara down low, small, a worm, a crawler,' " said Te Kemara at Waitangi, " 'No, no, no. O Governor!' " [16]

In the first two or three years after 1840 there were no difficulties to speak of; relations between the Maoris and the Europeans proceeded very favorably. The New Zealand Company started a colony in the North Island at New Plymouth (1841) and expanded its original settlement at Port Nicholson. Many of the company colonists went to Petre in Wanganui. In the north, Governor Hobson founded the official capital at Auckland (1841) and settlers began to gather there. Hundreds of Europeans settled independently on the fertile soil stretching up the river valleys toward the interior. By 1843, there were 11,489 white people in New Zealand, 8,326 of them in the North Island. This had been achieved with almost no friction between the two peoples.[17]

The fact was that there seemed at this time to be as good promise for the Maoris as for the Europeans. There is some evidence to

[15] Colenso, *Treaty of Waitangi,* p. 35; Buick, *Treaty of Waitangi,* p. 189; Hugh Carleton, *The Life of Henry Williams. Archdeacon of Waimate,* ed. and rev. J. Elliott (Wellington, 1948), p. 311.

[16] Colenso, *Treaty of Waitangi,* pp. 17, 18-27.

[17] Report of Andrew Sinclair, Colonial Secretary, March 23, 1845, *PP,* 1846, XXX, 45.

support the idea that the Maori population increased slightly after the Treaty of Waitangi as a result of the peaceful and stable conditions brought about by the end of war and of the evident British intentions of giving the Maoris leadership.[18] Tribes began to wander back to their old homes with a feeling of security, and to take an interest in their recently neglected children.[19]

Conversions came about in unprecedented numbers. The Church Missionary Society stopped estimating the "attendants on public worship" when the figure reached 35,000 in 1842. (It had been 8,760 in 1840.) For a while the number of communicants jumped a thousand every year. The number of scholars increased ninefold between 1840 and 1843. The situation was similar, as has been pointed out, for the other missionary societies. Only in the Urewera country and a few other interior backwaters were the Maoris still entirely heathen.

Not only was the rate of conversions at its peak, but the character of the Maoris seemed to be exemplary. "I think it is . . . conclusive," wrote George Clarke in 1842, "that we have to attribute our peace with the natives more to the good sense which actuates them than to the prudence and forbearance of Europeans." [20] Pointed remarks were dropped to the effect that heathen survivals were as common and as immoral in Christian England as in Christian New Zealand. In fact the greatest fear of the missionaries was of the contamination the Maoris might receive from the godless white settlers.

Even the Maoris near towns, however, appeared to benefit from the increase of British trade. They began to organize their activities along Western lines. A money economy made some headway, having been preceded and prepared for by the ubiquitous tobacco. In one case old tribal enemies cooperated to supply the British demand for foods, flax, and timber. Some tribes pooled money to create capital with which to buy mills for grinding wheat and ships for

[18] Report of Edmund Halswell, November 11, 1841, *PP*, 1844, XIII, appendix, p. 670.

[19] Report of Halswell, November 11, 1841, *PP*, 1844, XIII, appendix, p. 671; William Williams, *Christianity Among the New Zealanders* (London, 1867), p. 254.

[20] George Clarke, April 30, 1842, *PP*, 1844, XIII, appendix, p. 191.

transporting the heavy cargoes. The Maoris of Maketu, in the Bay of Plenty, clothed and fed themselves well by dressing flax. By August 1843, they had bought one small schooner and were about to buy another of twenty tons, at a price of five hundred pigs, so as to be able to trade directly with Auckland and the Bay of Islands.[21] It was indeed a golden age of Maori-white relations.

The extraordinarily propitious balance could not, however, be maintained indefinitely. Many of the European settlers became disenchanted with their situation only a few years after 1840. The missionaries and traders who had been in New Zealand in 1840 and had welcomed the Treaty of Waitangi had had for several years exaggerated importance because of their knowledge of Maori and the Maoris. This situation waned as the new settlers began to be able to deal with the Maoris themselves and as the increasing concentrations of white people brought other problems than the Maoris to the attention of the government. The new immigrants, meanwhile, who had found the Maoris helpful and easy to deal with at first, began to discover Maori opposition to the sale of lands and distrust on the part of Maori chiefs. They also found that the Maoris were not quite so "civilized" as had been advertised.

The Maoris themselves were disillusioned. They found their existence threatened by a series of pressures and difficulties which a few years before they had never imagined could occur.

One of the most troublesome problems, which has continued to the present day, concerned the sale of land. During the 1830's the Maoris were on the whole delighted to sell lands to white people because they not only received the purchase price in Western articles, but acquired a local European market, a source of supply for future exchanges of goods, and protection from enemy tribes. Many of the Maoris who sold land demanded that they be employed by the new owner, and the payments they received in this manner made them richer with less trouble than cultivating the land themselves could have done. When the British government arrived and began to look

[21] Edward Shortland, *Traditions and Superstitions of the New Zealanders: with Illustrations of their Manners and Customs,* 2nd ed. (London, 1856), p. 19; Edward Shortland, *PP,* 1844, XIII, appendix, p. 352.

over the more than one thousand European and American land claims, it discovered that 45,976,000 acres in two islands had apparently been transferred from the Maoris to the white settlers and speculators. Three of the claims were over a million acres each. Several others were over 25,000 acres, including those of Reverend William Fairburn (40,000 acres) and Reverend Richard Taylor (50,000 acres).

The Maori attitude toward the sale of land began to change when the extraordinary white demand for land after 1840 opened the Maoris' eyes to the fact that perhaps they were behaving foolishly to sell as readily as they did. This feeling was reinforced by the inevitable deterioration of the blankets, double-barreled guns, cows, umbrellas, and other bizarre articles which they had received as payment. The Maoris also saw what the white man could do with land. They had a growing desire to raise crops for the European market themselves. Fortunately the sale of lands had usually been carelessly made according to Maori custom, and there were loopholes in almost every case. If the whole tribe had not consulted on the sale, it was void. If all the claims had not been considered (besides heredity and conquest these included having had one's umbilical cord cut there, having been wounded there, having been cursed there, and other unlikely and tenuous connections) the sale was not complete. Thousands of Maori claimants sprang out of the bushes in the new climate of opinion. A potential source of Maori-white disharmony suddenly came to life.[22]

Another Maori problem was that of leadership, or, rather, the lack of it. In their understanding of the Treaty of Waitangi, the Maoris, by and large, had conceded the direction of relations between the Maoris and the white people to the colonial government. They expected to be able to run their own affairs themselves. The colonial government, however, was confused by legal problems

[22] Land and its problems: *PP*, 1837–38, XXI, 39, 343; *PP*, 1844, XIII, 177ff. and appendix, pp. 78–85, 355–59; Shortland, *Traditions and Superstitions,* pp. 285, 298; Buick, *Treaty of Waitangi,* p. 299; A. Ngata, "Maori Land Settlement," *Maori People Today,* pp. 96–154; Maning, *Old New Zealand,* pp. 69–75.

(how much of New Zealand is British? what are the legal rights of the colonists over the Maoris who did, and over those who did not, sign the Treaty of Waitangi? what are the land rights of the Maoris?) and by lack of coordination with the Colonial Office in London. While the Maoris expected to be told what to do and made to do it in certain areas of conduct and to be left alone in others, the colonial government, well-intentioned as it was, acted ineffectively in every area. When the government did apply its enlightened legal system to particular cases, the Maoris could not understand it. Furthermore, British concessions, inspired by generosity, implied to the Maoris a loss of British *mana*. The resulting failure of British leadership, with the already lowered prestige of the chiefs, began to produce a return to the confusion of the 1830's.[23]

The difficulties of land and leadership would not have been so pressing for the Maoris if the white settlers had not kept pushing and forcing their way into the interior. The destruction of pigs the Maoris thought were theirs, the trespass and spoliation of Maori crops by British cattle, the violation and disregard of *tapus,* the encroachment on Maori lands, the destructive cutting of kauri and other timber, not to mention the swearing and other offensive personal characteristics, combined to make the Maoris less certain of the advantages of white settlement.[24] When minor Maori depredations failed to receive white retaliation according to Maori custom, the prestige of the once awesome white settlers declined, and the depredations increased in frequency and degree—culminating in the Wairau massacre of 1843.

Christianity, meanwhile, which had been expected to save the Maoris and teach them civilized behavior, was losing adherents for reasons of its own. The number of Maoris interested in Christianity began to drop after 1842 or 1843. Backsliding increased among those actually baptized.[25] The debilitating influence of the new white

[23] See esp. G. Clarke, July 31, 1843, *PP,* 1844, XIII, appendix, pp. 346–50; Felton Mathew, Journal, *Founding of N.Z.,* pp. 219ff.

[24] G. Clarke, April 30, 1842, *PP,* 1844, XIII, appendix, p. 191.

[25] See, for example, *MR,* June 1843, p. 308, August 1845, pp. 368–69, and September 1846, pp. 407–408.

population was one reason for this, as the missionaries had feared it would be. This was not so much due to the godless example of the godless white people in the towns, however, as to the possibility which the white people seemed to present for the achievement of old Maori goals. Maoris rushed to the towns to satisfy their natural curiosity. They traded, even on the Sabbath, to acquire the articles they needed. Quarrels developed from the competition over lands; many Maoris thereby left the church since Christian Maoris were not expected to fight, although they not infrequently did. Wherever Christianity did not conform to traditional Maori goals, the Maoris were likely to treat it lightly.

A gradual decline of the missionaries' once awesome *mana* further weakened Christian sentiment. Soon after 1840 the Maoris realized that the missionaries were not regarded by other white people as the minor deities some of the Maoris had previously thought them. The Maoris resented and were confused by the constant bickering between the different denominations.[26] Large land purchases by members of the Church Missionary Society alienated many Maoris who felt, as the attitude toward land began to change, that they had been duped. The result of this was that at the same time that the white settlers denounced the missionaries for interfering with the sale of lands, on the one hand, the Maoris began, on the other, "to accuse the missionaries of having invited their white brethren to come and take possession of the country." [27]

William Williams later said that the reason large numbers of the Maoris had defected in the 1840's was because Christianity had been too much of a fad. He saw that in areas such as the East Cape, where there had been no contact with the white people to speak of, backsliding was as common as it was near Wellington or Auckland. He knew that many Maoris had turned to Christianity because of

[26] See letters of Rev. H. Hanson Turton, New Plymouth, to Rev. Dr. Selwyn, April 30, 1844, William Brown, *New Zealand and its Aborigines . . .* (London, 1845), pp. 253–74; and Polack, *Manners and Customs,* II, 237.

[27] Letter of Rev. J. Beecham, London, to Lord Stanley, March 7, 1844, *PP,* 1844, XIII, appendix, p. 179. The source of Beecham's thought is in a letter of S. Ironsides, on p. 184.

the prestige of those who had already done so and in the expectation
that Christianity could help stop the devastating wars. "The ex-
citement which followed upon the first introduction of the Gospel
was unnatural," he later wrote, "for nearly the whole population
became attendants upon Christian worship. It could not therefore
be expected that this state of things should be permanent." [28] He
thought the restraints imposed by Christianity—the repetitions of
meaningless phrases, the insistence on clothing and on premarital
chastity, etc.—became too onerous, and the converts lost enthusiasm.

The restraints might have been taken for granted, however, and
Christianity might have passed the novelty stage, if it had done all
the Maoris expected of it, if it had satisfied their basic needs. While
Christianity had indeed helped bring freedom from intertribal wars
and the excessive and now satiated practices of slavery and cannibalism, it did not provide a wholly sufficient replacement for them.
What William Colenso said about polygamy, slavery, and *tapu*
might be applied to war, cannibalism, and the other Maori customs
as well: "However distasteful these . . . things might be to an European and Christian, they were the life of the New Zealander.
They were perhaps the . . . rotten hoops around the old cask, but
they kept the cask together." [29]

While the Maoris were undoubtedly looking for justification to
abandon some of their Maori practices in any case, they had given
up more than they would have otherwise under the delusion that
Christianity was a superior way of fulfilling their traditional Maori
purposes. They felt that the benign and powerful Christian *atua*
could provide them with the order and the *mana* which they had
lost and desperately missed. But Christianity did not do this. Its
rewards are not of a Maori character. As the first, bright years faded
after 1842, and the Maoris felt the new pressures of land sales and
white immigration, it became obvious to them that Christian Maoris
were no more successful in solving the increasing problems than

[28] Williams, *Christianity,* p. 309; see also pp. 304–308. See also Williams,
MR, April 1844, p. 205, and November 1844, p. 493.
[29] William Colenso, "On the Maori Races of New Zealand," *TPNZI,* I
(1868), 72.

the heathen ones. Christianity was not, in short, the Maori panacea it had appeared; Maoris began to revert to practices they had been brought up with and which had been effective in the past. Tattooing was resumed. The *hahunga* once again became popular. Maori children were neglected. Maoris broke the Sabbath, danced again, and went to war.[30] This was especially true of the north, where there had been most white contact. In 1845, some of the Ngapuhi revolted openly against white leadership. The reason Christianity failed in the end was the same as the reason for which it had been accepted—the Maoris' perfectly understandable misconception of its essential nature.

Most of the claims of the missionaries and of the traders and whalers about each other were, as it turned out, largely beside the point. The traders and whalers were correct in their thought that the missionaries had failed to make well-integrated Christians out of the Maoris, but they were mistaken in blaming this either on missionary methods or on personal weaknesses. The missionaries were justified in stating that the whalers and traders had not "civilized" the Maoris with trade and had in fact contributed to the Maori disorganization, but they were mistaken in blaming this on specific Western vices. Both groups helped indirectly, and unconsciously, to produce the condition of the Maoris as it was in 1840. Neither group was so harmful as the other maintained; neither achieved what it claimed for itself.

Both the missionaries and the traders and whalers, in fact, though they would not have admitted it, were in large part indebted to each other so far as their own purposes were concerned. The missionaries had settled in the Bay of Islands after the *Boyd* massacre and showed that extensive trade with the Maoris was possible. The traders and whalers in turn had introduced Western elements which eventually helped make the first conversions possible. But the most important thing the two groups had in common was the fact that they made the same mistake, both in their approach to the Maoris

[30] For reversions to old ways see *MR*, July 1846, p. 329, July 1847, pp. 320, 323, and July 1848, pp. 324–25; and Williams, *Christianity*, pp. 319, 330–34, 347 *passim*.

and in their criticism of each other: they underestimated the durability of Maori habits of thought.

It was the mutual misunderstanding between the Europeans and the Maoris, in fact, which in the last analysis precipitated the difficulties of the years that followed. Except superficially, the Maoris of the 1840's were still Maori in their thought and outlook—no matter what the Europeans might think of them. Except for a few conventional concessions to Maori desires to help maintain the peace, the Europeans of later years were not concerned with achieving Maori goals—no matter what the Maoris might presume. The Europeans expected too much of the Maoris, and the Maoris expected too much of the Europeans. Each people mistakenly read into the minds of the other its own particular assumptions.

BIBLIOGRAPHICAL ESSAY

This bibliography does not attempt to include every source mentioned in the footnotes. It aims, rather, to give some general idea of the location and extent of unpublished materials as well as a brief description of the more important published works, both primary and secondary. More bibliographical details (and more complete documentation) may be found in my thesis in the Archives, Widener Library, Cambridge, Massachusetts, entitled: "New Zealand: 1769–1840. A Study of Maoris and Europeans."

MANUSCRIPTS

I. NEW ZEALAND

Without question the most valuable material for a study of New Zealand before 1840 is in the manuscript collection of the Hocken Library in Dunedin, N.Z. Mr. Thomas M. Hocken, of Dunedin, gathered a great quantity of records for a biography of Samuel Marsden, which he never wrote. There are hundreds of letters and journals of the different missionaries for the years between 1814 and 1840. John Butler, George Clarke, Richard Davis, William Hall, James Kemp, Thomas Kendall, John King, and Marsden himself are all represented to greater or lesser degree in manuscript volumes 54 to 73 with both letters and journals. In no case, however, are the journals without large gaps, and many of the letters (most of the approximately 450 by Marsden, for example) pertain more to administrative matters than to the Maoris. Some of the originals of Marsden's journals of his voyages to New Zealand are also in the Library. They are discussed in J. R. Elder's edition of Marsden's letters and journals, pp. 555–56.

The Hocken Library also has a copy of the "Transcript of New Zealand or Recollections of it," by the traveler Edward Markham in Ms vol. 85. There are two other manuscript copies of Markham's journal in New Zealand, each slightly different from the others, and it is unknown which is the original. Presumably the "Transcript" implies a copy, but the Hocken Library version has hand-painted illustrations and was probably done by the author at one time or another.

There are two valuable collections of typewritten copies of letters and journals in the Library. These are letters of Henry Williams (originals owned by his family) and some letters and a few journals of James Kemp (originals in the Auckland Public Library).

The Alexander Turnbull Library in Wellington has, among other items, the James Busby manuscript correspondence, 1833–39, and a collection of manuscript extracts of the letters and journals of Mr. and Mrs. Henry Williams and Mr. and Mrs. William Williams.

II. England

The library of the Church Missionary Society in London has a great many records of the early years in New Zealand. While there are some original papers, however, the main source of information is a series of manuscript copybooks into which, before 1880 (and more fully in the early years), C.M.S. secretaries copied letters and journals as they arrived from the missionaries overseas, to make reading easier for the members of the Society. Most of this material is a duplication of what can be found in New Zealand.

III. United States

The Peabody Museum in Salem, Massachusetts, has a number of whaling logs and other manuscript material which pertain to early New Zealand. Among the most useful of these is the journal of the Brig *Spy* of Salem, John B. Knights, Master, which is a long and pious description of the Bay of Islands in March and April, 1833. There is also the journal of John B. Williams in New Zealand, 1842–44. Williams was American consul at the Bay of Islands from 1842 to 1845, and a somewhat erratic one. His journal does have some pertinent material for the period before 1840. It has recently (1956) been edited by Robert W. Kenny, of Brown University, and published.

The Essex Institute in Salem, like the Peabody Museum, has a useful collection of the logs of traders and whalers, although there are none with a reference to New Zealand so extensive as that of Knights. Some information may be found in the journals of J. H. Eagleston in the *Emerald* (1833–36) and the *Mermaid* (1836–39), as well as the journal of George H. Cheever in the *Emerald* (1833–36).

The American consular records for the Bay of Islands from 1839 are deposited in the National Archives in Washington, D.C. Except for some remarks about the early shipping by J. B. Williams, however, and lists of American vessels in the Bay of Islands from 1839, there is little material pertaining to the period before 1840.

PUBLISHED PRIMARY SOURCES

I. OFFICIAL

The most important British official publication is the *Parliamentary Papers,* 1837–38 (680), XXI: Report from the Select Committee of the House of Lords, Appointed to Inquire into the Present State of New Zealand. . . This 376-page volume consists almost entirely of evidence given by nearly twenty witnesses on the current state of New Zealand, although many of the witnesses, particularly the Rev. John Beecham and Dandeson Coates—the two missionary society secretaries—had never been there. The Select Committee was established largely as the result of controversy between the New Zealand Association and the missionary interests, as the testimony reveals. Among the more knowledgeable witnesses were Mr. John Watkins, a surgeon who had been in New Zealand on and off in 1833 and 1834; Mr. John Tawell, a surgeon who traveled in New Zealand for two months in 1837; Mr. John Flatt, a missionary catechist who spent over two years (1834–37) in New Zealand; and J. S. Polack and R. FitzRoy (see published works below).

Another official British publication is *Parliamentary Papers,* 1844 (556), XIII: Report from the Select Committee on New Zealand. . . This immense volume (1119 pages) is concerned with a variety of New Zealand problems, particularly that of the quarrels between the New Zealand Company and the government of New Zealand, and it consists more of the papers of these two bodies than it does of testimony. There is little information on the period before 1840, but a great deal of material relating to 1840–44.

Among other Parliamentary Papers, one should mention *Parliamentary Papers,* 1846 (337), XXX: Papers Relative to New Zealand, which has useful statistics for the year 1845, and *Parliamentary Papers,* 1836 (538), VII: Report From the Select Committee on Aborigines, which contains some evidence of the missionary, Yate, about New Zealand.

The most useful New Zealand official publication is, without any doubt, the *Historical Records of New Zealand,* ed. Robert McNab (2 vols., Wellington, 1908–14). This collection of documents is concerned entirely with the period before 1840. The first volume consists simply of extracts from the *Historical Records of New South Wales* which have to do with New Zealand, a steady sequence up to 1840. The second volume has extracts from the early explorers (the French ones are particularly useful) and then skips abruptly to the 1830's and some American consular records.

The work of Francis D. Fenton, *Observations on the State of the Aboriginal Inhabitants of New Zealand* (Auckland, 1859), while discussing depopulation, is mostly concerned with a survey made in 1858. It has a great many statistical tables, a few useful statements of fact, and some bizarre conclusions.

II.   PERIODICALS

Some of the most valuable information about early New Zealand comes from missionary periodicals. Of the various publications of the Church Missionary Society, the most important is the *Missionary Register* (London, 1813——). This great repository of miscellaneous information contains running accounts of all the Protestant missionary societies, English and American, which means the C.M.S. and the W-M.M.S. so far as New Zealand is concerned. The information is irregular, but usually consists of comments by the editors illustrated with lengthy quotations (slightly edited) from the letters, journals, and reports of the missionaries abroad. The *Church Missionary Record* London, 1830——), a shorter publication, is devoted entirely to the missionaries of the C.M.S. It often duplicates the material in the *Missionary Register,* but does have a certain amount of other records, particularly statistical. The *Church Missionary Proceedings* (London, 1815——) deals primarily with administrative affairs but does, also, have some material pertaining to New Zealand not found elsewhere.

The periodicals of the Wesleyan-Methodist Missionary Society are not so useful as those of the C.M.S. The *Report of the Wesleyan-Methodist Missionary Society* (London, 1822——) and the *Wesleyan Missionary Notices,* however, do have some excerpts from the missionaries in New Zealand. The Catholic missionary journal, *Annales de la propagation de la foi,* XI (Lyons, 1838——) has some letters from the missionaries after 1838.

III.   MISSIONARIES: PUBLISHED WORKS AND RECENT COLLECTIONS

So far as Samuel Marsden is concerned, *The Letters and Journals of Samuel Marsden,* ed. J. R. Elder (Dunedin, 1932) is essential. The greatest part of it consists of Marsden's journals for his first four and his sixth voyages to New Zealand. The fifth and seventh, for which he left no journals, are pieced together by various accounts and letters. The other letters included, of which there are not many, deal primarily with administrative matters. Elder also edited a volume entitled *Marsden's Lieutenants* (Dunedin, 1934). It contains various letters and journals of Kendall, Hall, and King which are in the Hocken Library. Some of the more unpleasant passages have been deleted, but on the whole it is a careful job of editing. Most of the material is for the years 1814–23.

A descendant of John Butler, R. J. Barton, edited *Earliest New Zealand. The Journals and Correspondence of the Rev. John Butler* (Masterton, N.Z., 1927). The correspondence is extensive and the journals are virtually complete for the years 1819–23. The editor has interspersed the text with comments which are obviously designed to clear the reputation of his great-grandfather at the expense of Samuel Marsden, but these are clearly marked. The new edition of Hugh Carleton's, *The Life of Henry Williams. Archdeacon of Waimate,* ed. and rev. by James Elliott (Wellington, 1948), carries this sympathetic biography (Carleton was Williams' son-in-law) down to 1840. The book is most valuable for its long excerpts from Williams' diaries and letters.

Of books published by the missionaries, the most important is William Williams' *Christianity Among the New Zealanders* (London, 1867), written at the height of the Maori wars, no doubt to explain, or justify, the then apparently futile missionary efforts. The book is based on Church Missionary records and personal recollection. There is no mention of the mission musket trade or of Kendall's or Butler's dismissal, and the "uncivilized" character of the Maoris before 1814 is emphasized, perhaps in an unconscious effort to indicate the value of the missionary work. But Williams' book is generously unbiased. Most of it is devoted to the period before 1840, and it is indispensable. William Yate's *An Account of New Zealand; and of the Formation and Progress of the Church Missionary Society's Mission in the Northern Island* (London, 1835) systematically covers geography, flora and fauna, Maori customs, and the efforts of the missionaries. It is interesting and valuable, but not always reliable. William R. Wade, who was in New Zealand for several years, wrote *A Journey in the Northern Island of New Zealand: Interspersed with Various Information Relative to the Country and People* (Hobart Town, 1842) about a trip to the south in 1838. Wade was interested in botany and the Maoris, and he treated the matter of conversion in a straightforward fashion—without false optimism and without cynicism. Perhaps the most useful of the several works of

William Colenso is his long article, "On the Maori Races of New Zealand," in *The Transactions and Proceedings of the New Zealand Institute,* I (1868), 1–76 (separately paged). It is a long and careful antiquarian study of the pre-European Maoris which ends with some discussion of the effects of Western contact.

Catholic missionaries are represented with two books by Bishop Jean B. F. Pompallier: *Early History of the Catholic Church in Oceania* (Auckland, 1888) and *Notice historique et statistique de la mission de la nouvelle zélande. . .* (Anvers, 1850). These two short accounts overlap each other to some extent. The first is largely the historical part of Pompallier's report to the Holy See in 1846; the second is a typical piece of nineteenth-century didactic missionary propaganda. A poorly edited, but useful, collection of documents and letters of the early Catholic missionaries is *Fishers of Men,* ed. Peter McKeefry (N.Z., 1938), a centenary testimonial.

IV. EXPLORERS' ACCOUNTS: FRENCH, ENGLISH, AND AMERICAN

There are several accounts of the early explorers. Cook's journals have been conveniently collected in *Captain Cook in New Zealand. Extracts from the journals . . . ,* ed. A. H. and A. W. Reed (Wellington, 1951), which takes the pertinent extracts from modern editions which adhere (especially the first) more closely to the originals than did Hawkesworth. The first journal (1769–70) is the only one with much information on the North Island. George Forster's *A Voyage Round the World in His Britannic Majesty's Sloop, 'Resolution' . . .* (2 vols., London, 1777) has a few helpful passages. It is by the son of Cook's naturalist. *Crozet's Voyage to Tasmania, New Zealand, the Ladrone Islands, and the Philippines in the Years 1771–1772,* ed. and trans. H. Ling Roth (London, 1891) is interesting, but not always trustworthy. There is a short description of the Maoris and a long account of Marion's massacre.

After a lapse of almost fifty years, exploring expeditions began to visit New Zealand again in the 1820's. The French published extremely thorough accounts. The best of these is by M. J. Dumont D'Urville: *Voyage de la corvette l'Astrolabe . . . 1826–29 . . . Histoire du voyage* (5 vols. and an atlas, Paris, 1830–33). Dumont D'Urville was in New Zealand on this voyage from December 1826 to March 1827. Volumes II and III are devoted entirely to New Zealand with both text and compilations of other sources (Marsden, Nicholas, etc.). Dumont D'Urville made a long and careful examination of the northern coasts and spent a great deal of time in the Bay of Islands. His objective account is invaluable. He had already visited New Zealand with Duperrey in 1824, and there is a brief notice of the stop at the Bay of Islands in that year in vol. III, pp. 673–91, of this work. Dumont D'Urville visited New Zealand for the third time in 1840, but was disappointed and did not say much about it. René P. Lesson, who wrote *Voyage autour du monde . . . sur la corvette la Coquille* (2 vols., Paris, 1839), was a zoologist on the Duperrey expedition and was in the Bay of Islands in April 1824. Both his day-to-day account and his general section on the Maoris are quite sound, and they are particularly important because the official history of the voyage was never completed. M. C. P. T. Laplace's *Voyage autour du monde . . . sur la corvette de l'état la Favorite . . .* (4 vols. and an atlas, Paris, 1833–39) has, in vol. IV, about thirty pages on the Bay of Islands, where Laplace stopped briefly in October, 1831. Another French explorer, Abel Du Petit-Thouars, was at the Bay of Islands for about a month, late in 1838. His record, *Voyage autour du monde sur la frégate la Vénus . . .* (4 vols., Paris, 1839–41), devotes parts of vols. III and IV to general descriptions of the area—with a definite French bias and often statistical unreliability.

A British exploring expedition under Robert FitzRoy, which visited the Bay of Islands for about ten days in December 1835 was written up in Robert FitzRoy and others, *Narrative of the Surveying Voyages of His Majesty's Ships Adventure and Beagle . . . 1826–1836* (3 vols. and Appendix, London, 1839). Volume III ("Journal and Remarks") was by Charles Darwin, and in separate editions is his *Voyage of the Beagle*. The accounts are brief, but they are valuable because of their scientific approach. FitzRoy's discussion is more general than Darwin's. Both men liked the missionaries, but took a dim view of the Maoris. The American expedition under Charles Wilkes, described in his *Narrative of the United States Exploring Expedition during the Years 1838, 1839, 1840, 1841, 1842* (5 vols. and an atlas, Philadelphia, 1845), visited the Bay of Islands in the spring of 1840. In his account (vol. II, 369–414), Wilkes was generally unhappy about the Treaty of Waitangi, the Maoris, the missionaries, and so forth.

V. Miscellaneous: Traders, Whalers, Independent Travelers, and Others

There were a great many books written about New Zealand in its early years by people who were neither missionaries nor explorers. The first of these was John Savage's *Some Account of New Zealand; particularly the Bay of Islands, and Surrounding Country* . . . (London, 1807). This is a short, but nevertheless useful, description by a ship's surgeon. Savage was at the Bay of Islands in 1805, but only stayed briefly and did not stray far from his ship. The author of *Narrative of a Voyage to New Zealand* . . . (2 vols., London, 1817), John L. Nicholas, was a gentleman staying in Sydney who, with time on his hands, accompanied Marsden on his first trip to New Zealand, December 1814–February 1815. The narrative has many word pictures, details on the establishment of the mission, and descriptions of the leading Maoris (as the author saw them), but not a great deal of information. On the other hand, the shorter work of Richard A. Cruise, an army major, *Journal of a Ten Month's Residence in New Zealand,* 2nd ed. (London, 1824) is one of the most useful books on early New Zealand, although it has little literary style and a fairly rigid structure. Cruise was in New Zealand, mostly at the Bay of Islands and the Thames River area, for ten months in 1820. An ensign on the same ship, Alexander McCrae, wrote a *Journal Kept in New Zealand in 1820* . . . , ed. Sir F. R. Chapman (Wellington, 1928), a short, wry journal (not twenty pages) on the early part of the visit. Augustus Earle, the author of the controversial *A Narrative of a Nine Months' Residence in New Zealand, in 1827* . . . (London, 1832), visited Hokianga and the Bay of Islands between October 1827 and April 1828. This entertaining book, though critical of the missionaries, is one of the few detailed sources of information about the Bay of Islands in the 1820's. The two visits of Captain Peter Dillon to the Bay of Islands in 1827 are recorded in his *Narrative and Successful Result of a Voyage in the South Seas . . . to Ascertain the Actual Fate of La Pérouse's Expedition* . . . (2 vols., London, 1829). Dillon did not like the missionaries and his narrative is not always reliable.

More people visited New Zealand after 1830. One of the first was Peter Bays, who stayed at the Bay of Islands in February and March, 1830, on his way home from a wreck in the Tonga Islands. His account of the visit, in *A Narrative of the Wreck of the Minerva Whaler of Port Jackson* . . . (Cambridge, Eng., 1831) is short, but observant. Perhaps the most prolific author of the 1830's was Joel S. Polack, a trader who lived primarily at the Bay of Islands from 1831 to 1837. Polack was not liked by the missionaries, but always maintained he was one of the "respectable" traders at Kororareka. He wrote two books: *New*

Zealand: Being a Narrative of Travels and Adventures . . . , new ed. (2 vols., London, 1839) and *Manners and Customs of the New Zealanders* . . . (2 vols., London, 1840). The first is a compendium of miscellaneous information gathered from first- and second-hand sources and is a little more reliable than the second, which discusses the Maoris in more general terms and is something of a pot-boiler. In any case, Polack, though entertaining, is always slightly suspect, especially when he is not describing his own experiences. Another visitor who wrote two books about New Zealand was Ernest Dieffenbach, a surgeon and naturalist for the New Zealand Co. (1839–41). *New Zealand, and its Native Population* (London, 1841) is a thirty-page brochure about a visit in the Cook's Straits area. *Travels in New Zealand; with Contributions to the Geography, Geology, Botany, and Natural History of that Country* (2 vols., London, 1843) is a full-scale description. The classic book about the 1830's is F. E. Maning's *Old New Zealand* (Wellington, 1948; 1st ed. in 1863).

The establishment of permanent settlements after 1840 brought out a fresh spate of books by people who had been to New Zealand. William Brown, who wrote *New Zealand and its Aborigines* . . . (London, 1845), was a violently optimistic settler who hated his government. His book is uneven—the best part being the earlier chapters (written in 1840). Even these are not wholly reliable. John Logan Campbell, a friend of Brown's wrote *Poenamo. Sketches of the Early Days in New Zealand* . . . , "New Zealand" ed. (Wellington, 1953), a somewhat stilted, tiresome, and exaggerated book: useful, but overrated as literature. Campbell spent some time in the Hauraki Gulf area in 1840–41. R. G. Jameson, another author, was an independent traveler who was in New Zealand in 1839 and 1840, chiefly at the Bay of Islands and the Thames River area. His book, *New Zealand, South Australia, and New South Wales* . . . (London, 1842), is useful, but a little sanguine so far as the Maoris, trade, settlement, etc., are concerned. Charles Terry, the author of *New Zealand, its Advantages and Prospects, as a British Colony* . . . (London, 1842), was in New Zealand for over a year, in 1840–41, and was especially interested in the land problem. The only son of E. G. Wakefield, Edward Jerningham Wakefield, wrote *Adventure in New Zealand from 1839 to 1844. With some Account of the Beginning of the British Colonization of the Islands,* ed. R. Stout (Christchurch, 1908), which is vivid, but almost exclusively devoted to the Cook's Straits area. Edward Shortland, a Protector of the Aborigines in the early 1840's and a man who knew the Maoris well, wrote two useful books. These are *The Southern Districts of New Zealand; A Journal, with Passing Notices of the Customs of the Aborigines* (London, 1851) and *Traditions and Superstitions of the New Zealanders: with Illustrations of their Manners and Customs,* 2nd ed. (London, 1856). Like all the books described in this paragraph, however, Shortland's works pertain primarily to the period after 1840 and so make only occasional references to the earlier years.

The most important books by people who did not visit New Zealand are [George L. Craik], *The New Zealanders* (London, 1830), a well-known compilation relying on C.M.S. publications, Nicholas, etc. and featuring an at least partially fraudulent shipwreck account by a man named John Rutherford; and [E. G. Wakefield and John Ward], *The British Colonization of New Zealand; being an Account of the Principles, Objects, and Plans of the New Zealand Association* . . . (London, 1837), a typical production of a colonizing pressure group. A few of the articles are: Anonymous, "The Polynesians and New Zealand (by a N.Z. colonist)," *Edinburgh Review,* XCI (1850), 443–71, a generally unsound consideration of depopulation based on some useful observations; Saxe Bannister, "On the Population of New Zealand," *Journal of the Statistical Society of London,* I (1839), 362–76, concerned with the European, not the Maori population; and R. W. Hay, "Notices of New Zealand. From Original Documents in the Colonial Office," *The Journal of the Royal Geographical Society of London,* II (1831–32), 133–36, which is a collection of otherwise virtually unobtainable statistics.

There were countless other books and articles written about New Zealand in the early years. Some of these are mentioned in the notes. The most complete bibliography of them is that of T. M. Hocken, *A Bibliography of the Literature Relating to New Zealand* (Wellington, 1909), a superbly annotated list, by year, which other editors have continued. Another bibliography, one which includes material of all dates alphabetically, is C. R. H. Taylor's *A Pacific Bibliography. Printed matter relating to the Native Peoples of Polynesia, Melanesia, and Micronesia* (Wellington, 1951). This has a long section on New Zealand, largely devoted to material of anthropological interest.

SECONDARY WORKS

I. PERIODICALS

The *Journal of the Polynesian Society,* I——(Wellington, 1890——)

is an invaluable source of Maori anthropology. In spite of its general title, this periodical was at first devoted almost entirely to New Zealand, the Maoris, and the recording of Maori myths. It was the first place of publication of several later books by S. P. Smith and E. Best. More recently (especially since World War II) it has expanded to cover the rest of Polynesia. Since much of the early anthropology is now dated, however, some of the most valuable material is to be found in the later issues. *The Transactions and Proceedings of the New Zealand Institute,* I—— (Wellington, 1868——) is, in its earlier issues, a most useful source of information about the Maoris. Many of the early settlers were still alive when it began. Since the 1920's, however, the *Transactions* have emphasized chemistry, physics, biology, zoology, botany, etc.

II. WORKS PRIMARILY ANTHROPOLOGICAL

The two most famous students of Maori life are Elsdon Best and Peter H. Buck (Te Rangi Hiroa). Best's standard work was *The Maori* (2 vols., Wellington, 1924), based on years of specialized studies, such as can be found in *Forest Lore of the Maori* (Wellington, 1924), *The Pa Maori . . .* (Wellington, 1927), and *Tuhoe. The Children of the Mist* (2 vols., New Plymouth, N.Z., 1925). Best is still unmatched, save perhaps by Buck, in the detail of his descriptions of Maori material culture. The works of younger anthropologists, however, such as Beaglehole, Hawthorn, and others, have superseded many of his interpretations, and especially his too heavy reliance on Maori myths. The major work of Peter H. Buck is *The Coming of the Maori* (Wellington, 1949). Buck combined a scientific approach with personal anecdotes. The section on the origin of the Maoris is a little out of date. The rest of the book, on Maori material culture and social organization, is excellent. Buck also wrote *Vikings of the Sunrise* (Philadelphia, 1938), a book about the Polynesians which has a useful chapter on the Maori variation from the Polynesian norm.

Some of the older works about the Maoris are still worthwhile. *The Maoris of New Zealand* (Christchurch, 1910) was written by James Cowan, who collected his data from tribes in the middle of the North Island (Waikato, Te Arawa, etc.). This is a superbly written book, although somehow it manages to avoid the 1800–40 period and is, by now, in many respects out of date. William Baucke's *Where the White Man Treads* (Auckland, 1905) is a collection of newspaper articles in which the author gives a most sympathetic (and not always accurate) history of the Maoris before white contact, as well as a violent and verbose condemnation of current government policies. S. Percy Smith's *History and Traditions of the Maoris of the West Coast North Island of New Zealand Prior to 1840* (New Plymouth, N.Z., 1910) is more tradition than history and in no way comparable in value to his history of early Maori wars (see below). There were many articles on Maori depopulation in the late nineteenth century: it was a topical subject. Typical of them is Alfred K. Newman's "A Study of the Causes Leading to the Extinction of the Maori," *TPNZI*, XIV (1881), 459–77, a view that the Maori population was already declining when the white men arrived and that they only accelerated the process.

There are several valuable recent works. Raymond Firth's *Primitive Economics of the New Zealand Maori* (London, 1929) is organized around the functional concepts of Malinowski. One chapter at the end is devoted to the economic aspects of culture change resulting from western contact. In the first section of *The Changing Maori* (New Plymouth, N.Z., 1928), Felix M. Keesing presents some excellent psychological insights on the Maori of the past. Later sections, on the Maori present and future as of 1928, are only slightly out of date in the proposed policies. A short, but direct and valuable study, is "The Reaction of the Maori to the Impact of Civilization," *Journal of the Polynesian Society*, XLIV (1935), 216–43, by Bishop Herbert W. Williams of Waiapu. The article discusses specific culture traits, topic by topic.

A number of books have been written on the Maori in the modern period. Ernest and Pearl Beaglehole in *Some Modern Maoris* (Christchurch, 1946) and Harry B. Hawthorn in *The Maori. A Study in Acculturation* (Menasha, Wis., 1944) emphasize the persistence of traditional Maori traits. The most famous work, edited by I. L. G. Sutherland, *The Maori People Today. A General Survey* (London, 1940) is a series of twelve essays with an approach very sympathetic to the Maoris. The most pertinent history and the most objective attitude are to be found in the contributions of Sir Apirana Ngata: "Maori Land Settlement," "Maori Arts and Crafts," "Tribal Organization," and (with the editor) "Religious Influences." E. Beaglehole's "The Polynesian Maori" is useful anthropologically.

III. Historical Works on Special Topics

There are a variety of books which are concerned with New Zealand before 1840. Perhaps the most useful is the *Early History of New Zea-*

land, by R. A. A. Sherrin and J. H. Wallace (Auckland, 1890). This is an immense volume and a famous compilation of miscellaneous material about the early period which has frequent excerpts from the original sources. Another compiler of material was Robert McNab, who wrote several books on early Western visitors to New Zealand. McNab was not trying to interpret, but to collect sources for future historians. In this respect he succeeded very well, although there is no record for the origin of some of the material. Large portions of each volume are paraphrased from early accounts which may usually be found in the appendices or the *Historical Records of N.Z.* The only book on the North Island is *From Tasman to Marsden. A History of Northern New Zealand from 1642 to 1818* (Dunedin, 1914).

Several books have been written about Maori wars or warriors. Thomas W. Gudgeon's *The History and Doings of the Maoris, From the Year 1820 to the Signing of the Treaty of Waitangi in 1840* (Auckland, 1885) is a short work devoted primarily to battles on the west coast. S. Percy Smith's *Maori Wars of the Nineteenth Century . . . ,* 2nd and enlarged ed. (Christchurch, 1910) is a famous and detailed old narrative taken from missionary and other accounts. T. Lindsay Buick's *An Old New Zealander, or Te Rauparaha, the Napoleon of the South* (London, 1911) is a long detailed, and popular history.

A valuable book, by T. Lindsay Buick, is *The Treaty of Waitangi. How New Zealand Became a British Colony,* 3rd ed. (New Plymouth, N.Z., 1936). One of Eric Ramsden's books, *Marsden and the Missions. Prelude to Waitangi* (Sydney, 1936) pertains to the period 1830–1839 and is a partially digested mass of otherwise inaccessible material. It is built around a memoir of Martha Marsden, who went to New Zealand with her father in 1837. H. C. Fancourt's *The Advance of the Missionaries. Being the Expansion of the C.M.S. Missions South of the Bay of Islands, 1833–1840* (Dunedin, 1939) is occasionally useful. *The Early History of New Zealand* (Wellington, 1914), by Thomas M. Hocken, is devoted primarily to the settlement of Otago and Canterbury.

Three very recent volumes which bear with varying emphasis and point-of-view on early New Zealand history are Keith Sinclair's *A History of New Zealand* (Harmondsworth, Eng., 1959), E. J. Tapp's *Early New Zealand. A Dependency of New South Wales. 1788–1841* (Melbourne, 1958), and A. H. McLintock's *Crown Colony Government in New Zealand* (Wellington, 1958).

INDEX

Aborigines, Australian, 38, 109

Account of New Zealand, An, 43

Active, 22, 23, 86

Adultery, of Maoris, 73, 124

Akaroa, 29

Americans: early whaling near N.Z., 21; population in N.Z., 37; land claims, 196

Atua: in Maori explanations, 7, 60, 101, 154, 158; in Maori religion, 14; inadequacy of, 112, 183; and Maori conception of Christianity, 112, 150, 154, 159, 171, 172, 173–174, 180, 183, 199; relation of Europeans to, 149, 159; mentioned, 131, 142, 144

Auckland, N.Z., 93, 193, 195, 198

Australia, 19, 27, 38, 40, 46, 122, 131, 133, 187

Banks, Joseph, 6

Bay of Islands: first European settlement, 22, 38; C.M.S. station founded, 22, 38; population, 22–33, 37; weakness as economic depot, 28; description, 29; popularity, 29; Catholic mission, 48; venereal diseases, 63; liquor, 69–71; sexual laxity, 73; Maori health, 76; Maori arrogance, 117; center of religious changes, 157, 167; center of Maori teachers, 160; center of Maori reading, 174–175; economic dislocation, 189. *See also* Kororareka; Ngapuhi

Bay of Plenty, 12, 44, 45, 160, 195

Bays, Peter, 107, 130

Beagle, 31, 57, 67

Best, Elsdon, 9

Bibles. *See* Printed religious matter

Bishop of Australia, 57, 112

Boyd, 21–22, 46, 84, 86, 117, 200

Bream Head, 148

British and Foreign Bible Society, 53, 176

Brown, A. N., 170, 173

Brown, William, 72, 108, 111, 112

Buck, Sir Peter H., 9, 82

Buller, James, 97, 162, 175

Busby, James, opinions, 34, 71, 101, 122–123; mentioned, 26, 78

Bushmen, South African, 38, 109

Butler, John: description, 41; and musket trade, 88, 89; opinions, 78, 89, 122, 135, 136; mentioned, 131

Campbell, Maori chief, 156

Campbell, John Logan, 16, 72, 105

Cannibalism: pre-European, 17, 179; European descriptions, 105–106; increase, 118; Europeans not usually victims, 127; decline, 142, 143, 169, 181, 189; why abandoned, 178, 180, 181, 182, 199; mentioned, 38, 45, 60, 68, 77

Cape Horn, 21

Carlisle, William, 88

Chiefs, Maori: pre-European status, 17; and new type of wars, 96, 121–

122; Conversion, 150, 156–157, 164; decline of authority, 181, 182; status in 1840, 191. *See also* Hongi; Maoris

Christianity. *See* Maoris, conversion; Missionaries

Christian Rangi, 151, 153

Church Missionary Society: sponsors N.Z. mission, 22, 38; estimate of members in N.Z., 36–37; disputes with Methodists, 47, 48–49; attitude toward first missionaries, 86, 88; land purchases of members, 193, 198; mentioned, 23, 40, 42, 45, 109, 131, 136, 141, 194. *See also* Missionaries

Church of England, 38, 141, 164

Clarke, George: opinions, 36, 72, 122, 137, 138, 141, 148, 151–152, 165, 194; description, 42

Clarke, George, Jr., 72, 169

Clendon, James, 32

Cloudy Bay, 29

Coates, Dandeson, 79

Colenso, William: printer, 53; opinions, 62, 63, 127, 128, 176, 192, 199

Cook, James: visits N.Z., 3, 4; opinions, 4–5, 6, 59; Maori describes landing, 6–7; and introduction of venereal diseases, 63; and introduction of pigs, 65; and introduction of potatoes, 67; mentioned, 28, 62

Cook's Straits, 161, 164, 169

Coromandel Peninsula, 96, 173

Crozet, M.: and Dufresne massacre, 4; opinions, 5, 59, 69, 128

Cruise, Richard: publishes book on N.Z., 27; opinions, 69, 85, 87, 91, 105, 132, 134

Cumberland, Kenneth B., 11

Darwin, Charles, 31, 32, 67, 80, 100

Davis, Richard: description, 42; opinions, 51, 91, 100, 110, 112, 127, 138, 147, 153, 170, 176; mentioned, 154, 155

De Surville, Jean, 3

De Thierry, Charles, 34

Dieffenbach, Ernest, 80, 112

Diseases: pre-European Maori attitudes, 15, 58–60, 61, 158; and Maori depopulation, 20, 57, 58, 62–65, 78; estimate of Maori deaths by, 102; and conversion, 144, 151–152, 153–154, 159, 173; in interior, 157–158. *See also* Venereal diseases

Dromedary, 27

Du Clesmeur, M., 4, 59

Dufresne, Marion, 3, 4, 67

Du Petit-Thouars, Abel, **124**

D'Urville, M. J. Dumont, 92, 117

Earle, Augustus: description, 25; opinions, 25–26, 33, 70, 75, 76, 85, 110, 118, 130, 143, 149, 173

Earp, G. B., 72

East Cape: C.M.S. stations, 45, 161; Maori teachers, 45, 161–162, 176; mentioned, 12, 68, 83, 92, 160, 198

East India Company, 21

Endeavour, 7

England, 39, 40, 42, 44, 45, 93, 119, 131, 135

Europeans: first visits to N.Z., 3–6; Maoris' first impressions of, 6–7; early post-exploration contacts, 19, 21; estimates of general population in N.Z., 22–23, 36–37, 188–189, 193; and causes of Maori wars, 83–84, 119–122; responsibility of various groups for depopulation, 102; limitations in forming opinions of Maoris, 106–109, 113; changing Maori views of, 115–117, 149; elements of culture brought to N.Z., 125–126; dominated by

Maoris, 129–130, 133–139; cultural elements of disturb Maoris, 144–146; rarely seen inland, 158; mentioned, *passim.* *See also* Missionaries; Nonmissionary Europeans; Roman Catholics

Fairburn, William: opinions, 159, 175–176; mentioned, 159, 196
Fairfowl, Dr., 123
Fenton, Francis, 169
FitzRoy, Robert, 32, 57, 79, 106, 107
Flax: Maori clothing, 5, 13, 79, 190–191; European interest, 28; mentioned, 19, 34, 35, 77, 86, 87, 88, 158, 189, 194, 195
Ford, Dr. S. H., 65
Forster, Johan R., 4–5, 6, 11, 69

George IV, King of England, 97, 119, 136
Gordon, Charles, 88
Great Barrier Island, 191
Gregory XVI, Pope, 47
Gudgeon, Thomas, 182

Hadfield, Octavius, 37, 164
Hahunga, ceremony: at Bay of Islands, 142; decline, 168, 181–182, 189; resumption of, 200
Hakari, harvest feast, 168
Hall, Francis, 132, 136, 142, 155
Hall, William, 41, 87, 88, 89, 134
Hanson, Mr., 23
Hauraki Gulf, 24, 29, 93, 95
Hawaiians, 179
"Hawaiki," 6, 9, 14
Hay, R. W., 26, 33, 35
"Head of the Hokianga," 47
Herd expedition, 33
Hobbs, John, 47, 175
Hobson, William, 42, 78, 187, 193
Hokianga River: and N.Z. Company

(1825), 24, 25, 33; discovery, 33; European settlement and population, 33–34, 37; Methodists establish station, 38, 47; Catholics establish station, 47–48; venereal diseases, 63; consumption of liquor, 70–71; center of Maori reading, 174–175; economic dislocation, 189
Hone Heke, 192
Hongi: missionary dependency on, 41, 43, 46, 133, 135–137; campaigns, 92–96; character, 97; incidents in life, 97–99; death, 99, 136; wars, 119–121; mentioned, 86, 92–99 *passim,* 118, 131, 142, 155, 161
House of Lords, Select Committee, 36, 73

Indians, American, 118, 153, 174
Infanticide: and Maori depopulation, 57, 72–75, 80; pre-European, 73–74; decline of, 169, 178, 181, 182

Jameson, R. G., 79, 187–188, 189
Jews, and Maoris, 171–172

Kaipara Harbour (and district), 12, 35, 93, 96, 155, 161
Kaitaia: C.M.S. station, 44; mentioned, 58, 64, 170, 192
Kapiti Island, 35, 45
Kauri trees, 27, 33, 34, 76, 174
Kawhia, 35, 49
Kemp, James, 42, 90–91, 101, 138, 155
Kendall, Thomas: opinions, 23, 87, 88, 90, 91, 118–119, 134, 153, 179; visits Hokianga, 33; description, 40; accused of immorality, 41; removed from post, 41, 135; and musket trade, 88, 89, 134–135; and Hongi, 93, 135–136; enigma of, 134–135, 137

Kerikeri River; C.M.S. station, 41; and Hongi, 43, 136; mentioned, 44, 46

King, John: visits Hokianga, 33; description, 41; opinions, 138, 139, 151, 170; mentioned, 88, 155

King, Philip Gidley, 19, 65, 68

"King George," Maori chief, 23, 142, 143

Knights, John B., 31, 92

Kororareka: Marsden visit, 23; in 1820's, 23–26; modern views on, 26, 119; in 1830's, 30–32; missionary opinions of, 31, 107, 109–110; at end of 1830's, 32–33; Catholic station, 48; liquor, 70; "respectable" settlers' opinions of, 107; 1830 battle, 147, 154; in 1840, 33, 187–188; mentioned, 78, 113, 123, 130, 142. *See also* Nonmissionary Europeans

Kumaras. See Maoris, foods

Language: Kendall writes down Maori, 40; missionary teaching criticized, 111; Europeans' use of Maori, 129, 133; Maoris' use of English, 141–142; and missionary techniques, 150; and confusion of Maoris, 171

Laplace, M. C. P. T., opinions, 52, 190

Leigh, Samuel: founds Methodist mission, 46; opinions, 95

Lesson, René P., opinions, 70, 124, 190

L'Horne, Pottier de, opinions, 5

Linton, Ralph, 114

Liquor: modern opinions on effects in N.Z., 20, 69, 119; and Maori depopulation, 57, 65, 69–72, 78, 102; Maori distaste for, 69–70, 124, 127; mentioned, 109, 126

London, England, 21, 28, 42, 108, 126, 197

McCrae, Alexander, 69, 76, 87, 91, 117, 135

Maketu, place, 195

Maketu, witchcraft, 16, 191

Mana: in Maori life, 17–18, 82, 121, 146, 160, 181; of Europeans, 139, 149, 197, 198; disturbance of, 145, 146, 183, 199; mentioned, 125, 127, 174, 193

Mangakahia, 35, 47, 48

Mangapouri, 44, 45, 158

Mangungu, 47, 160

Maning, F. E., 35–36, 77

"Maori," origin of the term, 116

Maoris: physical characteristics, 5; suggested origins, 6, 9–10; tribal differences, 10–11; culture varies from Polynesian, 12–13; pre-European religion, 13–16, 60; pre-European social and political habits, 16–18; sexual habits, 20, 72–75, 119, 123–124; character, 106–109, 113–114; elements of culture similar to Europeans, 108–109; in 1840, 188–193

attitude toward Europeans; first impressions of, 6–8; effect of travel on, 115, 131–133, 143; early reactions to Europeans, 115–119; self-consciousness, 116, 158; self-confidence, 116–117; pursuit of traditional goals, 117–119; and swearing, 124–125, 127; and elements of European culture, 125–129, 133–134, 147–149; and domination of Europeans, 129–130, 133–139; of Europeanized Maoris, 131–133; and changes of habits, 141–143; and demoralization of Maoris, 144–149, 178–183; and land problems, 193, 195–196, 198; and official leadership, 196–197

foods of: pre-European, 5, 10,

12–13, 108; introduction of European plants, 8, 19, 29, 67, 68, 157–158; introduction of European animals, 8, 19, 29, 65, 66, 67, 157–158; lack of domestic animals, 10, 13; the potato, 11; European plants and Maori health, 58, 67–68, 76–77, 102, 190; European animals and Maori health, 65–67, 102; Maori plants, 66, 67, 68, 77

population: estimates, 6, 11, 101; pre-European, 11–12; distribution, 12; compared to European, 188–189; possible increase after 1840, 194

depopulation: extent, 11–12, 101–102; modern opinions, 20, 68, 69, 102; contemporary opinions, 57–58; pre-European Maori health, 58–59; favorable conditions, 59–61; diseases, 62–65, 78; European animals and plants, 65–68, 76–77; liquor, 65, 69–72, 78; sexual promiscuity, 72–75; clothing and blankets, 78–80; wars, 81–102 *passim;* Maori explanations, 101, 148; conclusions on, 101–102. *See also* Diseases; Liquor; Maoris, foods; Maoris, wars

conversion: slow at first, 39, 133–140; first baptism, 43, 151; statistics, 43, 44, 45–46, 47, 48, 49, 141, 152, 157, 161, 162 (table), 163, 194; contemporary nonmissionary opinions on effect, 110–113; influence of European articles, 138, 144–146, 150–151, 152–153, 158; influences of illnesses, 144, 151–152, 153–154; influence of wars, 146–147, 152, 154–155, 157, 159, 198–199; in interior, 157–163; Maori teachers, 159–162, 177–178; Maori enthusiasm, 163–165; missionaries concerned at nature, 164, 166, 170–171, 174; religious observances, 166–170, 178–183, 199–200; nature of Maori confusion, 171–178, 183, 198–201; prayer, 171, 173; Jews, 171–172; religious aberrations, 177–178; effectiveness, 183, 198–201; after 1840, 194, 197–201. *See also* *Atua;* Language; Missionaries; *Tapu*

wars: pre-European, 17, 75, 81–83, 179–180; causes, 17, 82–84, 119–122; effect on Maori crops, 77; decline, 84, 99–101, 169, 189; new kind, 92, 93, 119–122; Maori desire for peace, 93, 99–100, 152, 154–155, 180–181, 183, 198–199; extent of deaths, 95, 96, 97, 102; in the interior, 99–100, 159; why abandoned, 99–101, 146–147, 152, 178, 180–181; use of Bibles, 176–177; resumption, 200. *See also* Hongi; Ngapuhi

Markham, Edward, 30, 34, 36, 57, 70, 105

Marsden, Samuel: and *Boyd* massacre, 22; establishes C.M.S. mission in N.Z., 22, 38; opinions, 31, 32, 40, 42, 61, 77, 88, 89, 90, 98, 120–121, 135, 137, 152, 171–172, 190; character, 39–40; opinions on mission policy, 40, 42; distribution of muskets, 86–87, 88, 135; opposes musket trade, 87–89; Maoris of one district fear, 159; mentioned, 23, 38, 41, 93, 126, 127, 131, 134, 136, 183

Matakitaki, *pa,* 95

Matamata: C.M.S. station, 44, 45; mentioned, 64, 170, 173

Mathew, Mrs. Felton, 94

Matthews, Joseph, 58, 170

Mau-inaina, *pa,* 94

Maunsell, Robert, 163
Melanesians, 9
Mercury Bay, 62
Mere, 99, 106
Mermaid, 31, 32
Metal tools: Maori enthusiasm, 86, 90, 128, 137; use as weapons, 90–91; missionary techniques, 90–91, 150, 153; effect on Maori carving, 118, 189, 190; contribute to Maori confusion, 145–146
Methodists. *See* Wesleyan-Methodist Missionary Society
Missionaries: numbers, 22–23, 26–27, 36–37; musket trade, 39, 41–42, 86–90, 133; immorality, 39, 40, 41, 43, 122; individuals, 39–43; conversion techniques, 51, 149–152, 159; introduction of blankets, 78–79; agree with settlers about Maoris, 107; nonmissionary criticism, 110–113, 200–201; dominated by Maoris, 133–139; results of conversion techniques, 152–157; Maoris did not kill, 174; attitude to Treaty of Waitangi, 188; land purchases, 193, 198. *See also* Church Missionary Society; Europeans; Maoris, conversion of; Nonmissionary Europeans; Roman Catholics; Wesleyan-Methodist Missionary Society
Missionary Register, 156, 169
Moa, 13
Moehanga, 131
Mokoia, island, 95
Mokoia, *pa,* 93, 94, 159
Morgan, John, 158
Muru, 117, 142
Murupaenga, 93
Muskets: Maoris' first impressions, 7, 174; missionary trade, 39, 41–42, 86–90, 133; introduction and distribution, 76, 85–86, 91–92, 99–100, 159, 181; value to Maoris, 76, 87, 99, 128; impact of introduction, 83, 84; kinds, 84–85; early psychological effect, 84–85, 174; disturb Maori habits, 77, 92–93, 145–146, 190; Maoris unable to mend, 149; mentioned, 57, 83–102 *passim,* 109, 126, 138, 141, 143, 156

Napoleonic Wars, 21
Napoleonism: in Maori wars, 119–122
New Guinea, 179
New Plymouth, 193
New South Wales, 21, 22
New Zealand Company (1825), 24–25
New Zealand Company (1839), 193
Ngapuhi; characteristics, 10; changing attitudes toward war, 86, 92, 92–96, 99–100, 146–147, 154–155; most Westernized tribe, 149, 157, 189–192; increasingly Christian, 152; influence conversions in interior, 159–160; inferior arts and crafts, 190; revolt, 200; mentioned, 46, 47, 120, 131, 137, 146, 160. *See also* Bay of Islands; Hongi
Ngatimaru, 94, 120
Ngatipaoa, 93, 94, 120
Ngati-toa, 164
Ngati-whatua, 96, 120
Nicholas, John Liddard, 22, 69, 73, 86, 106, 107, 131
Nonmissionary Europeans; population in N.Z., 19–37 *passim,* 189, 193; whaling near N.Z., 19, 21, 23–24, 29–30, 143, 158; modern opinions, 20, 69, 119; missionary opinion, 31, 107, 109–110, 194; sexual immorality, 72–75, 78, 119, 122–125; criticize missionaries, 110–113; influence of Maoris, 129–130;

attitude to Treaty of Waitangi, 187; difficulty with Maoris after 1840, 195–198; relation to Maoris and missionaries, 200–201. *See also* Europeans; Kororareka; Maoris, depopulation of; Missionaries; Trading

Nopera, 192

Norfolk Island, 65

North Auckland peninsula, 4, 44, 47, 62

North Cape, 18, 64, 65, 86

Ohinemutu, 44, 45

Old New Zealand, 35

Opotiki, 45

Orton, Rev. Mr., 49

Otago, 29

Otamatea River, 96

Otawao, 35, 158

Owaiawai, 156

Paihia: C.M.S. station, 43, 109, 150; Maori teachers, 160

"Pakeha," 116

Pakeha Maoris, 35, 129

Papahurihia, 177–178

Parramatta, 177

Pas: pre-European, 5, 75; trade affects, 77; muskets affect, 77, 145; mentioned, 31, 82, 93, 94, 95, 96, 101, 120, 161, 177, 187

Petre, 193

Plants, American, in N.Z., 37. *See also* Flax, Kauri trees; Maoris, foods of

Polack, Joel, 35, 57, 110, 112, 129

Polygamy: Catholic policy, 51; decline, 167, 182; mentioned, 105, 199

Polynesia, 9–10, 12–13

Pomare, 32, 96

Pompallier, J. B. F., 47–48, 50–53, 172

Population. *See* Europeans; Maoris; Missionaries; Nonmissionary Europeans

Port Jackson, 100

Port Nicholson, 35, 177, 193

Preserved Maori heads, 6, 108, 146

Prince Regent, 33

Printed religious matter: early missionary activity, 44; weapon against Catholics, 52–53; statistics, 53, 176; sale, 111, 150; Maori attitudes, 174–177

Puriri, 44, 45, 159

Queen Charlotte Sound, 61

Raglan, 49

Raiatea, 9

Rangihoua, 41, 43, 133, 134

Rewha, 92, 121

Rewharewha, 62

Ripahu, 161

Roman Catholics: establish mission in N.Z., 38, 47–48; disputes with Protestants, 49–53; 1845 estimate of associated Maoris, 141; Maoris and ceremonies, 153; attitude to Bibles, 175; attitude to Treaty of Waitangi, 188. *See also* Missionaries

Rosanna, 24, 33

Rotorua, 12, 44, 45, 95, 96, 175

Roux, M. le St. Jean, 7

Royal Navy, 27, 28

Ruatara, 86, 127, 131

Savage, John, 21, 69, 76, 106, 107

Sealing, in N.Z., 19

Settlers. *See* Nonmissionary Europeans

Sexual immorality. *See* Maoris; Missionaries; Nonmissionary Europeans

Sharp, Andrew, 9–10

Shepherd, James, 170–171

Shortland, Edward, 164

Shunghee. *See* Hongi

Skinner, H. D., 10, 11

Slavery: pre-European, 18, 59, 82, 160, 179; slaughter of slaves increases, 118; missionary techniques, 150, 155–156, 157, 160–161; decline, 168, 178, 180, 181, 189, 199

Society Islands, 9

South Island: description, 4; Maori population, 12; sealing and whaling, 19, 29; Maori teachers, 162

Stack, James, 47, 142–143, 145

Stack, James (son), 72, 173

Sydney, Australia, 21, 22, 28, 29, 52, 76, 98, 136

Tahiti, 6, 63

Tapu: pre-European, 15–16, 60, 199; Maoris' changing attitudes toward, 112, 142, 143, 153–154, 182, 191; Maori conception of Christianity, 112, 149, 150, 152, 171, 172–173, 178, 180, 181, 182, 183; Europeans respect, 129, 130, 134, 140; mentioned, 83, 105, 127, 131, 157, 197

Taraia, 169

Taranaki, 12, 35, 62

Tasman, Abel Janszoon, 3, 4

Tattooing: described, 5; Catholic policy, 51; decline, 167, 178, 181, 189; resumption, 200; mentioned, 97, 124, 146

Taumatakura, 176–177

Taupo, 17, 97, 175

Tauranga: C.M.S. station, 44, 45; Catholic station, 48; mentioned, 35, 83, 147, 155, 158, 169, 170

Tawell, John, 110

Taylor, Richard, 37, 161, 196

Te Arawa, 11, 44, 95–96, 120

Te Atua Wera, 178

Te Hinaki, 94, 98

Te Ikaranganui, 96

Te Kemara, 193

Te Morenga, 91

Te Rauparaha, 35, 96, 121, 164

Te Reinga, 96, 99, 151

Terry, Charles, 57

Te Totara, 94, 120, 161

Te Waharoa, 45, 96

Thames River (and district), 44, 46, 62, 73, 86, 92, 159, 169, 175

Titore, 32, 92, 131–133

Tobacco: Maoris assimilate, 127–128; precedes money economy, 194; mentioned, 57, 109, 128, 149, 189, 193

Tohi, 150, 171

Tohungas: description, 16; Maori diseases, 60, 144, 154, 191–192; conversion, 150, 154, 156–157; present day, 191–192; mentioned, 129, 142, 157, 159

Tolaga Bay, 92

Trading: nature of first, 7–8; Maori depopulation, 65, 75–78; extent in 1830, 76; becomes easier, 141–143; disturbs Maori habits, 144–146; extent in 1840, 189; after 1840, 194–195, 197–198. *See also* Flax; Kauri trees; Nonmissionary Europeans

Tuhi, 92, 131–133

Tuhoe, 62

Turanga, 161

Turi, 98

Turner, Nathaniel, 49

Urewera, 194

Utu, 82, 116, 118, 121, 142

Venereal diseases: and Maori depopulation, 58, 63, 102; introduction into N.Z., 63; unrelated to moral problem, 124. *See also* Diseases; Maoris, depopulation of
Venus, 83–84, 117
Vicariate of Western Oceania, 47

Wade, William, 43, 164, 173
Waharoa. *See* Te Waharoa
Waikato, chief, 92, 93, 131
Waikato River (and district): and missionary societies, 44, 47, 49; mentioned, 12, 77, 95, 96, 120
Waimate: C.M.S. station, 43–44, 152; center of conversions, 44, 163; Maori teachers, 160; mentioned, 42, 70, 79, 109, 148, 154, 156, 168
Wairarapa, 191
Wairau, 197
Waitangi, district, 134
Waitangi, Treaty of: attitudes toward, 187–188; acceptance of, 192–193; problems arising from, 197; mentioned, 37, 78, 194, 195, 196
Waiwhariki, 120
Wakefield, Edward J., 111–112, 113
Wanganui, 175, 193
War of 1812, 21
Wars. *See* Maoris, wars of
Watkins, John, 130
Wellington, 24, 25
Wellington, N.Z., 12, 35, 198
Wesleyan-Methodist Missionary Society: 1839 estimate of members in N.Z., 37; established in N.Z., 38, 46–47; disputes with C.M.S.,

48–49; 1845 estimate of Maoris associated with, 141. See also Missionaries
"Wesleydale," 46
Westerners. *See* Europeans
Whakawhitira, 161
Whalers. *See* Nonmissionary Europeans
Whangarei, 12, 92
Whangaroa: and *Boyd* massacre, 21; Methodist station, 38, 46; Catholic station, 48; mentioned, 12, 35, 37, 86, 136
White man. *See* Europeans
Whiteley, John, 161
Wilkes, Charles, 71, 107
Williams, Henry: opinions, 24, 25, 34, 36–37, 46, 51, 70, 79, 87, 96–97, 99–100, 109–110, 137, 138, 147, 155, 161, 162, 163, 175, 176; 1839 estimate of European population in N.Z., 36–37; description, 42, 139–140; ideas on mission policy, 42; helps end musket trade, 42, 89; quarrel with Methodists, 49; on Catholics, 51; on nonmissionary Europeans, 109–110; on Marsden optimism, 137
Williams, Mrs. Henry, 139
Williams, William: description, 42; opinions, 100, 121–122, 151, 155, 181–182, 198–199; at East Cape, 161–162, 176
Woon, William, 51, 52

Yate, William: description, 42–43; opinions, 60–61, 65, 99, 155, 163, 174–175

Harvard Historical Monographs

1. Athenian Tribal Cycles in the Hellenistic Age. By W. S. Ferguson. 1932.
2. The Private Record of an Indian Governor-Generalship. The Correspondence of Sir John Shore, Governor-General, with Henry Dundas, President of the Board of Control, 1793–1798. Edited by Holden Furber. 1933.
3. The Federal Railway Land Subsidy Policy of Canada. By J. B. Hedges. 1934.
4. Russian Diplomacy and the Opening of the Eastern Question in 1838 and 1839. By P. E. Mosely. 1934.
5. The First Social Experiments in America. A Study in the Development of Spanish Indian Policy in the Sixteenth Century. By Lewis Hanke. 1935.*
6. British Propaganda at Home and in the United States from 1914 to 1917. By J. D. Squires. 1935.*
7. Bernadotte and the Fall of Napoleon. By F. D. Scott. 1935.
8. The Incidence of the Terror during the French Revolution. A Statistical Interpretation. By Donald Greer. 1935.
9. French Revolutionary Legislation on Illegitimacy, 1789–1804. By Crane Brinton. 1936.
10. An Ecclesiastical Barony of the Middle Ages. The Bishopric of Bayeaux, 1066–1204. By S. E. Gleason. 1936.
11. Chinese Traditional Historiography. By C. S. Gardner. 1938.*
12. Studies in Early French Taxation. By J. R. Strayer and C. H. Taylor. 1939.
13. Muster and Review. A Problem of English Military Administration 1420–1440. By R. A. Newhall. 1940.
14. Portuguese Voyages to America in the Fifteenth Century. By S. E. Morison. 1940.*
15. Argument from Roman Law in Political Thought, 1200–1600. By M. P. Gilmore. 1941.*
16. The Huancavelica Mercury Mine. A Contribution to the History of the Bourbon Renaissance in the Spanish Empire. By A. P. Whitaker. 1941.
17. The Palace School of Muhammad the Conqueror. By Barnette Miller. 1941.*
18. A Cistercian Nunnery in Mediaeval Italy: The Story of Rifreddo in Saluzzo, 1220–1300. By Catherine E. Boyd. 1943.
19. Vassi and Fideles in the Carolingian Empire. By C. E. Odegaard. 1945.
20. Judgment by Peers. By Barnaby C. Keeney. 1949.

21. The Election to the Russian Constituent Assembly of 1917. By O. H. Radkey. 1950.

22. Conversion and the Poll Tax in Early Islam. By Daniel C. Dennett. 1950.*

23. Albert Gallatin and the Oregon Problem. By Frederick Merk. 1950.

24. The Incidence of the Emigration during the French Revolution. By Donald Greer. 1951.*

25. Alterations of the Words of Jesus as Quoted in the Literature of the Second Century. By Leon E. Wright. 1952.*

26. Liang Ch'i Ch'ao and the Mind of Modern China. By Joseph R. Levenson. 1953.*

27. The Japanese and Sun Yat-sen. By Marius B. Jansen. 1954.

28. English Politics in the Early Eighteenth Century. By Robert Walcott, Jr. 1956.*

29. The Founding of the French Socialist Party (1893-1905). By Aaron Noland. 1956.

30. British Labour and the Russian Revolution 1917–1924. By Stephen Richards Graubard. 1956.

31. RKFDV: German Resettlement and Population Policy. By Robert L. Koehl. 1957.

32. Disarmament and Peace in British Politics, 1914–1919. By Gerda Richards Crosby. 1957.

33. Concordia Mundi: The Career and Thought of Guillaume Postel (1510–1581). By W. J. Bouwsma. 1957.

34. Bureaucracy, Aristocracy, and Autocracy. The Prussian Experience, 1660–1815. By Hans Rosenberg. 1958.

35. Exeter 1540–1640. The Growth of an English County Town. By Wallace T. MacCaffrey. 1958.

36. Historical Pessimism in the French Enlightenment. By Henry Vyverberg. 1958.

37. The Renaissance Idea of Wisdom. By Eugene F. Rice, Jr. 1958.

38. The First Professional Revolutionist: Filippo Michele Buonarroti (1761–1837). By Elizabeth L. Eisenstein. 1959.

39. The Formation of the Baltic States: A Study of the Effects of Great Power Politics upon the Emergence of Lithuania, Latvia, and Estonia. By Stanley W. Page. 1959.

40. Conservation and the Gospel of Efficiency: The Progressive Conservation Movement, 1890–1920. By Samuel P. Hays. 1959.

41. The Urban Frontier: The Rise of Western Cities, 1790–1830. By Richard C. Wade. 1959.

42. A Study of Early New Zealand: 1769–1840. By Harrison M. Wright. 1959.

43. Ottoman Imperialism and German Protestantism, 1521–1555. By Stephen A. Fischer-Galati. 1959.